EUREKA

Edgar Allan Poe

EUREKA

Edited with an Introduction,
Notes, and Textual Variants by

STUART LEVINE AND
SUSAN F. LEVINE

UNIVERSITY OF ILLINOIS PRESS
Urbana and Chicago

© 2004 by the Board of Trustees
of the University of Illinois
All rights reserved
Manufactured in the United States of America
C 5 4 3 2 1
∞ This book is printed on acid-free paper.

Library of Congress Cataloging-in-Publication Data
Poe, Edgar Allan, 1809–1849.
Eureka / Edgar Allan Poe ; edited with an introduction,
notes, and textual variants by
Stuart Levine and Susan F. Levine.
p.   cm.
Includes bibliographical references (p.) and index.
ISBN 0-252-02849-X (cloth : alk. paper)
1. Cosmology. I. Levine, Stuart. II. Levine, Susan F.
(Susan Fleming). III. Title.
PS2620.A2L48   2004
811'.3—dc21   2002152318

CONTENTS

ACKNOWLEDGMENTS

Colleagues in several departments at the University of Kansas have demonstrated again the worth of the old definition of a university, for they have consistently behaved like "a community of scholars." We are especially grateful to the classicists Michael Shaw, Oliver Phillips, and James Seaver; John A. Weir (deceased, 1997) of the Department of Physiology and Cell Biology; and Warner Morse (deceased, 1991), Richard DeGeorge, and Anthony Genova of the Department of Philosophy, but others helped as well.

Bruce Twarog's love for the history of his field, astronomy, was our good fortune. In five separate sessions, he patiently briefed us on the relationship between *Eureka* and the best scientific thinking of Poe's day. Our judgment that *Eureka* is sound in most of its astronomy history and in its introductions to what was known or hypothesized in the 1840s is really Bruce's. We should note that we are not the first to reach that conclusion. As Richard Hodgens said in a letter to us of May 11, 1985, "Poe's physical science was generally sound for the day."

Word processing for this edition was handled through the Wescoe Hall Word Processing Center at the University of Kansas. Denisa Brown, Sandee Kennedy, Pam LeRow, Lynn Porter, and Beth Ridenour each produced large portions of the text, staying cheerful and professional despite an airless office, the great complexity of this volume, SGL's handwriting, and a collapse of the university's mainframe computer. Pam LeRow's work has been especially concentrated. The project has gone on so long that these women have become connected to its texture; we admire them all and are very grateful.

Librarians have helped us early and late. We extend thanks to many staff members of the University of Kansas Libraries, especially to Sandra Brandt, Marilyn Clark, Eleanor Symons, Barbara Jones, and Rob Melton; to John Kirkpatrick and Cathy Henderson of the Harry Ransom Humanities Research Center, University of Texas at Austin; to Libby Chenault of the University of North Carolina Library; to Julius Barclay, Joan St. C. Crane, and George Riser of the Rare Books Department of the Alderman Library at the University of Virginia; to Paul Needham and Barbara Paulson at the Pierpoint Morgan Library in New York; to Dale Bentz and Frank Paluka at the University of Iowa Library; to Nancy J. Halli of the Historical Society of Pennsylvania; and to Evelyn Timberlake at the Library of Congress.

James C. Campbell, a doctoral student at the University of Kansas, took a directed readings course in Poe from SGL in 1987 and was good enough to do his reading of *Eureka* from word processor "batch" copies, proofreading as he went. The extra pair of eyes was most helpful.

The great generosity of Richard M. Hodgens must be acknowledged. He was good enough to share with us material used in his extensive comparison of the pamphlet publication of the Nichol lectures with the text of *Eureka*. The present edition of *Eureka* reflects his contribution in a number of places.

Originally conceived as a part of Burton Pollin's *The Collected Writings of Edgar Allan Poe*, this project bears evidence of his attention and suggestions. Moreover, his life's work on Poe has included important scholars' tools that greatly facilitated preparation of this edition and that will go on enriching subsequent work on Poe. Major scholarly reputations have rested on accomplishments less difficult and less useful than single reference volumes that Pollin has produced, and he has produced a number of them.

Our editorial work has been supported by a sabbatical granted to SGL by the University of Kansas and by a number of small awards: a grant from the General Research Fund, University of Kansas; a travel grant from the Travel to Collections Program, National Endowment for the Humanities, to work in the Harry Ransom Humanities Research Center Library, University of Texas at Austin (to work especially with the "Nelson-Mabbott" copy of the 1848 Putnam edition of *Eureka*); and a travel grant from the Hall Center for the Humanities, University of Kansas, to aid with the expenses of a trip to the Pierpont Morgan Library in New York (to work especially with the "Hurst-Wakeman" copy of the same edition). The Graduate School of the University of Kansas has twice allowed SFL to take extended leaves from her duties in that office to dedicate extra time to the project.

In 1985 David M. Katzman of the University of Kansas, and in early

ACKNOWLEDGMENTS

1988 Theodore M. Hovet of the University of Northern Iowa and Nancy Walker of Vanderbilt University, members of the editorial board of *American Studies,* were good enough to take on portions of what were normally SGL's duties as editor of that journal. Their generosity expedited work on this edition.

INTRODUCTION

A longing swept him like the wind of the muse to understand and trans-
form his beginnings: to see the indestructible nucleus and redemption
of creation, the remote and the abstract image and correspondence,
in which all things and events gained their substance and universal
meaning. However far from him, however distant and removed, he
longed to see, *he longed to see* the atom, the very nail of moment in the
universe.

—Wilson Harris, *Palace of the Peacock* (London, 1960)

Poe's *Eureka* is a product of the age that also produced Carlyle's *Sartor
Resartus,* Melville's *Moby-Dick* and *Pierre,* Thoreau's *Walden,* the music of
Liszt and Wagner, Whitman's *Leaves of Grass,* and Humboldt's *Kosmos,*
startlingly unconventional works difficult to confine to convenient cate-
gories, works intended, indeed, to dissolve boundaries between catego-
ries that their creators felt to be oppressive. To some of their creators Poe
has direct intellectual ties, to which this introduction and the notes al-
lude, but the larger context, the milieu in which such explosive artifacts
were invented, must be borne in mind lest *Eureka* appear an isolated
anomaly, an inexplicable freak. Mention, no more, is all that is appropri-
ate here. Understand that the list of unconventional and rebellious works
of that age is arbitrary; the reader may think of others. That was an era
of such things.

These introductory remarks are an attempt to characterize one of this
group of strange mid-century works. The reader should keep in mind that
these comments were written by an editor who, in the course of annotat-
ing *Eureka,* came to see many aspects of how it had been put together.
Knowing its seams and stitches, acutely aware of its patchwork fabric, he
is perhaps too close to it, too liable to underestimate its impact on those
who come to it with less foreknowledge of Poe's methods. Poe intended
that impact to be powerful.

For certainly many readers have been moved by *Eureka.* Paul Valéry said
that he was grateful to Poe for the scientific briefing and for a glimpse of
the emotion behind scientific discovery. "These sciences," he wrote, "now

taught so coldly were founded and developed by men with a passionate interest in their work. *Eureka* made me feel some of this passion." The great underlying unity for which *Eureka* argues has of course been deeply appealing to many. Valéry again put it well: "The universe is formed on a plan the profound symmetry of which is present, as it were, in the inner structure of our minds. Hence, the poetic instinct will lead us blindly to the truth."[1]

This introduction must stress the strong connections between *Eureka*, the works that Poe used in preparing it, and the rest of his writing. Explaining these connections, however, does not demonstrate that *Eureka* is merely a collage of ideas and language assembled from the writings of others and from Poe's own work, for it connects to his poetry, criticism, and fiction in another way as well: in it, as in all his best writing, Poe remembered the importance of dramatic impact, of memorable effect. Poe had selected the largest of topics—matter and spirit, science and inspiration, the nature and meaning of the universe, the history and destiny of the world. He meant to bring it all off grandly. If much of the substance of *Eureka* comes from borrowings familiar to the specialist in Poe, much of its rhetorical tone and its occasional exaltation come from the same sources as that tone and that mood when they appear in work of Melville, Whitman, Wagner, or other inventors of new forms.

This is not to imply that there were no precedents. When Poe called *Eureka* a poem, he was placing it in a very long tradition of writings that were poetic and were at the same time attempts to grasp the nature of things. In translation, at first hand or through secondary accounts, Poe was familiar with at least some such works. Humboldt's *Kosmos,* to whose author *Eureka* is dedicated but that Poe may not have read thoroughly, was a modern example, at once a scientific treatise and a highly charged emotional poetic response to the cosmic environment. Equally emotional was the religiously moralizing scientific rhetoric of J. P. Nichol, much less important intellectually but very well known to Poe, as we shall see.

What Poe engaged in is an ancient, honorable venture. Parmenides of Elea, for example, around 470 B.C.E.—the date is very tenuous—similarly presented his great findings as a poem. Carried by a chariot "on to the resounding road of the Goddess" of Truth, he reported what the goddess

1. The quotations are from Malcom Cowley's translation of "Au sujet d'Eurêka," quoted in Carlson, ed., *Recognition,* 103–10 (quotations on 105 and 106), from *Variety* 1 (1927): 123–37. Cowley's text was Valéry's preface to the Baudelaire translation of *Eurêka* (1921) from *Variété* 1 (1923).

had spoken, axioms about the nature of existence, spirit, matter, oneness, and the heavenly bodies. Poe would not have accepted Parmenides—paragraph 17 of *Eureka,* indeed, perhaps even alludes to his dicta as examples of axioms that should be challenged—but like Parmenides he began his truth-giving poem with a dramatized journey in quest of knowledge, dealt with the nature of being, and attempted to tie all understanding to a physics and astronomy that showed unity. "Thought and being are the same," says Parmenides' goddess. Poe's, too.

There is philosophical precedent as well for Poe's idea of multiple universes and multiple gods (¶87) in the thinking of the presocratic philosopher Anaximander (ca. 610–ca. 546) as his ideas have been transmitted by later Greek and Roman compilers and doxographers. Simplicius (sixth century C.E.), for example, reported, "Those who believed in an unlimited number of worlds, as Anaximander and his associates did, regarded them as coming-to-be and passing away throughout unlimited time" (Wheelwright, *The Presocratics,* 57). Cicero, in *De Natura Deorum,* said, "It was the opinion of Anaximander that the gods come into existence and perish, rising and setting at long intervals, and that there are countless worlds" (ibid., 59). In St. Augustine's *Civitas Dei,* Anaximander is said to have "believed that the worlds, . . . are indefinite in number, and they contain everything that would grow upon them by nature. He held further [as Poe would, too] that those worlds are subject to perpetual cycles of alternating dissolution and regeneration" (ibid., 59).

Poe scholars quarrel about how well he knew the classics. Perhaps he knew very little about other than major figures. The matter of parallels with ancient Anaximander, however, suggests several points. First, it shows that *Eureka,* although strange, was by no means isolated; there is a long tradition of similar works that unify poetic, religious, and scientific approaches to truth. Sometimes they are even congruent in major details. Comparison also suggests that Poe may have had a sense that the Greek philosophy he knew (even his knowledge of Plato seems suspect to some modern scholars, in part because in Poe's era Plato was read differently) was only a flawed remnant of a direct visionary truth that people once had enjoyed intuitively. Poe seems to have toyed with the idea of the existence of a golden age. The ideal creative artist Ellison, in Poe's "The Domain of Arnheim" (1842–47), speaks of how nature as we see it now shows but the flawed remnant of the ideal beauty it once might have embodied. Monos, in the visionary story "The Colloquy of Monos and Una" (1841), says that seer-poets "ponder piningly, yet not unwisely, upon the ancient days," when Nature spoke directly. The passage moves, appropriately, to a wistful call for "the pure contemplative spirit and majestic intuition of Plato" (*Short Fiction,* 108–9, 119–24, esp. 120, 146–47).

It is unlikely that Poe knew what is known or believed of the early Milesian philosopher and cosmologist Anaximander. His name is never mentioned in Poe's work, although there is an allusion to the Ionic school of philosophers to which Aniximander belonged in Poe's satire "How to Write a Blackwood Article" (1838). But because *Eureka* is dedicated to Humboldt, whose *Kosmos* is a beautiful and poetic modern scientific work that attempts to unify diverse fields of knowledge, and because Poe seems to have felt that the "proper spirit" for scientific inquiry existed once in ancient Greece, it is worth noting places in which *Eureka* for whatever reason actually intersects ancient speculative thought. This is because, although available evidence will not support claims of influence or knowledge, it seems likely that Poe had the "ancients" in mind as he wrote *Eureka.* Monos, in the story just mentioned, explains how occasionally in human history "the poetic intellect—that intellect which we now feel to have been the most exalted of all" has revealed truths that were not available to "the unaided reason" (*Short Fiction,* 120). The motto of this story is the Greek Μέλλοντα ταῦτα, "Mellonta Tauta," the title of the story Poe incorporated into the opening portions of *Eureka* (¶11 and ¶174n).

There is no question, then, of at least the association of ideas. Ancient Greece suggested the unity of poetic and scientific vision. The same passage in "The Colloquy of Monos and Una," incidentally, alludes to "the mystic parable" of the tree of knowledge. Poe had at hand a part of Humboldt's *Kosmos;* he was cobbling together evidence to support a cosmological insight. Perhaps, to mix metaphors, the ancient vein was open again.

Poe's calling *Eureka* a prose-poem gives some readers pause. Several overlapping explanations might justify the term. *Eureka* could be called a poem, first, for reasons that Poe states very plainly in the course of it: "Man cannot long or widely err, if he suffer himself to be guided by his poetical . . . instincts." Moreover, "the Universe . . . is . . . the most sublime of poems. . . . Poetry and Truth are one" (¶237). Supernal beauty and supernal truth are identical, and they are identical with us, because we are made of the stuff of the eternal unity: the particles that constitute us and all the universe began as "unparticled" matter. Mankind carries in its being, then, knowledge of its origin and destiny; Poe's universe is even now returning to unity. Through the ages, Poe writes, occasional sages have brilliantly sensed the nature of reality. He created fictional sages of his own, who speak in some of his visionary stories. They, like the scientists he admires and like all of Poe's truth-givers, are poetically inspired.

Poetic truth-givers appear in stories other than visionary tales as well. Thus in the detective story "The Purloined Letter" (1844) Poe pointedly reveals that the detective Dupin is also a poet. It is he, using poetic gifts, who can solve mysteries that elude the dead and unpoetic logic of the prefect of police. In "The Domain of Arnheim" (1842–47), Ellison can transform the environment to make it embody the Edenic beauty that was the earth's in remote times past. Ellison is a landscape architect because, the narrator explains, the creation of landscape provides the freest scope for the poet. So because poetic inspiration gives truth and is in itself founded in the essence of the universe, *Eureka,* a book that offers inspired revelation of the true nature of the universe, is a poem.

As the annotations make clear, *Eureka* is closely intertwined with both Poe's prose and his poetry. The notes point to numerous echoes of his poems, but there are also echoes of his poetic theory. In his criticism, Poe explains how poets deliberately play upon readers' minds, making associations and constructing effects. In paragraph 188 and elsewhere, he confesses that *Eureka* is built the same way, poetically, through *"graduated impression"* rather than through a "merely natural . . . arrangement." One more sense, then, in which it is a "poem," despite Poe's famous dictum that a long poem is impossible.

At a stage at which Poe seemed not yet to have devised the subtitle *A Prose Poem,* the notion that *Eureka* was a poem occurred to a journalist. Hence it is also possible that Poe did not think to call *Eureka* a poem until the idea was given him by a reviewer in the *New York Express,* who said, "The work has all the completeness and oneness of plot required in a poem" (Pollin, "Contemporary Reviews of *Eureka,* " 27).[2]

The notes locate and discuss those sections in *Eureka* that refer to its poetic nature. This essay, however, seems the proper place to mention a famous contradiction: Poe says emphatically in his criticism that a long poem cannot exist, for no reader can remain for long in the state of high

2. Burton R. Pollin (BRP) also points out a number of passages in *Eureka* in which Poe uses language poetically. Of the phrase "partial and pain-intertangled pleasures" in paragraph 266, for example, he writes, "This phrase, based on its poignant Poe-created compound, is composed of iambic rhythms and cleverly mingles plosives (e.g., 'p' and 't') which help toward the general "prose poem" effect that Poe promised in his subtitle." Both kindly and conscientious is Barbara Cantalupo's *"Eureka:* Poe's 'Novel Universe,'" a discussion of reactions to *Eureka.* It covers this debate about how to classify *Eureka* and other areas of confusion.

elevation of soul that is (to Poe) the nature of true poetic response. *Eureka* cannot be read in one sitting. Yet Poe called it a poem. No matter. If his entitling *Eureka* a poem is inconsistent with such statements in his criticism, the criticism itself is sometimes contradictory, too. Indeed, Poe's *arguments* are frequently contradictory throughout his writings.

Yet while the major criticism is sometimes contradictory, it consistently makes use of the same allusions, references, citations, quotations, pet sayings, and turns of phrase. *Eureka* does as well. Poe's criticism, his other nonfiction prose, and his fiction as well are built from a single storehouse of material. Indeed, Poe sometimes uses the same "example" in different places to support opposite sides of an argument. The relationship between *Eureka* and Poe's statements of literary theory is especially close, as the notes show.

Four characteristics unite most of Poe's work: the presence of a body of reusable ideas, phrases, allusions, and quotations; an apparent belief in supernal inspiration; a craftsmanlike concern with strong effect; and high intelligence. The first is not substantive, the second is sometimes undercut or parodied. The third and fourth are almost always in evidence. All four are present in *Eureka,* and their interaction needs to be assessed.

Poe complains in various pieces about transcendentalism in general and about Ralph Waldo Emerson in particular, but he is often philosophically very close to Emerson. Paragraph 22 provides a convenient illustration. In it, Poe's narrator speaks of "the great thoroughfare—the majestic highway of the *Consistent.* "In his great poem "Blight," Emerson uses "same" to mean just about what Poe does in paragraph 22 by "consistent":

> The old men studied magic in the flowers,
> And human fortunes in astronomy,
> And an omnipotence in chemistry,
> Preferring things to names, for these were men,
> Were unitarians of the united world,
> And, wheresoever their clear eye-beams fell,
> They caught the footsteps of the SAME. Our eyes
> Are armed, but we are strangers to the stars. . . .
> (*Poems,* ed. Emerson, 140)

Emerson in fact deals with science just the way Poe does. The complaint of "Blight" is the complaint of Poe's "Sonnet—To Science." Specialized research by itself is sterile. It lacks the unifying poetic vision that Humboldt and other visionary scientist-artists share. The sources of the vision are in the nature of the universe itself: we poets sense sameness or consistency because all matter is also spirit, part of the original oneness.[3] Indeed, even Emerson's famous comment about consistency and hobgoblins is worth comparing to Poe, as are the equally famous lines from Emerson's poetic disciple Walt Whitman: "Do I contradict myself? / Very well then I contradict myself, / (I am large, I contain multitudes)." Both are matched in paragraph 22; Poe reserves to his poet-scientist the right to be inconsistent, as "our Keplers—our Laplaces" sometimes are. But he is sure that the universe itself is consistent.

To the extent that it is serious, *Eureka* is a transcendental treatise. If it sounds in passages more like scripture than like scientific exposition, that is just the point. Emerson's scholar, scientist, priest were all the same enlightened person. Poe's, too.

Eureka contains a good deal of satire, but it would not be accurate to call it "a satire"; it has too many other purposes for that label to be appropriate. Much of the material in the early portion of *Eureka* is used both here and in Poe's satirical story "Mellonta Tauta," but the satire is by no means limited to the material which *Eureka* shares with the story. Poe remains playful even in what one would imagine were the most serious passages in *Eureka*.

In the opening of the story "The Imp of the Perverse" (1845), Poe has a reliable-sounding narrator explain the logical danger of imposing upon reality—in this case, the nature of the human mind—properties that it would be reasonable to expect to find, instead of beginning with properties that can be observed. Poe says in the passage following paragraphs 238 and 239 in *Eureka* that astronomers make a similar mistake. His rhet-

3. Speaking of paragraphs 215, 235, and 236, BRP has asked whether the basic mood of *Eureka* is euphoric or pessimistic because the "'fulfillment' of God's plan will mean the death of the universe and the extinction of human life. This accords with the frequent tone of despair, with the contemplation of the happiness of man's soul only after death (as in the 'Heavenly Dialogue' tales) and with the sickly and morbid nature and tone of many of his characters and settings, both in fiction and poetry. By maintaining an astronomic distance—as the observer in *Eureka*— he manages to adduce a rapturous appreciation of the divine plot, but it must encompass the termination, as Poe held true also, of man's artistic planning." BRP wonders why Poe "excludes ordinary human considerations from his contemplation of the 'perfect plot' of creation which leads back to the 'unity' of the original particle. He therefore ignores the death of all species, including the human, as being a deplorable consummation of the creative plan." The answer is easy to provide, although, of course, it is not satisfactory to the reader who does not accept Poe's mystical-materialistic premises. If man is of the stuff of the original atom and that atom and the godhead are the same, if matter and spirit are one, then man is not destroyed when the universe returns to its original state; he rather is reunited ("rëunited"?). Matter and spirit "go hand in hand," as they do in mystical thought and in Poe's apocalyptic tales.

INTRODUCTION

oric in this section strongly reminds one of the argument in the short story: it seems reasonable that there exists a resisting ether; by analogy, one *ought* to exist. But there is none. In "The Imp of the Perverse," the plausible narrator who explained the fallacy to us turns out to be insane, a homicidal maniac. Now, the parallel logic in two passages on the nature of scientific assumptions does not prove anything; it would be rash to claim, dogmatically, that Poe gleefully inserted this argument in order to undermine everything he was advocating in *Eureka*. But one cannot entirely rule out the possibility that the parallel situation was in his mind, either. The notes to *Eureka* identify so many places where Poe quotes literally from his criticism, his fiction, or his satirical prose or reuses allu- . sions or quotations that had for him connotations that seem foreign to their contexts in this work, that one wonders about his attitude.

To put it differently: one can prove that Poe is playing private literary games in so many places in *Eureka* that one questions whether to trust anything in the book. Poe played such games throughout his career. It seems to have tickled him to deck out some old trouper of a passage in new clothes and send it onstage in a fresh role. This practice is further evidence of the complexity of his attitude toward *Eureka*. It should make the reader wary.

Indeed, Poe's practices as a writer raise fundamental questions about his attitude. One has the right to ask whether sometimes his sleight of hand implies a certain underlying contempt for the reader. Was Poe thinking, "The fools will never notice that my great scientific-philosophic-poetic *Eureka* is really a collage, pasted together from scraps lifted from other writers and my own miscellaneous writings on totally different, mostly inappropriate, subjects"? That is too simple, however. No one such explanation will account for the strangeness of *Eureka*.

Portions of *Eureka*, moreover, are simply wild. Paragraph 185, for example, begins with an extended sexual metaphor and ends with a deliberately obscure sentence on genius and madness. This is interesting, for Poe is normally very precise in syntax. When he is not, his "error" is intentional, as when he makes up a syntactically ambiguous title for a work on duelling in his story "Mystification" (*Short Fiction*, 469). The writing error is deliberate; it is there to "say" that justifications of duelling are nonsense. The plot says the same. Poe is very different in this from the early Melville, whose syntax in the novels published between 1846 and 1852 was splendidly enthusiastic and energetic but not always correct, abounding especially in dangling sentence elements. Melville's prose becomes almost bookishly correct in his magazine work during the 1850s and in the post-humous and incompletely revised *Billy Budd*. Perhaps this later Melville is instructive for *Eureka*. One suspects that the few dangling modifiers that remain in *Billy Budd* are deliberate because they come in places at which Melville had philosophical reasons for obscuring meaning. That may be what is going on in paragraph 185 of *Eureka*. *Caveat lector.*

Eureka also contains some bad writing. Poe is so good a craftsman that only readers who know him well will remember comparable lapses.[4] Sometimes the sloppy sections in *Eureka* deal with issues that seem important to him. Poe's comments on the size of the universe, for instance, are revealing. At the close of the book, in paragraph 266, he says that he feels the universe to be finite in size but that there may be infinite numbers of other universes. That seems consistent with his philosophical stance. In the earlier discussion of the enormous size of the universe (see ¶193, ¶194, and the passages surrounding them), however, Poe was plainly padding, reworking material of only journalistic interest. A sentence or two would have said as much and not have so impeded the flow of the argument. The reader thinks of similarly nonfunctional padding: the pages of deadwood in "The Mystery of Marie Rogêt" or the section in Poe's only completed novel, *The Narrative of Arthur Gordon Pym* (1837–38), wherein he goes on for pointless pages explaining the proper method of stowing cargo in the hold of a ship and then fails to use the exposition in his plot. On the subject of cosmic size, Poe could have said that it is hard to visualize such immense distances and let it go at that. The passage he included might be reasonably effective as a popular magazine article or a Sunday feature-section filler but strikes one as inappropriate in a visionary "Poem." We wonder again about seriousness and intention.

Questioned about the target of some of his fictional satires, Poe responded that the satires did not have just one target but that he was rather hitting out in a number of directions. It is enlightening to bear that in mind in reading *Eureka*. Poe was likely doing a number of things.

It is impossible ever to be sure when Poe is truly committed to an idea. *Eureka* comes with serious credentials; Poe made a number of statements about how deeply he believed what he had found. One senses perhaps that to some extent the satire and play are present because they serve to

---

4. BRP, who certainly knows Poe well, points out numerous instances in *Collected Writings of Edgar Allan Poe* (e.g., the Introduction to *The Narrative of Arthur Gordon Pym*, 1:7–8 passim). This is a different matter, probably, from the complaints of critics who simply find Poe's writing overdone, excessive, and vulgar. Aldous Huxley's *Vulgarity in Literature* is a case in point.

"protect him," to allow him to say, in effect, "I'm just kidding," in case what he had done seemed foolish in the eyes of readers and authorities.

Yet such a conclusion is hardly congruent with an important characteristic of this unusual book, its skill and accuracy as scientific summary. Valéry was right—Poe is very good at briefing lay readers on the state of knowledge in several fields. Throughout *Eureka* Poe makes a reasonably conscientious effort to bring his book into line with the latest available information about the nature of the cosmos. This was a difficult job, because in 1848 there was a great deal of "late-breaking news," even about such seemingly elementary matters as the number of planets and moons in our solar system or in such basic information such as whether nebulae existed.

Poe attempts also to stake out a little factual and interpretive scientific turf he can call his own. This accounts for the occasional quibbling with authorities and with the popularizer J. P. Nichol. Were *Eureka* more unified in intention, the quibbling would be unnecessary; Poe could confine himself to a main argument and not bother with fussbudget points on which, as often as not, he is wrong. The "main argument," we take it, is the one about the essential underlying unity of creation and the rhythm of universal expansion and contraction. Poe argues that gravity is the force by which all matter tries to return to its "normal" state of oneness. Only God's "Volition" caused matter to "radiate" in the first place. So the universe of matter is finite in size and in age and is currently in its second, final, contracting phase. (There may, however, be other universes, other "gods" as already noted—see the very end of *Eureka*.) Given the grandeur of this scheme, there is inconsistency of tone whenever Poe feels compelled to insist, somewhat shrilly, that he can hold his own with anyone in explaining and interpreting physics and astronomy.

Poe's summary of scientific matters is in general excellent; he understood most available astronomical theory. His summaries of the arguments of different scientists, as the notes indicate, are very competent. The scientific speculation and theorizing are consistently intelligent and no more rhetorically overblown than other comparable statements of the era: Nichol gushes, and Humboldt is very florid. There exists a literature by Poe fans about how Poe predicted twentieth-century physics and astronomy. This does not strike us as a fruitful argument; Poe did not magically predict Einstein or intuit subatomic physics. One can, however, at least say that Poe knew the sorts of basic questions that science was going to face. He did think through intelligently the implications of what was known in his day. Our notes compare the hypotheses and data in *Eureka* with contemporary (2004) theory.

Poe had a strong sense that nature would turn out to be unified by some very basic principle. So did Einstein, but that conviction seems to have betrayed Einstein when it came to quantum mechanics. Moreover, at the present writing, the characteristics of the strange new particles being discovered make scientists unsure whether in fact one is going to be able to make broad statements about the ultimate "unity" and nature of either basic processes or of matter. Certainly, Poe does not anticipate "Superstring" theory, the controversial ten-dimensional hypothesis we read about today. But in paragraph 57 he does say that science has not yet named what is most basic to the makeup of the cosmos.

Poe is surprisingly good on some issues. Bruce Twarog, our scientific consultant, says that Poe's understanding of space and time is unusually advanced for his day. His notion that electricity is only part of a complex of forces is also prescient.[5] As Poe's general scheme may loosely be said to be equivalent to the "Big Bang" theory, so his notion of the "reciprocity" of matter and energy (see ¶¶252–53 especially, where Poe is explicit) is *roughly* akin to the modern understanding of the relationship represented by Einstein's $e = mc^2$. In paragraph 251, Poe even says that if all matter came together, it could not continue to exist: a reader inclined to press the issue could claim that Poe was intuiting something roughly like a black hole.[6] Poe comes close to anticipating astrophysical speculation that the universe is ultimately going to coalesce because it lacks sufficient energy to escape its own gravity. But in general, one cannot take his science and project it literally toward the present. One is not saying

5. Might Poe have seen comparable ideas in the writings of Michael Faraday (1791–1861) (BRP)? That is possible, reports Twarog, who adds that because Faraday's "suggestions were quite original and primarily conjecture," Poe's statements would show an unusual degree of insight even were they in response to Faraday. The mathematical work that carried Faraday's speculation beyond conjecture was done much later, long after Poe's death, by James Clerk Maxwell (1831–79).

6. Black holes in a sense much closer to the modern concept had been postulated before *Eureka,* as BRP points out. Laplace, in the early editions of *The System of the World* (Paris, 1796, 1799 and later; in English, London, 1809, 1830, etc.) speculated about the possibility of a star so large and dense that its gravitational field would prevent the escape of its own light: "any light emitted from the surface of the star would be dragged back by the star's gravitational attraction before it could get very far." We quote the summary of the issue given by Hawking (*A Brief History of Time,* 82). Hawking points out (81–82) that the idea had been suggested independently by John Mitchell in 1783. But in fact that is not what Poe was saying in paragraph 251; Poe is talking about the end of the universe, the final coalescence with the godhead.

anything very bad about Poe in pointing out that some of his predictions and generalizations are wrong. His well-informed contemporaries, including those in the sciences, made errors as gross as his. Poe's universe contracts; ours is still expanding. But *Eureka* is very successful as a brief introduction to good mid-century knowledge of the cosmos. Poe was a solid journalist and knew how to gather and splice material of this sort.

Poe also speaks of something he calls the "spiritual ether," which includes electricity and other forces. Poe's idea of seeing electricity as one among several other forces, as yet not well defined, is an interesting guess or projection; it is not totally unlike what is being learned about the functions of sub-atomic particles. At the present writing, science is more than a little uncertain about whether research is indeed going to find one clear and underlying particle, principle, or unity or whether "first causes" will turn out to be ambiguous, relativistic, and changeable, depending on how the scientist approaches them. Such ambiguity seems to run counter to Poe's assumptions, for he equates God with unity and regularity. On this subject, then, one cannot say, "Poe loosely predicted our present understanding." At best, one can say, "Poe loosely predicted much of what science believed a few years ago."

All things considered, it is fair to say that Poe, despite the bunko in *Eureka,* was thinking in the right directions, certainly speculating creatively.

Moreover, this aspect of *Eureka* is fascinating, for it lets the reader see how far a good mind furnished with a decent understanding of the best relevant science of the 1840s, and making philosophical assumptions characteristic of that era, could go. During Poe's lifetime the sciences were, by necessity, becoming specialized; earlier, one informed person could be simultaneously at the forefront of what we now consider several sciences; he might also, like Franklin or Jefferson, be important in fields outside of science. Specialization changed all this as Poe and his contemporaries watched. That Poe was a freshman at Jefferson's university and may well have seen the old man when he visited the campus shows with what terrible speed the world had advanced, for multifaceted careers on Jefferson's scale had come to be impossible. Indeed, the Romantic movement in literature was largely a protest against just that specialization, an attempt by artists to reassert the power of the arts as a path not just to beauty but to universal truths as well. Hence Shelley's "A Defense of Poetry" (1822), Emerson's "Blight," and many of the Poe works cited in the notes. They are cited generally because *Eureka* shares ideas, phrases, allusions, strings of association, and in one case entire pages of prose with them. As already noted, this connection shows how Poe reuses material, but it may indicate more. Many of the works that echo in *Eureka* are about the nature of inspiration and the perception of truth, beauty, and ultimate knowledge. (Poe, however, is also on the other side; always contradictory, it is he who asserts that "Beauty," not "Truth," is a poet's province, thus apparently accepting for the poet the specialized role of producer of pretties and no more.)

Eureka must in part be seen as a component of the movement to reclaim the artist's credentials: the artist alone could see underlying unities. Poe's praise for figures in science history—such as Humboldt—who had the poetic gift and could therefore generalize powerfully is important; Poe unquestionably hopes that *Eureka* will put him in their number—while at the same time hedging in order to protect his psyche in case *Eureka* fails.

Poetic insight was indispensable if science were to be creative. But Poe knew that the sciences were bestowing benefits, too. He speaks in *Eureka* of how spirit and matter are one. It seemed to most informed people in Poe's day that science was in fact providing material proof of spirituality. The popularized embodiments of the idea—quack Mesmerism, spiritualism, and, a little later, Christian Science—suggest how widespread such notions were. That electricity played a large part in the workings of the human nervous system was well known and very suggestive. The telegraph, developed and implemented in Poe's maturity, was understood as an analogous device. The relationship of magnetism to electricity had been long since established. Perhaps "animal magnetism," studied seriously before it fell to charlatans, was based on a cosmic principle of the greatest importance: spirit and matter indeed would turn out to be the same. The passages in paragraphs 132 and 154, in which Poe repeats his idea about the relationship between gravity and electricity, are important for understanding the sense of educated people in Poe's generation that science would shortly prove spirituality. As Poe writes, "The Body and the Soul walk hand in hand."

The idea that science provided material proof of spirituality received widespread circulation in the century preceding *Eureka*. As George Woodberry[7] and Carol Maddison ("Poe's *Eureka*") point out, Roger Joseph Boscovich's *Theoria Philosophiae Naturalis redacta ad unicam legem virium in*

7. For Woodberry, see Poe, *The Works of Edgar Allan Poe*, ed. Edmund Clarence Stedman and George Woodberry.

natura existentium (Vienna, 1758), which speculated about attraction and repulsion in an attempt to reconstruct a godly universe out of hints in Newton, was enormously popular and widely known. Maddison does not establish that Poe knew it; indeed, Poe nowhere mentioned Boscovich's name (Pollin, *Dictionary of Names and Titles*), and, in point of fact, Boscovich's theory is not very much like the theory of repulsion as "soul" that Poe develops in paragraph 55 and following (see especially ¶58). But it is simply true that romantic intellectuals thought along such lines: Newtonian gravity suggested "holistic" theories for the cosmos; electricity seemed at once physical and spiritual.

The overthrow of the phlogiston theory and its replacement by a chemistry that recognized oxygen serves to symbolize transformations in a number of basic sciences at approximately the turn of the nineteenth century. Modernization theorists point out that that is also the era in which the characteristics of modernization—such as specialization, industrialization, and urbanization—begin to transform our society.[8] *Eureka* is a document of the first generation in human history to have the new sciences, instantaneous communication, machine-powered transportation. It is an attempt, whatever its seriousness, to generalize broadly and poetically as great science had in the past, to deal with the bewildering torrent of new data in terms that would allow a position of honor and power to the truth-giver, the inspired poet-scientist.

It is thus akin to such diverse attempts to understand the changed world as Humboldt's *Kosmos,* romantic poetry, transcendentalism, and even the new religions that sprang up in the United States at mid-century. Its contents and its argument would not have been as shocking for many readers as one might suppose; many people were in fact accustomed to encountering the idea that science and spirit might be compatible. What is known of the reception of lecture and book bear this out, as does the fact that *Eureka* did not cause nearly the sensation that Poe hoped it would.

Readers are familiar with popularized accounts of the appearances of masterpieces that say that contemporary critical reception was hostile because the works ruffled feathers or because reviewers were somehow not ready for or unable to understand them. Herman Melville again provides convenient comparison, for older discussions of Melville generally make such statements about the contemporary reception of *Moby-Dick.* But

8. A full discussion of Poe in terms of Modernization Theory appears in Levine, "Poe and Society," which includes explanation of relevant aspects of Modernization Theory and a list of introductory works in the field.

to tell the truth, although the great book of course failed to find a large contemporary audience, a close look at all the reviews that greeted it shows that some were more accurate than one might expect. Although *Moby-Dick* did receive hostile notices, it also received several that were very favorable; some individual readers, moreover, fully understood what Melville had set out to do. Hawthorne understood, and Melville responded with a supremely exultant letter.

It is by no means clear that *Eureka* is a comparable masterpiece. But as a matter of fact, although Poe was done an injustice, contemporary reception of *Eureka* by and large will strike many modern readers as just and accurate. There exists an excellent overview of the contemporary reviews (Pollin, "Contemporary Reviews of *Eureka*"). The *Home Journal* said, "Poe boldly disavows induction for his theory of the universe in favor of scientific inspiration. All is attraction and repulsion in this suggestive work of phantasy, sounding like the *Vestiges of Creation* and close in ideas to Swedenborg's." A Swedenborgian publication notes ways in which Poe approximates Emanuel Swedenborg but complains about "pantheism." There is a strongly laudatory review in the *New York Evening Express,* which Pollin summarizes: "The most elaborate and profound lecture ever heard, unified in thought and 'in plot' like 'a poem' but with the detail and accuracy of a scientific lecture. Summarizes the theory and argument in florid metaphors and calls it an extraordinary work of 'Art,' of searching analysis, metaphysical acumen, and unsurpassed passion for ideals, from a man whose uncommon powers are still growing." Even a generally condemnatory long review in the *Literary World* by John H. Hopkins, Jr., is wary because Hopkins thinks that *Eureka* might "be a scientific hoax from the ingenious narrator of 'The Maelstrom.'" There is similar hedging in a review by an Amherst student, John Milton Emerson, in a college magazine, the Amherst *Indicator;* the review is snide, but the reviewer confesses uncertainty in matters scientific (Walker, *Edgar Allan Poe*).

Pollin writes that the space accorded in New York City newspapers to Poe's lecture is small when one compares it to the space awarded to coverage of J. P. Nichol's series of talks on astronomy or to another course of lectures, this on biblical history by a man named Enoch Cobb Wines, running at the same time. Still, looking over the reviews and thinking both of the very peculiar nature of Poe's lecture and book and the spate of puzzling new works that appeared at that time, it is hard not to feel that contemporary reviewers on the whole did a very decent job of describing and assessing *Eureka*.

The Publication of *Eureka*

A useful article by Burton R. Pollin reviews what is known about how *Eureka* was published ("Contemporary Views of *"Eureka"*): what was to have been a lecture tour to promote a magazine that Poe had been trying to found was reduced to a single talk in New York. The content of the presentation perhaps changed from Poe's essay "The Rationale of Verse" to his nearly completed *Eureka* (or, as Pollin jokes, "from verse to universe").

Poe enlisted friends to help fund and publicize the event, but dreadful weather, competing lectures, and a colleague's forgetfulness limited the turnout. Still, some hardy journalists who had press passes attended, and there were write-ups in the newspapers. Pollin judiciously calls these "mildly favorable," but they might have convinced Poe to take the manuscript when he completed it to the publisher, Putnam. There is some epistolary evidence (Poe, *Letters of Edgar Allan Poe,* ed. Ostrom, 361, 363, 364, 365) of Poe's publication plans. The talk came on February 3, 1848, a book contract in May, and the book appeared in late June.

Variations in the title, Pollin figures, reflect first, the lecture title (on the spine, the book is called *Eureka or the Universe*); and, second, a phrase from one of the reviews—"The work has all the completeness and oneness of plot required in a poem." (On the half-title page the wording is *Eureka: A Prose Poem*) (Poe, *The Works of Edgar Allan Poe,* ed. Stedman and Woodberry, 376.)

Moreover, Pollin was correct in saying that if Poe is behind the differences between the full title (*Eureka: An Essay on the Material and Spiritual Universe*) and the title given in the Putnam advertisements (*Eureka: A Prose Poem. Or the Physical and Metaphysical Universe*), the difference is important.

The Pollin article also points to the language of a review in the *New-World* in which the writer speaks of Poe's "select and nervous diction" and "lofty language" ("Empedocles in Poe," 378). Those phrases very forcibly suggest the famous passage in chapter sixteen of *Moby-Dick* that includes the phrase "a bold and nervous lofty language." There is likely a trail running between the two passages, for Melville, like Poe, had strong ties to New York journalism. That issue is beyond the proper scope of this introduction but serves to remind readers again that *Eureka* is of its time and place.

Considering connections, influences, and borrowings should not diminish *Eureka* but rather make it less strange. It is plainly a product of the science of the day and of a moment in the history of science when the promise of science seemed cosmically bright. It is a product of the history of philosophy. It is a product of a critical moment in literary history as well, when the artist felt threatened as never before. If its tone seems to modern readers to run to excess, they should compare it to the contemporary documents to which it refers. The *Kosmos* of Humboldt is at least as passionate and poetic. Nothing in *Eureka* approaches the craziness of the writings of F. M. C. Fourier. When Joseph Wood Krutch wrote that Poe's "works bear no conceivable relation, either external or internal, to the life of any people" and that "it is impossible to account for them on the basis of any social or intellectual tendencies or as the expression of the spirit of any age," he was simply wrong (*Edgar Allan Poe,* 192, 193). *Eureka* is a window on the 1840s.

ABBREVIATIONS FOR BOOKS AND AUTHORITIES CITED

Frequently used sources for which we use initials or abbreviated titles in notes and commentaries. Further bibliographical data appear in the Bibliography.

BRP	Notes and suggestions from Burton R. Pollin, who went over drafts of this edition, adding numerous suggestions, and making queries.
Complete Works	Edgar Allan Poe, *Complete Works of Edgar Allan Poe,* ed. James A. Harrison.
Short Fiction	Edgar Allan Poe, *The Short Fiction of Edgar Allan Poe: An Annotated Edition,* ed. Stuart Levine and Susan F. Levine.
Thirty-Two Stories	Edgar Allan Poe, *Edgar Allan Poe / Thirty-Two Stories,* ed. Stuart Levine and Susan F. Levine.
TOM	Thomas Ollive Mabbott, notes in the Special Collections Department, University of Iowa Library, Iowa City.
Twarog	Consultations with Bruce Twarog, professor of physics and astronomy, University of Kansas.
Collected Works	Edgar Allan Poe, *Collected Works of Edgar Allan Poe,* ed. Thomas Ollive Mabbott. See Bibliography. One printing of this edition uses consecutive volume numbers, the other does not.
Collected Writings	Edgar Allan Poe, *Collected Writings of Edgar Allan Poe,* ed. Burton R. Pollin, vols. 1–4.

EDITORIAL METHOD

A Note on the Text

There are four copies of the 1848 Putnam edition of *Eureka* in which Poe wrote changes; sometimes he also jotted down notes to himself, such as "Here describe the whole process as one instantaneous flash," which comes at the end of paragraph 96. We have followed Nelson's sensible suggestion to prefer readings from the last and most extensive revision, the "Hurst-Wakeman" copy that Poe annotated in the summer of 1849, and our text incorporates those.

The changes are not very numerous or extensive, but they do make it impossible to duplicate the page and line number system that Richard P. Benton added in his facsimile edition. So we decided, at Burton R. Pollin's suggestion, to number the paragraphs as T. O. Mabbott had done in preparation for the edition he planned. Note, however, that Poe decided to begin a new paragraph (see ¶105) in one of his penciled emendations.

Small letters in the text identify places in which our text differs from the 1848 Putnam edition or in which Poe made annotations of any sort. Lettered footnotes show what occurred at each place where alteration or note appears. See also "A Note on Variant Readings," below.

A Note on Poe's Notes

Where Poe made corrections or additions to the text, we accepted his changes, indicating each with a small raised letter that guides the reader to a comparison of alteration and original in the list of variants. Poe also added some new footnotes, most including asterisks. We accepted these as well, placing each on the page where it occurs, just as he treated his published footnotes. After each new footnote we add an explanation in parentheses. These footnotes are not listed among the variants.

Poe penciled in some notes to himself as well. We reproduce these also on the pages where they occur rather than in the variants and provide explanations in parentheses.

The note at the close of paragraph 140 is especially interesting. Nelson suggests that it is Poe's memorandum to himself. Knowing Poe's fondness for claiming to have predicted events, we think he meant to use it in a revised edition by way of bragging.

A Note on Variant Readings

Lettered footnotes identify variant readings in places in which Poe annotated his own text in order to correct typographical errors, to alter words, phrases, or paragraphing, to add new footnotes, or to jot down notes to himself. See "A Note on the Text" for an explanation of our policy for establishing a critical text.

In the lettered footnotes,

P   = The 1848 Putnam edition, available in a facsimile edition (Benton).

O   = The Osborne copy, annotated in July 1848, now in rare book department, Alderman Library, University of Virginia.

W   = The Whitman copy, annotated in October 1848, now in the Lilly Library at Indiana University.

NM = The Nelson-Mabbott copy, annotated in January and June 1849, now in the Harry Ransom Humanities Research Center at the University of Texas, Austin.

HW = The Hurst-Wakeman copy, annotated in the summer of 1849, now in the Pierpont Morgan Library in New York City.

To make the lettered footnotes as uniform and easy to use as possible, we list in each case all readings, chronologically, with the one we adopted in italics and with explanations when appropriate immediately following. For example, had Poe used "green" in Putnam, "blue" in Nelson-Mabbott, and "purple" in Hurst-Wakeman, we would select "purple," and the item would read: P green / NM blue / HW *purple*. In cases in which Poe intended italics, we add the bracketed word [italics] for clarity. In a few cases, we made changes for consistency in places which Poe and earlier editors seem to have missed. We list these here: In paragraph 209, a word Poe several times hyphenated, "cannon-ball," occurs at the line's end without a hyphen. In several places in *Eureka,* Poe restored hyphens in similar situations when the printer left them out; several times he spelled "cannon-ball" with a hyphen, so we restored it, assuming Poe missed one here. In paragraph 23, he neglected to close a quotation within a quotation; we closed it in brackets. Similarly, in paragraph 58, where Poe added capital letters on "Matter," "Attraction," and "Repulsion," he missed one, which we added in brackets.

In some cases we made decisions by analogy, looking for similar cases in Poe's fiction because the fiction has been word-indexed by Pollin (*Word Index to Poe's Fiction*). In paragraph 218: "washer-womanish" does not appear in the fiction, so it is not in Pollin's *Word Index* (its use here in *Eureka* is duly noted in Pollin, *Poe, Creator of Words*). But the similar "old-womanish" does appear in the fiction, so we retained the hyphen. In paragraph 221 we hyphenated "non-luminous." It is in Pollin's *Word Index* but not in Nelson ("Apparatus for a Definitive Edition"). It plainly should be hyphenated; it appears with a hyphen later in the same paragraph.

In paragraph 246 appears the word *climacic*. Some editors have altered it to "climactic," but because Pollin (*Poe, Creator of Words*) lists both "climacic" and "climacing," we assume that Poe coined and intended it. And in paragraph 178, Poe writes "excentrically." Although Pollin (*Word Index to Poe's Fiction*) shows that Poe usually spelled the word "eccentrically," we let the odd spelling stand because it appears in one of his sources for *Eureka*. The matter is explained in the note to paragraph 178.

For the convenience of readers using Nelson's "Apparatus for a Definitive Edition," we have also added (in parentheses) indications of places in which that list of variants seems in error and of readings he decided to reject but we reproduce as variants. Neither is intended as criticism of Nelson. The latter is simply a matter of editorial policy. And as for apparent errors: these sometimes creep in after a document has left an editor's control. Would that we could be certain our own work were without errors.

James A. Harrison's edited *Complete Works* (16:319–36) includes a listing of Poe's handwritten material from the Hurst-Wakeman copy, and Nelson warns that he "noted ten errors when comparing the Harrison [i.e., *Complete Works*] list to the actual variants as found in the Hurst-Wakeman copy" (178). Our text of *Eureka* differs from that in *Complete Works* in that when it was plain that Poe had caught an error or intended to change his published text we accepted his corrections and alterations in our text and presented the rejected published version in the Variants. Harrison, in contrast, presented the 1848 published volume as his text and reproduced the Hurst-Wakeman corrections and notes separately. He did not offer a list of handwritten material in the Osborne or Nelson-Mabbott copies.

It seemed preferable in the lettered footnotes to add a few words of explanation as needed rather than to design an elaborate code. In this way a reader can determine what are the features of a given text or passage without undue leafing back and forth.

EUREKA:

A PROSE POEM.

by

EDGAR A. POE.

New-York:

Geo. P. Putnam

of Late Firm of "Wiley & Putnam,"

155 Broadway.

MDCCCXLVIII.

Leavitt, Trow & Co Prs.
33 Ann-street

WITH VERY PROFOUND RESPECT,

This Work is Dedicated

TO

ALEXANDER VON HUMBOLDT.

PREFACE.

To the few who love me and whom I love—to those who feel rather than to those who think—to the dreamers and those who put faith in dreams as in the only realities—I offer this Book of Truths, not in its character of Truth-Teller, but for the Beauty that abounds in its Truth; constituting it true. To these I present the composition as an Art-Product alone:—let us say as a Romance; or, if I be not urging too lofty a claim, as a Poem.

What I here propound is true:—therefore it cannot die:—or if by any means it be now trodden down so that it die, it will "rise again to the Life Everlasting."

Nevertheless it is as a Poem only that I wish this work to be judged after I am dead.

E.A.P.

EUREKA:

AN ESSAY ON THE MATERIAL AND SPIRITUAL UNIVERSE

1   It is with humility really unassumed—it is with a sentiment even of awe—that I pen the opening sentence of this work;[a] for of all conceivable subjects I approach the reader with the most solemn—the most comprehensive—the most difficult—the most august.

2   What terms shall I find sufficiently simple in their sublimity—sufficiently sublime in their simplicity—for the mere enunciation of my theme?

3   I design to speak of the *Physical, Metaphysical and Mathematical—of the Material and Spiritual Universe:—of its Essence, its Origin, its Creation, its Present Condition and its Destiny.* I shall be so rash, moreover, as to challenge the conclusions, and thus, in effect, to question the sagacity, of many of the greatest and most justly reverenced of men.

4   In the beginning, let me as distinctly as possible announce—not the theorem which I hope to demonstrate—for, whatever the mathematicians may assert, there is, in this world at least, *no such thing* as demonstration—but the ruling idea which, throughout this volume, I shall be continually endeavoring to suggest.

5   My general proposition, then, is this:—*In the Original Unity of the First Thing lies the Secondary Cause of All Things, with the Germ of their Inevitable Annihilation.*

6   In illustration of this idea, I propose to take such a survey of the Universe that the mind may be able really to receive and to perceive an individual impression.

7   He who from the top of Ætna casts his eyes leisurely around, is affected chiefly by the *extent* and *diversity* of the scene. Only by a rapid whirling on his heel could he hope to comprehend the panorama in the sublimity of its *oneness*. But as, on the summit of Ætna, *no* man has thought of whirling on his heel, so no man has ever taken

a. P work: / HW *work*. See p. xxxii for explanation and key to abbreviations.

into his brain the full uniqueness of the prospect; and so, again, whatever considerations lie involved in this uniqueness, have as yet no practical existence for mankind.

8   I do not know a treatise in which a survey of the *Universe*—using the word in its most comprehensive and only legitimate acceptation—is taken at all:—and it may be as well here to mention that by the term "Universe," wherever employed without qualification in this essay, I mean in most cases[a] to designate *the utmost conceivable expanse of space, with all things, spiritual and material, that can be imagined to exist within the compass of that expanse.* In speaking of what is *ordinarily* implied by the expression, "Universe," I shall in most cases, again[b] take a phrase of limitation—"the Universe of Stars."[c] Why this distinction is considered necessary, will be seen in the sequel.

9   But even of treatises on the really limited, although always assumed as the *un*limited, Universe of *Stars,*[d] I know none in which a survey, even of this limited Universe, is so taken as to warrant deductions from its *individuality.* The nearest approach to such a work is made in the "Cosmos" of Alexander Von Humboldt. He presents the subject, however, *not* in its individuality but in its generality. His theme, in its last result, is the law of *each* portion of the merely physical Universe, as this law is related to the laws of *every other* portion of this merely physical Universe. His design is simply synœretical. In a word, he discusses the universality of material relation, and discloses to the eye of Philosophy whatever inferences have hitherto lain hidden *behind* this universality. But however admirable be the succinctness with which he has treated each particular point of his topic, the mere multiplicity of these points occasions, necessarily, an amount of detail, and thus an involution of idea, which preclude all *individuality* of impression.

10   It seems to me that, in aiming at this latter effect, and, through it, at the consequences—the conclusions—the suggestions—the speculations—or, if nothing better offer itself, the mere guesses which may result from it—we require something like a mental gyration on the heel. We need so rapid a revolution of all things about the central point of sight that, while the minutiæ vanish altogeth-

a. P mean / HW *mean in most cases*
b. P shall / HW *shall in most cases, again*
c. P stars / HW *Stars*
d. P *stars* [italics] / HW *Stars* [italics] [Nelson omits italics in both. We follow HW.]

er, even the more conspicuous objects become blended into one. Among the vanishing minutiæ, in a survey of this kind, would be all exclusively terrestrial matters. The Earth would be considered in its planetary relations alone. A man, in this view, becomes Mankind; Mankind[a] a member of the cosmical family of Intelligences.

11   And now, before proceeding to our subject proper, let me beg the reader's attention to an extract or two from a somewhat remarkable letter, which appears to have been found corked in a bottle and floating on the *Mare Tenebrarum*—an ocean well described by the Nubian geographer, Ptolemy Hephestion, but little frequented in modern days unless by the Transcendentalists and some other divers for crotchets. The date of this letter, I confess, surprises me even more particularly than its contents; for it seems to have been written in the year *two* thousand eight hundred and forty-eight. As for the passages I am about to transcribe, they, I fancy, will speak for themselves.

12   "Do you know, my dear friend," says the writer, addressing, no doubt, a contemporary—"Do you know that it is scarcely more than eight or nine hundred years ago since the metaphysicians first consented to relieve the people of the singular fancy that there exist *but two practicable roads to Truth?* Believe it if you can! It appears, however, that long, long ago, in the night of Time, there lived a Turkish philosopher called Aries and surnamed Tottle." [Here, possibly, the letter-writer means Aristotle; the best names are wretchedly corrupted in two or three thousand years.] "The fame of this great man depended mainly on[b] his demonstration that sneezing is a natural provision, by means of which over-profound thinkers are enabled to expel superfluous ideas through the nose; but he obtained a scarcely less valuable celebrity as the founder, or at all events as the principal propagator, of what was termed the *dæductive* or *à priori* philosophy. He started with what he maintained to be axioms, or self-evident truths:—and the now well understood fact that *no* truths are *self*-evident, really does not make in the slightest degree against his speculations:—it was sufficient for his purpose that the truths in question were evident at all. From axioms he proceeded, logically, to results. His most illustrious disciples were one Tuclid, a geometrician," [meaning Euclid] "and one Kant, a Dutchman, the origi-

a. P mankind; mankind / HW *Mankind; Mankind*
b. P upon / HW *on*

nator of that species of Transcendentalism which, with the change merely of a C for a K, now bears his peculiar name.

13   "Well, Aries Tottle flourished supreme, until the advent of one Hog, surnamed 'the Ettrick shepherd,' who preached an entirely different system, which he called the *à posteriori* or *in*ductive. His plan referred altogether to sensation. He proceeded by observing, analyzing, and classifying facts—*instantiæ Naturæ,* as they were somewhat affectedly called—and arranging them into general laws. In a word, while the mode of Aries rested on *noumena,* that of Hog depended on *phenomena;* and so great was the admiration excited by this latter system that, at its first introduction, Aries fell into general disrepute. Finally, however, he recovered ground, and was permitted to divide the empire of Philosophy with his more modern rival:—the savans[a] contenting themselves with proscribing all *other* competitors, past, present, and to come; putting an end to all controversy on the topic by the promulgation of a Median law, to the effect that the Aristotelian and Baconian roads are, and of right ought to be, the sole possible avenues to knowledge:—'Baconian,' you must know, my dear friend," adds the letter-writer at this point, "was an adjective invented as equivalent to Hog-ian, while[b] more dignified and euphonious.

14   "Now I do assure you most positively"—proceeds the epistle—"that I represent these matters fairly; and you can easily understand how restrictions so absurd on their very face must have operated, in those days, to retard the progress of true Science, which makes its most important advances—as all History will show—by seemingly intuitive *leaps.* These ancient ideas confined investigation to crawling; and I need not suggest to you that crawling, among varieties of locomotion, is a very capital thing of its kind;—but because the snail[c] is sure of foot, for this reason must we clip the wings of the eagles? For many centuries, so great was the infatuation, about Hog especially, that a virtual stop was put to all thinking, properly so called. No man dared utter a truth for which he felt himself indebted to his soul alone. It mattered not whether the truth was even demonstrably such; for the dogmatizing philosophers of that epoch regarded only *the road* by which it professed to have been attained. The end, with them, was a

a. P *savans.* [No variants in Poe. We include it here because some editors correct it to read *savants.* Poe does not italicize savans.]
b. P and at the same time / HW *while*
c. P tortoise / HW *snail*

point of no moment, whatever:—'the means!' they vociferated—'let us look at the means!'—and if, on scrutiny of the means, it was found to come neither under the category Hog, nor under the category Aries (which means ram), why then the savans went no farther, but, calling the thinker 'a fool'[a] and branding him a 'theorist,' would never, thenceforward, have any thing to do either with *him* or with his truths.

15   "Now, my dear friend," continues the letter-writer, "it cannot be maintained that by the crawling system, exclusively adopted, men would arrive at the maximum amount of truth, even in any long series of ages; for the repression of imagination was an evil not to be counterbalanced even by *absolute* certainty in the snail processes. But their certainty was very far from absolute. The error of our pro-genitors was quite analogous with that of the wiseacre who fancies he must necessarily see an object the more distinctly, the more closely he holds it to his eyes. They blinded themselves, too, with the impal-pable, titillating Scotch snuff of *detail;* and thus the boasted facts of the Hog-ites were by no means always facts—a point of little impor-tance but for the assumption that they always *were.* The vital taint, however, in Baconianism—its most lamentable fount of error—lay in its tendency to throw power and consideration into the hands of merely perceptive men—of those inter-Tritonic minnows, the micro-scopical savans—the diggers and pedlers of minute *facts,* for the most part in physical science—facts all of which they retailed at the same price on[b] the highway; their value depending, it was supposed, sim-ply upon the *fact of their fact,* without reference to their applicability or inapplicability in the development of those ultimate and only le-gitimate facts, called Law.

16   "Than the persons"—the letter goes on to say—"Than the persons thus suddenly elevated by the Hog-ian philosophy into a station for which they were unfitted—thus transferred from the sculleries into the parlors of Science—from its pantries into its pulpits—than these in-dividuals a more intolerant—a more intolerable set of bigots and ty-rants never existed on the face of the earth. Their creed, their text and their sermon were, alike, the one word *'fact'*—but, for the most part, even of this one word, they knew not even the meaning. On those who ventured to *disturb* their facts with the view of putting them in order

a. P a fool / HW *'a fool'*
b. P upon / HW *on*

and to use, the disciples of Hog had no mercy whatever. All attempts at generalization were met at once by the words 'theoretical,' 'theory,' 'theorist'—all *thought,* to be brief, was very properly resented as a personal affront to themselves. Cultivating the natural sciences to the exclusion of Metaphysics, the Mathematics, and Logic, many of these Bacon-engendered philosophers—one-idead, one-sided and lame of a leg—were more wretchedly helpless—more miserably ignorant, in view of all the comprehensible objects of knowledge, than the veriest unlettered hind who proves that he knows something at least, in admitting that he knows absolutely nothing.

17   "Nor had our forefathers any better right to talk about *certainty,* when pursuing, in blind confidence, the *à priori* path of axioms, or of the Ram. At innumerable points this path was scarcely as straight as a ram's-horn. The simple truth is, that the Aristotelians erected their castles on[a] a basis far less reliable than air; *for no such things as axioms ever existed or can possibly exist at all.* This they must have been very blind, indeed, not to see, or at least to suspect; for, even in their own day, many of their long-admitted 'axioms' had been abandoned:—'*ex nihilo nihil fit,*' for example, and a 'thing cannot act where it is not,' and 'there cannot be antipodes,' and 'darkness cannot proceed from light.' These and numerous similar propositions formerly accepted, without hesitation, as axioms, or undeniable truths, were, even at the period of which I speak, seen to be altogether untenable:—how absurd in these people, then, to persist in relying upon a basis, as immutable, whose mutability had become so repeatedly manifest!

18   "But, even through evidence afforded by themselves against themselves, it is easy to convict these *à priori* reasoners of the grossest unreason—it is easy to show the futility—the impalpability of their axioms in general. I have now lying before me"—it will be observed that we still proceed with the letter—"I have now lying before me a book printed about a thousand years ago. Pundit assures me that it is decidedly the cleverest ancient work on its topic, which is 'Logic.' The author, who was much esteemed in his day, was one Miller, or Mill; and we find it recorded of him, as a point of some importance, that he rode a mill-horse whom he called Jeremy Bentham:—but let us glance at the volume itself!

19   "Ah!—'Ability or inability to conceive,' says Mr. Mill very proper-

a. P upon / HW *on*

ly, 'is *in no case* to be received as a criterion of axiomatic truth.' Now, that this is a palpable truism no one in his senses will deny. *Not* to admit the proposition, is to insinuate a charge of variability in Truth itself, whose very title is a synonym of the Steadfast. If ability to conceive be taken as a criterion of Truth, then a truth to *David* Hume would very seldom be a truth to *Joe;* and ninety-nine hundredths of what is undeniable in Heaven would be demonstrable falsity upon Earth. The proposition of Mr. Mill, then, is sustained. I will not grant it to be an *axiom;* and this merely because I am showing that *no* axioms exist; but, with a distinction which could not have been cavilled at even by Mr. Mill himself, I am ready to grant that, *if* an axiom *there be,* then the proposition of which we speak has the fullest right to be considered an axiom—that no *more* absolute axiom *is*—and, consequently, that any subsequent proposition which shall conflict with this one primarily advanced, must be either a falsity in itself—that is to say no axiom—or, if admitted axiomatic, must at once neutralize both itself and its predecessor.

20   "And, now, by the logic of their own propounder, let us proceed to test any one of the axioms propounded. Let us give Mr. Mill the fairest of play. We will bring the point to no ordinary issue. We will select for investigation no common-place axiom—no axiom of what, not the less preposterously because only impliedly, he terms his secondary class—as if a positive truth by definition could be either more or less positively a truth:—we will select, I say, no axiom of an unquestionability so questionable as is to be found in Euclid. We will not talk, for example, about such propositions as that two straight lines cannot enclose a space, or that the whole is greater than any one of its parts. We will afford the logician *every* advantage. We will come at once to a proposition which he regards as the acme of the unquestionable—as the quintessence of axiomatic undeniability. Here it is:—'Contradictions cannot *both* be true—that is, cannot cöexist in nature.' Here Mr. Mill means, for instance,—and I give the most forcible instance conceivable—that a tree must be either a tree or *not* a tree—that it cannot be at the same time a tree *and* not a tree:—all which is quite reasonable of itself and will answer remarkably well as an axiom, until we bring it into collation with an axiom insisted upon a few pages before—in other words—words which I have previously employed—until we test it by the logic of its own propounder. 'A tree,' Mr. Mill asserts, 'must be either a tree or *not* a tree.' Very

well:—and now let me ask him, *why*. To this little query there is but one response:—I defy any man living to invent a second. The sole answer is this:—'Because we find it *impossible to conceive* that a tree can be any thing else than a tree or not a tree.' This, I repeat, is Mr. Mill's sole answer:—he will not *pretend* to suggest another:—and yet, by his own showing, his answer is clearly no answer at all; for has he not already required us to admit, *as an axiom,* that ability or inability to conceive is *in no case* to be taken as a criterion of axiomatic truth? Thus all—absolutely *all* his argumentation is at sea without a rudder. Let it not be urged that an exception from the general rule is to be made, in cases where the 'impossibility to conceive' is so peculiarly great as when we are called upon to conceive a tree *both* a tree and *not* a tree. Let no attempt, I say, be made at urging this sotticism; for, in the first place, there are no *degrees* of 'impossibility,' and thus no one impossible conception can be *more* peculiarly impossible than another impossible conception:—in the second place, Mr. Mill him-self, no doubt after thorough deliberation, has most distinctly, and most rationally, excluded all opportunity for exception, by the em-phasis of his proposition, that, *in no case,* is ability or inability to con-ceive, to be taken as a criterion of axiomatic truth:—in the third place, even were exceptions admissible at all, it remains to be shown how any exception is admissible *here*. That a tree can be both a tree and not a tree, is an idea which the angels, or the devils, *may* enter-tain, and which no doubt many an earthly Bedlamite, or Transcen-dentalist, *does*.

21   "Now I do not quarrel with these ancients," continues the letter-writer, *"so much* on account of the transparent frivolity of their logic—which, to be plain, was baseless, worthless and fantastic altogether—as on account of their pompous and infatuate proscription of all *other* roads to Truth than the two narrow and crooked paths—the one of creeping and the other of crawling—to which, in their ignorant perversity, they have dared to confine the Soul—the Soul which loves nothing so well as to soar in those regions of illimitable intuition which are utterly incognizant of *'path.'*

22   "By the bye, my dear friend, is it not an evidence of the mental sla-very entailed upon those bigoted people by their Hogs and Rams, that in spite of the eternal prating of their savans about *roads* to Truth, none of them fell, even by accident, into what we now so distinctly perceive to be the broadest, the straightest and most available of all

mere roads—the great thoroughfare—the majestic highway of the *Consistent?* Is it not wonderful that they should have failed to deduce from the works of God the vitally momentous consideration that *a perfect consistency can be nothing but an absolute truth?* How plain—how rapid our progress since the late announcement of this proposition! By its means, investigation has been taken out of the hands of the ground-moles, and given as a duty, rather than as a task, to the true— to the *only* true thinkers—to the generally-educated men of ardent imagination. These latter—our Keplers—our Laplaces—'speculate'— 'theorize'—these are the terms—can you not fancy the shout of scorn with which they would be received by our progenitors, were it possible for them to be looking over my shoulders as I write? The Keplers, I repeat, speculate—theorize—and their theories are merely correct-ed—reduced—sifted—cleared, little by little, of their chaff of incon-sistency—until at length there stands apparent an unencumbered *Consistency*—a consistency which the most stolid admit—because it is a consistency—to be an absolute and an unquestionable *Truth.*

23   "I have often thought, my friend, that it must have puzzled these dogmaticians of a thousand years ago, to determine, even, by which of their two boasted roads it is that the cryptographist attains the so-lution of the more complicate cyphers—or by which of them Cham-pollion guided mankind to those important and innumerable truths which, for so many centuries, have lain entombed amid the phonet-ical hieroglyphics of Egypt. In especial, would it not have given these bigots some trouble to determine by which of their two roads was reached the most momentous and sublime of *all* their truths—the truth—the fact of *gravitation?* Newton deduced it from the laws of Kepler. Kepler admitted that these laws he *guessed*—these laws whose investigation disclosed to the greatest of British astronomers that principle, the basis of all (existing) physical principle, in going be-hind which we enter at once the nebulous kingdom of Metaphysics. Yes!—these vital laws Kepler *guessed*—that is to say, he *imagined* them. Had he been asked to point out either the *de*ductive or *in*ductive route by which he attained them, his reply might have been—'I know noth-ing about *routes*—but I *do* know the machinery of the Universe. Here it is. I grasped it with *my soul*—I reached it through mere dint of *in-tuition*.['] Alas, poor ignorant old man! Could not any metaphysician have told him that what he called 'intuition' was but the conviction resulting from *de*ductions or *in*ductions of which the processes were

so shadowy as to have escaped his consciousness, eluded his reason, or bidden defiance to his capacity of expression? How great a pity it is that some 'moral philosopher' had not enlightened him about all this! How it would have comforted him on his death-bed to know that, instead of having gone intuitively and thus unbecomingly, he had, in fact, proceeded decorously and legitimately—that is to say Hog-ish-ly, or at least Ram-ishly—into the vast halls where lay gleaming, untended, and hitherto untouched by mortal hand—unseen by mortal eye—the imperishable and priceless secrets of the Universe!

24 "Yes, Kepler was essentially a *theorist;* but this title, *now* of so much sanctity, was, in those ancient days, a designation of supreme contempt. It is only *now* that men begin to appreciate that divine old man—to sympathize with the prophetical and poetical rhapsody of his ever-memorable words. For *my* part," continues the unknown correspondent, "I glow with a sacred fire when I even think of them, and feel that I shall never grow weary of their repetition:—in concluding this letter, let me have the real pleasure of transcribing them once again:— *'I care not whether my work be read now or by posterity. I can afford to wait a century for readers when God himself has waited six thousand years for an observer. I triumph. I have stolen the golden secret of the Egyptians. I will indulge my sacred fury.'"*

25 Here end my quotations from this very unaccountable if not[a] impertinent epistle; and perhaps it would be folly to comment, in any respect, upon the chimerical, not to say revolutionary, fancies of the writer—whoever he is—fancies so radically at war with the well-considered and well-settled opinions of this age. Let us proceed, then, to our legitimate thesis, *The Universe.*

26 This thesis admits a choice between two modes of discussion:— We may *a*scend[b] or *de*scend. Beginning at our own point of view— at the Earth on which we stand—we may pass to the other planets of our system—thence to the Sun—thence to our system considered collectively—and thence, through other systems, indefinitely outwards; or, commencing on high at some point as definite as we can make it or conceive it, we may come down to the habitation of Man. Usually—that is to say, in ordinary essays on Astronomy—the first of these two modes is, with certain reservation, adopted:—this for the obvious reason that astronomical *facts,* merely, and principles, being

a. P and, perhaps, somewhat / HW *if not*
b. P *a*scend / HW *a*scend [italics on *a*] [Nelson does not show italics on *a* in HW.]

the object, that object is best fulfilled in stepping from the known because proximate, gradually onward to the point where all certitude becomes lost in the remote. For my present purpose, however,—that of enabling the mind to take in, as if from afar and at one glance, a distinct conception of the *individual* Universe—it is clear that a descent to small from great—to the outskirts from the centre (if we could establish a centre)—to the end from the beginning (if we could fancy a beginning) would be the preferable course, but for the difficulty, if not impossibility, of presenting, in this course, to the unastronomical, a picture at all comprehensible in regard to such considerations as are involved in *quantity*—that is to say, in number, magnitude and distance.

27   Now, distinctness—intelligibility, at all points, is a primary feature in my general design. On important topics it is better to be a good deal prolix than even a very little obscure. But abstruseness is a quality appertaining to no subject in itself.[a] All are alike, in facility of comprehension, to him who approaches them by properly graduated steps. It is merely because a stepping-stone, here and there, is heedlessly left unsupplied in our road to the Differential Calculus, that this latter is not altogether as simple a thing as a sonnet by Mr. Solomon Seesaw.

28   By way of admitting, then, no *chance* for misapprehension, I think it advisable to proceed as if even the more obvious facts of Astronomy were unknown to the reader. In combining the two modes of discussion to which I have referred, I propose to avail myself of the advantages peculiar to each—and very especially of the *iteration in detail* which will be unavoidable as a consequence of the plan. Commencing with a descent, I shall reserve for the return upwards those indispensable considerations of *quantity* to which allusion has already been made.

29   Let us begin, then, at once, with that merest of words, "Infinity." This, like "God," "spirit," and some other expressions of which the equivalents exist in nearly[b] all languages, is by no means the expression of an idea—but of an effort at one. It stands for the possible attempt at an impossible conception. Man needed a term by which to point out the *direction* of this effort—the cloud behind which lay,

a. P *per se* [italics] / HW *in itself* [Rom.]
b. P in / HW *in nearly*

forever invisible, the *object* of this attempt. A word, in fine, was demanded, by means of which one human being might put himself in relation at once with another human being and with a certain *tendency* of the human intellect. Out of this demand arose the word, "Infinity;" which is thus the representative but of the *thought of a thought.*

30   As regards *that* infinity now considered—the infinity of space—we often hear it said that "its idea is admitted by the mind—is acquiesced in—is entertained—on account of the greater difficulty which attends the conception of a limit." But this is merely one of those *phrases* by which even profound thinkers, time out of mind, have occasionally taken pleasure in deceiving *themselves.* The quibble lies concealed in the word "difficulty." "The mind," we are told, "entertains the idea of *limitless,* through the greater *difficulty* which it finds in entertaining that of *limited,* space." Now, were the proposition but fairly *put,* its absurdity would become transparent at once. Clearly, there is no mere *difficulty* in the case. The assertion intended, if presented *according* to its intention and without sophistry, would run thus:—"The mind admits the idea of limitless, through the greater *impossibility* of entertaining that of limited, space."

31   It must be immediately seen that this is not a question of two statements between whose respective credibilities—or of two arguments between whose respective validities—the *reason* is called upon to decide:—it is a matter of two conceptions, directly conflicting, and each avowedly impossible, one of which the *intellect* is supposed to be capable of entertaining, on account of the greater *impossibility* of entertaining the other. The choice is *not* made between two difficulties;—it is merely *fancied* to be made between two impossibilities. Now of the former, there *are* degrees—but of the latter, none:—just as our impertinent letter-writer has already suggested. A task *may be* more or less difficult; but it is either possible or not possible:—there are no gradations. It might[a] be more *difficult* to overthrow the Andes than an ant-hill; but it can[b] be no more *impossible* to annihilate the matter of the one than the matter of the other. A man may jump ten feet with less *difficulty* than he can jump twenty, but the *impossi-*

a. P *might* [italics] / HW *might* [Rom.] [Poe indicates that he wants italics removed in a number of instances in HW. His proofreading method of doing so is to underscore the word to be changed and write "Rom." "Rom" or "Rom:" in the margin. We follow HW in such cases.]
b. P *can* [italics] / HW *can* [Rom. See ¶31 note a. We follow HW.]

bility of his leaping to the moon is not a whit less than that of his leaping to the dog-star.

32   Since all this is undeniable: since the choice of the mind is to be made between *impossibilities* of conception: since one impossibility cannot be greater than another: and since, thus, one cannot be preferred to another: the philosophers who not only maintain, on the grounds mentioned, man's *idea* of infinity but, on account of such supposititious idea, *infinity itself*—are plainly engaged in demonstrating one impossible thing to be possible by showing how it is that some one other thing—is impossible too. This, it will be said, is nonsense; and perhaps it is:—indeed I think it very capital nonsense—but forego all claim to it as nonsense of mine.

33   The readiest mode, however, of displaying the fallacy of the philosophical argument on this question, is by simply adverting to a *fact* respecting it which has been hitherto quite overlooked—the fact that the argument alluded to both proves and disproves its own proposition. "The mind is impelled," say the theologians and others, "to admit a *First Cause,* by the superior difficulty it experiences in conceiving cause beyond cause without end." The quibble, as before, lies in the word "difficulty"—but *here* what is it employed to sustain? A First Cause. And what is a First Cause? An ultimate termination of causes. And what is an ultimate termination of causes? Finity—the Finite. Thus the one quibble, in two processes, by God knows how many philosophers, is made to support now Finity and now Infinity— could it not be brought to support something besides? As for the quibblers—*they,* at least, are insupportable. But—to dismiss them:— what they prove in the one case is the identical nothing which they demonstrate in the other.

34   Of course, no one will suppose that I here contend for the absolute impossibility of *that* which we attempt to convey in the word "Infinity." My purpose is but to show the folly of endeavoring to prove Infinity itself, or even our conception of it, by any such blundering ratiocination as that which is ordinarily employed.

35   Nevertheless, as an individual, I may be permitted to say that *I cannot* conceive Infinity, and am convinced that no human being can. A mind not thoroughly self-conscious—not accustomed to the introspective analysis of its own operations—will, it is true, often deceive itself by supposing that it *has* entertained the conception of which we speak. In the effort to entertain it, we proceed step beyond step—

we fancy point still beyond point; and so long as we *continue* the effort, it may be said, in fact, that we are *tending* to the formation of the idea designed; while the strength of the impression that we actually form or have formed it, is in the ratio of the period during which we keep up the mental endeavor. But it is in the act of discontinuing the endeavor—of fulfilling (as we think) the idea—of putting the finishing stroke (as we suppose) to the conception—that we overthrow at once the whole fabric of our fancy by resting upon some one ultimate and therefore definite point. This fact, however, we fail to perceive, on account of the absolute coincidence, in time, between the settling down upon the ultimate point and the act of cessation in thinking.—In attempting, on the other hand, to frame the idea of a *limited* space, we merely converse the processes which involve the impossibility.

36   We *believe* in a God. We may or may not *believe* in finite or in infinite space; but our belief, in such cases, is more properly designated as *faith*, and is a matter quite distinct from that belief proper—from that *intellectual* belief—which presupposes the mental conception.

37   The fact is, that, upon the enunciation of any one of that class of terms to which "Infinity" belongs—the class representing *thoughts of thought*—he who has a right to say that he thinks *at all*, feels himself called on,[a] *not* to entertain a conception, but simply to direct his mental vision toward some given point, in the intellectual firmament, where lies a nebula never to be solved.[b] To solve it, indeed, he makes no effort; for with a rapid instinct he comprehends, not only the impossibility, but, as regards all human purposes, the *inessentiality*, of its solution. He perceives that the Deity has not *designed* it to be solved. He sees, at once, that it lies *out* of the brain of man, and even *how*, if not exactly *why*, it lies out of it. There *are* people, I am aware, who, busying themselves in attempts at the unattainable, acquire very easily, by dint of the jargon they emit, among those thinkers-that-they-think with whom darkness and depth are synonymous, a kind of cuttle-fish reputation for profundity; but the finest quality of Thought is its self-cognizance; and, with some little equivocation, it may be said that no fog of the mind can well be greater than that which, extending to the very boundaries of the mental domain, shuts out even these boundaries themselves from comprehension.

a. P upon / HW *on*
b. P resolved / HW *solved*

38   It will now be understood that, in using the phrase, "Infinity of Space," I make no call upon the reader to entertain the impossible conception of an *absolute* infinity. I refer simply to the *"utmost conceivable expanse"* of space—a shadowy and fluctuating domain, now shrinking, now swelling,[a] with the vacillating energies of the imagination.

39   Hitherto,[b] the Universe of Stars[c] has always been considered coincident[d] with the Universe proper, as I have defined it in the commencement of this Discourse. It has been always either directly or indirectly assumed—at least since the dawn of intelligible Astronomy—that, were it possible for us to attain any given point in space, we should still find, on all sides of us, an interminable succession of stars. This was the untenable idea of Pascal when making perhaps the most successful attempt ever made, at periphrasing the conception for which we struggle in the word "Universe." "It is a sphere," he says, "of which the centre is everywhere, the circumference, nowhere." But although this intended definition is, in fact, *no* definition of the Universe of *Stars*,[e] we may accept it, with some mental reservation, as a definition (rigorous enough for all practical purposes) of the Universe *proper*—that is to say, of the Universe of *space*. This latter, then, let us regard as *"a sphere of which the centre is everywhere, the circumference nowhere."* In fact, while we find it impossible to fancy an end[f] to space, we have no difficulty in picturing to ourselves any one of an infinity of beginnings.[g]

40   As our starting-point, then, let us adopt the *Godhead*. Of this Godhead, *in itself,* he alone is not imbecile—he alone is not impious who propounds——nothing. *"Nous ne connaissons rien,"* says the Baron de Bielfeld— *"Nous ne connaissons rien de la nature ou de l'essence de Dieu:— pour savoir ce qu'il est, il faut être Dieu même."*—"We know absolutely *nothing* of the nature or essence of God:—in order to comprehend what he is, we should have to be God ourselves."

41   *"We should have to be God ourselves!"*—With a phrase so startling as

a. P swelling, in accordance / HW *swelling,*
b. P *Hitherto* [italics] / HW *Hitherto* [Rom. See ¶31, note a. We follow HW.]
c. P stars / HW *Stars*
d. P as coincident / NM, HW *coincident.* [But see ¶59, note i; Poe seems to have preferred cöincident but to have been inconsistent.]
e. P *stars* [italics] / HW *Stars* [italics] [We follow HW.]
f. P *end* [italics] / HW *end* [Rom. See ¶31, note a. We follow HW.]
g. P *beginnings* [italics] / HW *beginnings* [Rom. See ¶31, note a. We follow HW.]

this yet ringing in my ears, I nevertheless venture to demand if this our present ignorance of the Deity is an ignorance to which the soul is *everlastingly* condemned.

42   By *Him,* however—*now,* at least, the Incomprehensible—by Him—assuming him as *Spirit*—that is to say, as *not Matter*—a distinction which, for all intelligible purposes, will stand well instead of a definition—by Him, then, existing as Spirit, let us content ourselves[a] with supposing to have been *created,* or made out of Nothing, by dint of his Volition—at some point of Space which we will take as a centre—at some period into which we do not pretend to inquire, but at all events immensely remote—by Him, then again, let us suppose to have been created——*what?* This is a vitally momentous epoch in our considerations. *What* is it that we are justified—that alone we are justified in supposing to have been[b] primarily[c] *created?*

43   We have attained a point where only *Intuition* can aid us:—but now let me recur to the idea which I have already suggested as that alone which we can properly entertain of intuition. It is but *the conviction arising from those inductions or deductions of which the processes are so shadowy as to escape our consciousness, elude our reason, or defy our capacity of expression.* With this understanding, I now assert—that an intuition altogether irresistible, although inexpressible, forces me to the conclusion that what God originally created—that that Matter which, by dint of his Volition, he first made from his Spirit, or from Nihility, *could* have been nothing but Matter in its utmost conceivable state of——what?—of *Simplicity.*[d]

44   This will be found the sole absolute *assumption* of my Discourse. I use the word "assumption" in its ordinary sense; yet I maintain that even this my primary proposition, is[e] very far indeed[f] from being really a mere assumption. Nothing was ever more certainly—no human conclusion was ever, in fact, more regularly—more rigorously *de*duced:—but, alas! the processes lie out of the human analysis—at all events are beyond the utterance of the human tongue. If, however, in the course of this Essay, I succeed in showing that, out of Matter in its extreme of Simplicity, all things *might* have been con-

---

a. P ourselves, to-night, / NM, HW *ourselves*
b. P been, / HW *been*
c. P and solely, / HW [*deleted*]
d. P *Simplicity?* [italics] / NM, HW *Simplicity.* [italics] [We follow HW.]
e. P is very, / HW *is*
f. P indeed, / HW *indeed*

structed, we reach directly the inference that they *were* thus constructed, through the impossibility of attributing supererogation to Omnipotence.[a]

45   Let us now endeavor to conceive what Matter must be, when, or if, in its absolute extreme of *Simplicity*. Here the Reason flies at once to Imparticularity—to a particle—to *one* particle—a particle of *one* kind—of *one* character—of *one* nature—of *one size*—of one form— a particle, therefore, *"without* form and void"—a particle positively a particle at all points—a particle absolutely unique, individual, undivided, and not indivisible only because He who *created* it, by dint of his Will, can by an infinitely less energetic exercise of the same Will, as a matter of course, divide it.

46   *Oneness,* then, is all that I predicate of the originally created Matter; but I propose to show that this *Oneness is a principle abundantly sufficient to account for the constitution, the existing phænomena and the plainly inevitable annihilation of at least the material Universe.*

47   The willing into being the primordial Particle,[b] has completed the act, or more properly the *conception,* of Creation. We now proceed to the ultimate purpose for which we are to suppose the Particle created—that is to say, the ultimate purpose so far as our considerations *yet* enable us to see it—the constitution of the Universe from it, the Particle.

48   This constitution has been effected by *forcing* the originally and therefore normally *One* into the abnormal condition of *Many*. An action of this character implies rëaction. A diffusion from Unity, under the conditions, involves a tendency to return into Unity—a tendency ineradicable until satisfied. But on these points I will speak more fully hereafter.

49   The assumption of absolute Unity in the primordial Particle includes that of infinite divisibility.[*c] Let us conceive the Particle, then, to be only not totally exhausted by diffusion into Space. From the

---

*Show this in another edition. [Poe's handwritten memo, HW.]

a. P tongue. / HW tongue. *If, however, in the course of this Essay, I succeed in showing that, out of Matter in its extreme of Simplicity, all things might* [italics] *have been constructed, we reach directly the inference that they were* [italics] *thus constructed, through the impossibility of attributing supererogation to Omnipotence.* [The Nelson entry omits the comma after "If," does not capitalize "Essay," and does not put *might* and *were* in italics. Poe himself wrote and then crossed out, after "Simplicity," the following: "or out of of an absolute Particle,"]
b. P particle, / HW *Particle,*
c. P divisibility. / HW *divisibility*.* [Poe added asterisk and note.]

one Particle, as a centre, let us suppose to be radiated[a] spherically—in all directions—to immeasurable but still to definite distances in the previously vacant Space[b]—a certain inexpressibly great yet limited number of unimaginably yet not infinitely minute atoms.

50   Now, of these atoms, thus diffused, or on[c] diffusion, what conditions are we permitted—not to assume, but to infer, from consideration as well of their source as of the character of the design apparent in their diffusion? *Unity* being their source, and *difference from Unity* the character of the design manifested in their diffusion, we are warranted in supposing this character to be at least generally[d] preserved throughout the design, and to form a portion of the design itself:—that is to say, we shall be warranted in conceiving continual differences at all points from the uniquity and simplicity of the origin. But, for these reasons, shall we be justified in imagining the atoms heterogeneous, dissimilar, unequal, and inequidistant? More explicitly—are we to consider no two atoms as, at their diffusion, of the same nature, or of the same form, or of the same size?—and, after fulfilment of their diffusion into Space, is absolute inequidistance, each from each, to be understood of all of them? In such arrangement, under such conditions, we most easily and immediately comprehend the subsequent most feasible carrying out to completion of any such design as that which I have suggested—the design of multiplicity[e] out of unity—diversity out of sameness—heterogeneity out of homogeneity—complexity out of simplicity—in a word, the utmost possible multiplicity of *relation* out of the emphatically irrelative *One*. Undoubtedly, therefore, we *should* be warranted in assuming all that has been mentioned, but for the reflection, first, that supererogation is not presumable of any Divine Act; and, secondly, that the object supposed in view, appears as feasible when some of the conditions in question are dispensed with, in the beginning, as when all are understood immediately to exist. I mean to say that some are involved in the rest, or so instantaneous a consequence of them as to make the distinction inappreciable. Difference of *size,* for example, will at once be brought about through the tendency of one

---

a. P irradiated / NM, HW *radiated*
b. P space / HW *Space*
c. P upon / HW *on*
d. P *generally* [italics] / HW *generally* [Rom.] See ¶31, note a.
e. P variety / HW *multiplicity*

atom to a second, in preference to a third, on account of particular inequidistance; which is to be comprehended as *particular inequidistances between centres of quantity, in neighboring atoms of different form*—a matter not at all interfering with the generally-equable distribution of the atoms. Difference of *kind,* too, is easily conceived to be merely a result of differences in size and form, taken more or less conjointly:—in fact, since the *Unity* of the Particle Proper implies absolute homogeneity, we cannot imagine the atoms, at their diffusion, differing in kind, without imagining, at the same time, a special exercise of the Divine Will, at the emission of each atom, for the purpose of effecting, in each, a change of its essential nature:—and[a] so fantastic an idea is the less to be indulged, as the object proposed is seen to be thoroughly attainable without such minute and elaborate interposition. We perceive, therefore, on[b] the whole, that it would be supererogatory, and consequently unphilosophical, to predicate of the atoms, in view of their purposes, any thing more than *difference of form* at their dispersion, with particular inequidistance after it—all other differences arising at once out of these, in the very first processes of mass-constitution:—We thus establish the Universe on a purely *geometrical* basis. Of course, it is by no means necessary to assume absolute difference, even of form, among *all* the atoms radiated[c]—any more than absolute particular inequidistance of each from each. We are required to conceive merely that no *neighboring* atoms are of similar form—no atoms which can ever approximate, until their inevitable rëunion at the end.

51   Although the immediate and perpetual *tendency* of the disunited atoms to return into their normal Unity, is implied, as I have said, in their abnormal diffusion; still it is clear that this tendency will be without consequence—a tendency and no more—until the diffusive energy, in ceasing to be exerted, shall leave *it,* the tendency, free to seek its satisfaction. The Divine Act, however, being considered as determinate, and discontinued on fulfilment of the diffusion, we understand, at once, a *rëaction*—in other words, a *satisfiable* tendency of the disunited atoms to return into *One.*

52   But the diffusive energy being withdrawn, and the rëaction having commenced in furtherance of the ultimate design—*that of the*

a. P nature:—so /HW *nature:—and so*
b. P upon / HW *on*
c. P irradiated / NM, HW *radiated*

utmost possible Relation—this design is now in danger of being frustrated, in detail, by reason of that very tendency to return which is to effect its accomplishment in general. *Multiplicity* is the object; but there is nothing to prevent proximate atoms, from lapsing *at once,* through the now satisfiable tendency—*before* the fulfilment of any ends proposed in multiplicity—into absolute oneness among themselves:—there is nothing to impede the aggregation of various *unique* masses, at various points of space:—in other words, nothing to interfere with the accumulation of various masses, each absolutely One.

53   For the effectual[a] completion of the general design, we thus see the necessity for a repulsion of limited capacity—a separative *something* which, on withdrawal of the diffusive Volition, shall at the same time allow the approach, and forbid the junction, of the atoms; suffering them infinitely to approximate, while denying them positive contact; in a word, having the power—*up to a certain epoch*—of preventing their *coalition,* but no ability to interfere with their *coalescence* in any respect *or degree.* The repulsion, already considered as so peculiarly limited in other regards, must be understood, let me repeat, as having power to prevent absolute coalition, *only up to a certain epoch.* Unless we are to conceive that the appetite for Unity among the atoms is doomed to be satisfied *never;*—unless we are to conceive that what had a beginning is to have no end—a conception which cannot *really* be entertained, however much we may talk or dream of entertaining it—we are forced to conclude that the repulsive influence imagined, will, finally—under pressure of the Uni-tendency[b] *collectively* applied, but never and in no degree *until,* on fulfilment of the Divine purposes, such collective application shall be naturally made—yield to a force which, at that ultimate epoch, shall be the superior force precisely to the extent required, and thus permit the universal subsidence into the inevitable, because original and therefore normal, *One.*[c] The conditions here to be reconciled are difficult indeed:—we cannot even comprehend the possibility of their conciliation;—nevertheless, the apparent impossibility is brilliantly suggestive.

54   That the repulsive something actually exists, *we see.* Man neither

a. P effectual and thorough / HW *effectual*

b. P *Uni-tendency* [italics] / NM, HW *Uni-tendency* [Rom.; See ¶31, note a. Hyphen at end of line. We retain it because Poe often hyphenated such words: see Pollin, *Word Index.*]

c. P *One.*— [italics] / HW *One.* [italics] [Both P and HW are in italics; Poe deleted the dash. Nelson does not show italics on P. We follow HW.]

employs, nor knows, a force sufficient to bring two atoms into contact. This is but the well-established proposition of the impenetrability of matter. All Experiment proves—all Philosophy admits it. The *design* of the repulsion—the necessity for its existence—I have endeavored to show; but from all attempt at investigating its nature have religiously abstained; this on account of an intuitive conviction that the principle at issue is strictly spiritual—lies in a recess impervious to our present understanding—lies involved in a consideration of what now—in our human state—is *not* to be considered—in a consideration of *Spirit in itself.* I feel, in a word, that here the God has interposed, and here only, because here and here only the knot demanded the interposition of the God.

55   In fact, while the tendency of the diffused atoms to return into Unity, will be recognized, at once, as the principle of the Newtonian Gravity, what I have spoken of as a repulsive influence prescribing limits to the (immediate) satisfaction of the tendency, will be understood as *that* which we have been in the practice of designating now as heat, now as magnetism, now as *electricity;* displaying our ignorance of its awful character in the vacillation of the phraseology with which we endeavor to circumscribe it.

56   Calling it, merely for the moment, electricity, we know that all experimental analysis of electricity has given, as an ultimate result, the principle, or seeming principle, *heterogeneity. Only* where things differ is electricity apparent; and it is presumable that they *never* differ where it is not developed at least, if not apparent. Now, this result is in the fullest keeping with that which I have reached unempirically. The design of the repulsive influence I have suggested[a] to be that of preventing immediate Unity among the diffused atoms; and these atoms are represented as different each from each. *Difference* is their character—their essentiality—just as *no-difference* was the essentiality of their source. When we say, then, that an attempt to bring any two of these atoms together would induce an effort, on the part of the repulsive influence, to prevent the contact, we may as well use the strictly convertible sentence that an attempt to bring together any two differences will result in a development of electricity. All existing bodies, of course, are composed of these atoms in proximate contact, and are therefore to be considered as mere assemblages of

a. P maintained / HW *suggested*

more or fewer differences; and the resistance made by the repulsive spirit, on bringing together any two such assemblages, would be in the ratio of the two sums of the differences in each:—an expression which, when reduced, is equivalent to this:—*The amount of electricity developed on the approximation of two bodies, is proportional with*[a] *the difference between the respective sums of the atoms of which the bodies are composed.* That *no* two bodies are absolutely alike, is a simple corollary from all that has been here said. Electricity, therefore, existing always, is *developed* whenever *any* bodies, but *manifested* only when bodies of appreciable difference, are brought into approximation.

57 To electricity—so, for the present, continuing to call it—we *may* not be wrong in referring the various physical appearances of light, heat and magnetism; but far less shall we be liable to err in attributing to this strictly spiritual principle the more important phænomena of vitality, consciousness and *Thought.* On this topic, however, I need pause *here* merely to suggest that these phænomena, whether observed generally or in detail, seem to proceed *at least in the ratio of the heterogeneous.*

58 Discarding now the two equivocal terms, "gravitation" and "electricity," let us adopt the more definite expressions, *"Attraction"*[b] and *"Repulsion."*[c] The former is the body; the latter the soul: the one is the material; the other the spiritual, principle of the Universe. *No other principles exist. All* phænomena are referable to one, or to the other, or to both combined. So rigorously is this the case—so thoroughly demonstrable is it that Attraction[d] and Repulsion[e] are the *sole* properties through which we perceive the Universe—in other words, by which Matter is manifested to Mind—that, for all merely argumentative purposes, we are fully justified in assuming that Matter[f] *exists* only as Attraction[g] and Repulsion[h]—that Attraction[i] and Repulsion[j] *are* [M]atter:—there being no conceivable case in

a. P to / NM, HW *with*
b. P *"attraction"* [italics] / HW *"Attraction"* [italics] [We follow HW.]
c. P *"repulsion"* [italics] / HW *"Repulsion"* [italics] [We follow HW.]
d. P attraction / HW *Attraction*
e. P repulsion / HW *Repulsion*
f. P matter / HW *Matter*
g. P attraction / HW *Attraction*
h. P repulsion / HW *Repulsion*
i. P attraction / HW *Attraction*
j. P repulsion / HW *Repulsion*

which we may not employ the term "Matter"[a] and the terms "Attraction"[b] and "Repulsion,"[c] taken together, as equivalent, and therefore convertible, expressions in Logic.

59   I said, just now, that what I have described as the tendency of the diffused atoms to return into their original Unity,[d] would be understood as the principle of the Newtonian law of Gravity:[e] and, in fact, there can be little difficulty in such an understanding, if we look at the Newtonian Gravity[f] in a merely general view, as a force impelling Matter[g] to seek Matter;[h] that is to say, when we pay no attention to the known *modus operandi* of the Newtonian force. The general cöincidence[i] satisfies us; but, on[j] looking closely, we see, in detail, much that appears *in*cöincident,[k] and much in regard to which no cöincidence,[l] at least, is established. For example; the Newtonian Gravity,[m] when we think of it in certain moods, does *not* seem to be a tendency to *oneness* at all, but rather a tendency of all bodies in all directions—a phrase apparently expressive of a tendency to diffusion. Here, then, is an *in*cöincidence.[n] Again; when we reflect on the mathematical *law* governing the Newtonian tendency, we see clearly that no cöincidence[o] has been made good, in respect of the *modus operandi*, at least, between Gravity[p] as known to exist and that seemingly simple and direct tendency which I have assumed.

60   In fact, I have attained a point at which it will be advisable to strengthen my position by reversing my processes. So far, we have gone on *à priori*, from an abstract consideration of *Simplicity,* as that quality most likely to have characterized the original action of God.

---

a. P matter / HW *Matter*
b. P attraction / HW *Attraction*
c. P repulsion / HW *Repulsion*
d. P unity / HW *Unity*
e. P gravity / HW *Gravity*
f. P gravity / HW *Gravity*
g. P matter / HW *Matter*
h. P matter / HW *Matter*
i. P coincidence / HW *cöincidence*
j. P upon / HW *on*
k. P *in*coincident [*in* italicized] / HW *in*cöincident [*in* italicized] [We follow HW.]
l. P coincidence / HW *cöincidence*
m. P gravity / HW *Gravity*
n. P *in*coincidence [*in* italicized] / HW *in*cöincidence [*in* italicized] [We follow HW.]
o. P coincidence / HW *cöincidence*
p. P gravitation / HW *Gravity*

Let us now see whether the established facts of the Newtonian Gravitation may not afford us, *à posteriori,* some legitimate inductions.

61   What does the Newtonian law declare?—That all bodies attract each other with forces proportional with[a] their quantities of matter and inversely proportional with[b] the squares of their distances. Purposely, I have here given, in the first place, the vulgar version of the law; and I confess that in this, as in most other vulgar versions of great truths, we find little of a suggestive character. Let us now adopt a more philosophical phraseology:—*Every atom, of every body, attracts every other atom, both of its own and of every other body, with a force which varies inversely as the squares of the distances between the attracting and attracted atom.*—Here, indeed, a flood of suggestion bursts upon the mind.

62   But let us see distinctly what it was that Newton *proved*—according to the grossly irrational definitions of *proof* prescribed by the metaphysical schools. He was forced to content himself with showing how thoroughly the motions of an imaginary Universe, composed of attracting and attracted atoms obedient to the law he announced, coincide with those of the actually existing Universe so far as it comes under our observation. This was the amount of his *demonstration*—that is to say, this was the amount of it, according to the conventional cant of the "philosophies." His successors[c] added proof multiplied by proof—such proof as a sound intellect admits—but the *demonstration* of the law itself, persist the metaphysicians, had not been strengthened in any degree. *"Ocular, physical* proof," however, of Attraction,[d] here upon Earth, in accordance with the Newtonian theory, was, at length, much to the satisfaction of some intellectual grovellers, afforded. This proof arose collaterally and incidentally (as nearly all important truths have arisen) out of an attempt to ascertain the mean density of the Earth. In the famous Maskelyne, Cavendish and Bailly experiments for this purpose, the attraction of the mass of a mountain*[e] was seen, felt, measured, and found to be mathematically consistent with the theory[f] of the British astronomer.

63   But in spite of this confirmation of that which needed none—in

---

*Schehallien, in Wales. [New footnote inscribed in pencil, HW.]

a. P to / NM, HW *with*
b. P to / NM, HW *with*
c. P successes / O, W, NM successor [Nelson rejects this reading.] / HW *successors*
d. P attraction / HW *Attraction*
e. P *mountain.* / HW *mountain** [Poe added asterisk and note.]
f. P immortal theory / HW *theory*

spite of the so-called corroboration of the "theory" by the so-called "ocular and physical proof"—in spite of the *character* of this corroboration—the ideas which even really philosophical men cannot help imbibing of Gravity[a]—and, especially, the ideas of it which ordinary men get and contentedly maintain, are *seen* to have been derived, for the most part, from a consideration of the principle as they find it developed—*merely in the planet on*[b] *which they stand.*

64   Now, to what does so partial a consideration tend—to what species of error does it give rise? On the Earth we *see* and *feel*, only that Gravity[c] impels all bodies towards the *centre* of the Earth. No man in the common walks of life could be *made* to see or to feel anything else—could be made to perceive that anything, anywhere, has a perpetual, gravitating tendency in *other* direction than to the centre of the Earth; yet (with an exception hereafter to be specified) it is a fact that every earthly thing (not to speak now of every heavenly thing) has a tendency not *only* to the Earth's centre but in every conceivable direction besides.

65   Now, although the philosophic cannot be said to *err with* the vulgar in this matter, they nevertheless permit themselves to be influenced, without knowing it, by the *sentiment* of the vulgar idea. "Although the Pagan fables are not believed," says Bryant, in his very erudite "Mythology," "yet we forget ourselves continually and make inferences from them as from existing realities." I mean to assert that the merely *sensitive perception* of Gravity[d] as we experience it on Earth, beguiles mankind into the fancy of *concentralization* or *especiality* respecting it—has been continually biasing towards this fancy even the mightiest intellects—perpetually, although imperceptibly, leading them away from the real characteristics of the principle; thus preventing them, up to this date, from ever getting a glimpse of that vital truth which lies in a diametrically opposite direction—behind the principle's *essential* characteristics—those, *not* of concentralization or especiality—but of *universality* and *diffusion*. This "vital truth" is *Unity* as the *source* of the phænomenon.

66   Let me now repeat the definition of Gravity:[e]—*Every atom, of every*

---

a. P gravity / HW *Gravity*
b. P upon / HW *on* [italics]
c. P gravity / HW *Gravity*
d. P gravity / HW *Gravity*
e. P gravity / HW *Gravity*

body, attracts every other atom, both of its own and of every other body, with a force which varies inversely as the squares of the distances of the attracting and attracted atom.

67   Here let the reader pause with me, for a moment, in contemplation of the miraculous—of the ineffable—of the altogether unimaginable complexity of relation involved in the fact that *each atom attracts every other atom*—involved merely in this fact of the Attraction,[a] without reference to the law or mode in which the Attraction[b] is manifested—involved *merely* in the fact that each atom attracts every other atom *at all,* in a wilderness of atoms so numerous that those which go to the composition of a cannon-ball, exceed, probably, in mere point of number, all the stars which go to the constitution of the Universe.

68   Had we discovered, simply, that each atom tends[c] to some one favorite point, a favorite with all[d]—to some especially attractive atom—we should still have fallen upon a discovery which, in itself, would have sufficed to overwhelm the mind:—but what is it that we are actually called on[e] to comprehend? That each atom attracts—sympathizes with the most delicate movements of every other atom, and with each and with all at the same time, and forever, and according to a determinate law of which the complexity, even considered by itself solely, is utterly beyond the grasp of the imagination.[f] If I propose to ascertain the influence of one mote in a sunbeam on[g] its neighboring mote, I cannot accomplish my purpose without first counting and weighing all the atoms in the Universe and defining the precise positions of all at one particular moment.[h] If I venture to displace, by even the billionth of a part of an inch, the microscopical speck of dust which lies now on[i] the point of my finger, what is the character of that act upon which I have adventured? I have done a deed which shakes the Moon in her path, which causes the Sun to be no longer the Sun, and which alters forever the destiny of the multitudinous myriads of stars that roll and glow in the majestic presence of their Creator.

a. P attraction / HW *Attraction*
b. P attraction / HW *Attraction*
c. P tended / HW *tends*
d. P favorite point—to some especially attractive atom / HW *point, a favorite with all*
e. P upon / HW *on*
f. P imagination of man / HW *imagination*
g. P upon / HW *on*
h. P moment / NM, HW *moment*
i. P upon / HW *on*

69   *These* ideas—conceptions such as *these*—unthoughtlike thoughts—soul-reveries rather than conclusions or even considerations of the intellect:—ideas, I repeat, such as these, are such as we can alone hope profitably to entertain in any effort at grasping the great principle, *Attraction.*

70   But now,—*with* such ideas—with such a *vision* of the marvellous complexity of Attraction fairly in his mind—let any person competent of thought on such topics as these, set himself to the task of imagining a *principle* for the phænomena observed—a condition from which they sprang.

71   Does not so evident a brotherhood among the atoms point to a common parentage? Does not a sympathy so omniprevalent, so ineradicable, and so thoroughly irrespective, suggest a common paternity as its source? Does not one extreme impel the reason to the other? Does not the infinitude of division refer to the utterness of individuality? Does not the entireness of the complex hint at the perfection of the simple? It is *not* that the atoms, as we see them, are divided or that they are complex in their relations—but that they are inconceivably divided and unutterably complex:—it is the extremeness of the conditions to which I now allude, rather than to the conditions themselves. In a word, is it not because the atoms were, at some remote epoch of time, even *more than together*—is it not because originally, and therefore normally, they were *One*—that now, in all circumstances—at all points—in all directions—by all modes of approach—in all relations and through all conditions—they struggle *back* to this absolutely, this irrelatively, this unconditionally *One?*[a]

72   Some person may here demand:—"Why—since it is to the *One* that the atoms struggle back—do we not find and define Attraction as merely 'a[b] general tendency to a centre?'—why, in especial, do not *your* atoms—the atoms which you describe as having been radiated[c] from a centre—proceed at once, rectilinearly, back to the central point of their origin?"

73   I reply that *they do;* as will be distinctly shown; but that the cause of their so doing is quite irrespective of the centre *as such.* They all tend rectilinearly towards a centre, because of the sphericity[d] with which

a. P *one?* [italics] / HW *One?* [italics] [We follow HW.]
b. P 'a merely general / HW *as merely* 'a *general*
c. P irradiated / NM, HW *radiated*
d. P sphereicity / NM, HW *sphericity*

they have been radiated[a] into space. Each atom, forming one of a generally uniform globe of atoms, finds more atoms in the direction of the centre, of course, than in any other, and in that direction, therefore, is impelled—but is *not* thus impelled because the centre is *the point of its origin.* It is not to any *point* that the atoms are allied. It is not any *locality,* either in the concrete or in the abstract, to which I suppose them bound. Nothing like *location* was conceived as their origin. Their source lies in the principle, *Unity. This* is their lost parent. *This* they seek always—immediately—in all directions—wherever it is even partially to be found; thus appeasing, in some measure, the ineradicable tendency, while on the way to its absolute satisfaction in the end. It follows from all this, that any principle which shall be adequate to account for the *law,* or *modus operandi,* of the attractive force in general, will account for this law in particular:—that is to say, any principle which will show why the atoms should tend to their *general centre of radiation*[b] with forces inversely proportional with[c] the squares of the distances, will be admitted as satisfactorily accounting, at the same time, for the tendency, according to the same law, of these atoms each to each:—*for* the tendency to the centre *is* merely the tendency each to each, and not any tendency to a centre as such.—Thus it will be seen, also, that the establishment of my propositions would involve no *necessity* of modification in the terms of the Newtonian definition of Gravity, which declares that each atom attracts each other atom and so forth, and declares this merely; but (always under the supposition that what I propose be, in the end, admitted) it seems clear that some error might occasionally be avoided, in the future processes of Science, were a more ample phraseology adopted:—for instance:—"Each atom tends to every other atom &c. with a force &c.: *the general result being a tendency of all, with a similar force, to a general centre.*"

74   The reversal of our processes has thus brought us to an identical result; but, while in the one process *Intuition*[d] was the starting-point, in the other it was the goal. In commencing the former journey I could only say that, with an irresistible Intuition,[e] I *felt* Simplicity to have been the characteristic of the original action of God:—in ending the latter

a. P irradiated / NM, HW *radiated*
b. P *irradiation* [italics] / NM, HW *radiation* [italics] [We follow HW.]
c. P to / NM, HW *with*
d. P *intuition* [italics] / HW *Intuition* [italics] [We follow HW.]
e. P intuition / HW *Intuition*

I can only declare that, with an irresistible Intuition,[a] I perceive Unity to have been the source of the observed phænomena of the Newtonian Gravity.[b] Thus, according to the schools, I *prove* nothing. So be it:—I design but to suggest—and to *convince* through the suggestion. I am proudly aware that there exist many of the most profound and cautiously discriminative intellects[c] which cannot *help* being abundantly content with my—suggestions. To these intellects—as to my own—there is no mathematical demonstration which *could* bring the least additional *true proof* of the great *Truth* which I have advanced—*the truth of Original Unity as the source—as the principle of the Universal Phænomena.* For my part, I am not so sure that I speak and see—I am not so sure that my heart beats and that my soul lives:—of the rising of to-morrow's sun—a probability that as yet lies in the Future—I do not pretend to be one thousandth part as sure—as I am of the irretrievably by-gone *Fact* that All Things and All Thoughts of Things, with all their ineffable Multiplicity of Relation, sprang at once into being from the primordial and irrelative *One.*

75   Referring to the Newtonian Gravity, Dr. Nichol, the eloquent author of "The Architecture of the Heavens," says:—"In truth we have no reason to suppose this great Law, as now revealed, to be the ultimate or simplest, and therefore the universal and all-comprehensive, form of a great Ordinance. The mode in which its intensity diminishes with the element of distance, has not the aspect of an ultimate *principle;* which always assumes the simplicity and self-evidence of those axioms which constitute the basis of Geometry."

76   Now, it is quite true that "ultimate principles," in the common understanding of the words, always assume the simplicity of geometrical axioms—(as for "self-evidence," there is no such thing)—but these principles are clearly *not* "ultimate;" in other terms what we are in the habit of calling principles are no principles, properly speaking—since there can be but one *principle,* the Volition of God. We have no right to assume, then, from what we observe in rules that we choose foolishly to name "principles," anything at all in respect to the characteristics of a principle proper. The "ultimate principles" of which Dr. Nichol speaks as having geometrical simplicity, may and do have this geometrical turn, as being part and parcel of a vast geometrical sys-

a. P intuition / HW *Intuition*
b. P gravitation / HW *Gravity*
c. P discriminative human intellects / HW *discriminative intellects*

tem, and thus a system of simplicity itself—in which, nevertheless, the *truly* ultimate principle is, *as we know,* the consummation of the complex—that is to say, of the unintelligible—for is it not the Spiritual Capacity of God?

77   I quoted Dr. Nichol's remark, however, not so much to question its philosophy, as by way of calling attention to the fact that, while all men have admitted *some* principle as existing behind the Law of Gravity, no attempt has been yet made to point out what this principle in particular *is:*—if we except, perhaps, occasional fantastic efforts at referring it to Magnetism, or Mesmerism, or Swedenborgianism, or Transcendentalism, or some other equally delicious *ism* of the same species, and invariably patronized by one and the same species of people. The great mind of Newton, while boldly grasping the Law itself, shrank from the principle of the Law. The more fluent and comprehensive at least, if not the more patient and profound, sagacity of Laplace, had not the courage to attack it. But hesitation on the part of these two astronomers it is, perhaps, not so very difficult to understand. They, as well as all the first class of mathematicians, were mathematicians *solely:*—their intellect, at least, had a firmly-pronounced mathematico-physical tone. What lay not distinctly within the domain of Physics, or of Mathematics, seemed to them either Non-Entity or Shadow. Nevertheless, we may well wonder that Leibnitz, who was a marked exception to the general rule in these respects, and whose mental temperament was a singular admixture of the mathematical with the physico-metaphysical, did not at once investigate and establish the point at issue. Either Newton or Laplace, seeking a principle and discovering none *physical,* would have rested contentedly in the conclusion that there was absolutely none; but it is almost impossible to fancy, of Leibnitz, that, having exhausted in his search the physical dominions, he would not have stepped at once, boldly and hopefully, amid his old familiar haunts in the kingdom of Metaphysics. Here, indeed, it is clear that he *must* have adventured in search of the treasure:—that he did not find it after all, was, perhaps, because his fairy guide, Imagination, was not sufficiently well-grown, or well-educated, to direct him aright.

78   I observed, just now, that, in fact, there had been certain vague attempts at referring Gravity to some very uncertain *isms.* These attempts, however, although considered bold and justly so considered,

looked no farther than to the generality—the merest generality—
of the Newtonian Law. Its *modus operandi* has never, to my knowledge,
been approached in the way of an effort at explanation. It is, there-
fore, with no unwarranted fear of being taken for a madman at the
outset, and before I can bring my propositions fairly to the eye of
those who alone are competent to decide on[a] them, that I here de-
clare the *modus operandi* of the Law of Gravity to be an exceedingly
simple and perfectly explicable thing—that is to say, when we make
our advances towards it in just gradations and in the true direction—
when we regard it from the proper point of view.

79   Whether we reach the idea of absolute *Unity* as the source of All
Things, from a consideration of Simplicity as the most probable
characteristic of the original action of God;—whether we arrive at
it from an inspection of the universality of relation in the gravitat-
ing phænomena;—or whether we attain it as a result of the mutual
corroboration afforded by both processes;—still, the idea itself, if
entertained at all, is entertained in inseparable connection with
another idea—that of the condition of the Universe of Stars[b] as we
now perceive it—that is to say, a condition of immeasurable *diffusion*
through space. Now a connection between these two ideas—unity
and diffusion—cannot be established unless through the entertain-
ment of a third idea—that of *radiation*.[c] Absolute Unity being taken
as a centre, then the existing Universe of Stars[d] is the result of *radi-
ation*[e] from that centre.

80   Now, the laws of radiation[f] are *known*. They are part and parcel
of the *sphere*. They belong to the class of indisputable geometrical
properties.[g] We say of them, "they are true—they are evident." To
demand *why* they are true, would be to demand why the axioms are
true upon which their demonstration is based. Nothing[h] is demon-
strable, strictly speaking; but if[i] anything *be*, then the properties—
the laws in question are demonstrated.

a. P upon / HW *on*
b. P stars / HW *Stars*
c. P *irradiation* [italics] / NM, HW *radiation* [italics] [We follow HW.]
d. P stars / HW *Stars*
e. P *irradiation* [italics] / NM, HW *radiation* [italics] [We follow HW.]
f. P irradiation / NM, HW *radiation*
g. P *indisputable geometrical properties* [italics] / HW *indisputable geometrical properties* [Rom. See ¶31,
note a.]
h. P *Nothing* [italics] / HW *Nothing* [Rom. See ¶31, note a. We follow HW.]
i. P *if* [italics] / HW *if* [Rom. See ¶31, note a. We follow HW.]

81   But these laws—what do they declare? Radiation[a]—how—by what steps does it proceed outwardly from a centre?

82   From a *luminous* centre, *Light* issues by radiation;[b] and the quantities of light received upon any given plane, supposed to be shifting its position so as to be now nearer the centre and now farther from it, will be diminished in the same proportion as the squares of the distances of the plane from the luminous body, are increased; and will be increased in the same proportion as these squares are diminished.

83   The expression of the law may be thus generalized:—the number of light-particles (or, if the phrase be preferred, the number of light-impressions) received upon the shifting plane, will be *inversely* proportional with the squares of the distances of the plane. Generalizing yet again, we may say that the diffusion—the scattering—the radiation,[c] in a word—is *directly* proportional with the squares of the distances.

84   For example: at the distance B, from the luminous centre A, a certain number of particles are so diffused as to occupy the surface B. Then at double the distance—that is to say at C—they will be so

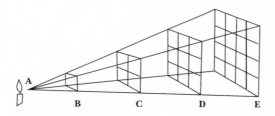

much farther diffused as to occupy four such surfaces:—at treble the distance, or at D, they will be so much farther separated as to occupy nine such surfaces:—while, at quadruple the distance, or at E, they will have become so scattered as to spread themselves over sixteen such surfaces—and so on forever.

85   In saying, generally, that the radiation[d] proceeds in direct proportion with the squares of the distances, we use the term radiation[e] to

a. P Irradiation / NM, HW *Radiation*

b. P irradiation / NM, HW *radiation*

c. P irradiation / NM, HW *radiation*

d. P irradiation / NM, HW *radiation*

e. P irradiation / NM, HW *radiation*

express *the degree of the diffusion* as we proceed outwardly from the centre. Conversing the idea, and employing the word "concentralization" to express *the degree of the drawing together* as we come back toward the centre from an outward position, we may say that concentralization proceeds *inversely* as the squares of the distances. In other words, we have reached the conclusion that, on the hypothesis that matter was originally radiated[a] from a centre and is now returning to it, the concentralization, in the return, proceeds *exactly as we know the force of gravitation to proceed.*

86   Now here, if we could be permitted to assume that concentralization exactly represents[b] the *force of the tendency to the centre*—that the one is[c] exactly proportional with[d] the other, and that the two proceed[e] together—we should have shown all that is required. The sole difficulty existing, then, is to establish a direct proportion between "concentralization" and the *force* of concentralization; and this is done, of course, if we establish such proportion between "radiation"[f] and the *force* of radiation.[g]

87   A very slight inspection of the Heavens assures us that the stars have a certain general uniformity, equability, or equidistance, of distribution through that region of space in which, collectively, and in a roughly globular form, they are situated:—this species of very general, rather than absolute, equability, being in full keeping with my deduction of inequidistance, within certain limits, among the originally diffused atoms, as a corollary from the design[h] of infinite complexity of relation out of irrelation. I started, it will be remembered, with the idea of a generally uniform but particularly *un*uniform distribution of the atoms;—an idea, I repeat, which an inspection of the stars, as they exist, confirms.

88   But even in the merely general equability of distribution, as regards the atoms, there appears a difficulty which, no doubt, has already suggested itself to those among my readers who have borne in mind that I suppose this equability of distribution effected through

---

a. P irradiated / NM, HW *radiated*
b. P represented / HW *represents*
c. P was / HW *is*
d. P to / NM, HW *with*
e. P proceeded / HW *proceed*
f. P "irradiation" / NM, HW *"radiation"*
g. P irradiation / NM, HW *radiation*
h. P from the evident design / HW *from the design*

EUREKA.

radiation[a] *from a centre.* The very first glance at the idea, radiation,[b] forces us to the entertainment of the hitherto unseparated and seemingly inseparable idea of agglomeration about a centre, with dispersion as we recede from it—the idea, in a word, of *in*equability of distribution in respect to the matter radiated.[c]

89   Now, I have elsewhere[*] observed that it is by just such difficulties as the one now in question—such peculiarities—such roughnesses[d]— such protuberances above the plane of the ordinary—that Reason feels her way, if at all, in her search for the True. By the difficulty— the "peculiarity"—now presented, I leap at once to *the* secret—a secret which I might never have attained *but* for the peculiarity and the inferences which, *in its mere character of peculiarity,* it affords me.

90   The process of thought, at this point, may be thus roughly sketched:—I say to myself—"Unity, as I have explained it, is a truth— I feel it. Diffusion is a truth—I see it. Radiation,[e] by which alone these two truths are reconciled, is a consequent truth—I perceive it. *Equability* of diffusion, first deduced *à priori* and then corroborated by the inspection of phænomena, is also a truth—I fully admit it. So far all is clear around me:—there are no clouds behind which *the* secret—the great secret of the gravitating *modus operandi*—can possibly lie hidden;—but this secret lies *hereabouts,* most assuredly; and *were* there but a cloud in view, I should be driven to suspicion of that cloud." And now, just as I say this, there actually comes a cloud into view. This cloud is the seeming impossibility of reconciling my truth, *radiation,*[f] with my truth, *equability of diffusion.* I say now:—"Behind this *seeming* impossibility is to be found what I desire." I do not say *"real* impossibility;" for invincible faith in my truths assures me that it is a mere difficulty after all—but I go on to say, with unflinching confidence, that, *when* this *difficulty* shall be solved, we shall find, *wrapped up in the process of solution,* the key to the secret at which we aim. Moreover—I *feel* that we shall discover *but one* possible solution of the difficulty; this for the reason that,

---

[*] *"Murders in the Rue Morgue"*—p. *133.*

a. P *irradiation* [italics] / NM, HW *radiation* [italics] [We follow HW.]
b. P irradiation / NM, HW *radiation*
c. P irradiated / HW *radiated*
d. P —such roughnesses—such peculiarities— / HW —*such peculiarities—such roughnesses*—
e. P Irradiation / NM, HW *Radiation*
f. P *irradiation* [italics] / NM, HW *radiation* [italics] [We follow HW.]

were there two, one would be supererogatory—would be fruitless—
would be empty—would contain no key—since no duplicate key
can be needed to any secret of Nature.

91   And now, let us see:—Our usual notions of radiation[a]—in fact *all*
our distinct notions of it—are caught merely from the process as we
see it exemplified in *Light.* Here there is a *continuous* outpouring of
ray-streams, and *with a force which we have at least no right to suppose varies
at all.* Now, in any such radiation[b] *as this*—continuous and of unvary-
ing force—the regions nearer the centre must *inevitably* be always more
crowded with the radiated[c] matter than the regions more remote. But
I have assumed no[d] such radiation[e] as this.[f] I assumed no *continuous*
radiation;[g] and for the simple reason that such an assumption would
have involved, first, the necessity of entertaining a conception which
I have shown no man *can* entertain, and which (as I will more fully
explain hereafter) all observation of the firmament refutes—the con-
ception of the absolute infinity of the Universe of Stars[h]—and would
have involved, secondly, the impossibility of understanding a rëac-
tion—that is, gravitation—as existing now—since, while an act is con-
tinued, no rëaction, of course, can take place. My assumption, then—
or[i] rather my inevitable deduction from just premises—was that of a
determinate radiation[j]—one finally *dis*continued.

92   Let me now describe the sole possible mode in which it is conceiv-
able that matter could have been diffused through space, so as to
fulfil the conditions at once of radiation[k] and of generally equable
distribution.

93   For convenience of illustration, let us imagine, in the first place,
a hollow sphere of glass, or of anything else, occupying the space
throughout which the universal matter is to be thus equably[l] dif-

a. P irradiation / NM, HW *radiation*
b. P irradiation / NM, HW *radiation*
c. P irradiated / NM, HW *radiated*
d. P *no* [italics] / HW *no* [Rom. See ¶31, note a.]
e. P irradiation [italics] / HW *radiation* [Rom. See ¶31, note a.]
f. P *as this.* [italics] / HW *as this.* [Rom. See ¶31, note a. We follow HW.]
g. P Irradiation / NM, HW *radiation*
h. P stars / HW *Stars*
i. P then, / HW *then*—
j. P irradiation / NM, HW *radiation*
k. P irradiation / NM, HW *radiation*
l. P equally / NM, HW *equably*

fused, by means of radiation,[a] from the absolute, irrelative, uncon-
ditional Particle,[b] placed in the centre of the sphere.

94   Now, a certain exertion of the diffusive power (presumed to be the
Divine Volition)—in other words, a certain *force*—whose measure is
the quantity of matter—that is to say, the number of atoms—emitted;
emits, by radiation,[c] this certain number of atoms; forcing them in
all directions outwardly from the centre—their proximity to each
other diminishing as they proceed—until, finally, they are distribut-
ed, loosely, over the interior surface of the sphere.

95   When these atoms have attained this position, or while proceed-
ing to attain it, a second and inferior exercise of the same force—
or a second and inferior force of the same character—emits, in the
same manner—that is to say, by radiation[d] as before—a second stra-
tum of atoms which proceeds to deposit itself upon the first; the
number of atoms, in this case as in the former, being of course the
measure of the force which emitted them; in other words the force
being precisely adapted to the purpose it effects—the force and the
number of atoms sent out by the force, being *directly proportional*.

96   When this second stratum has reached its destined position—or
while approaching it—a third still inferior exertion of the force, or
a third inferior force of a similar character—the number of atoms
emitted being in *all* cases the measure of the force—proceeds to
deposit a third stratum upon the second:—and so on, until these
concentric strata, growing gradually less and less, come down at
length to the central point; and the diffusive matter, simultaneously
with the diffusive force, is exhausted.[*][e]

97   We have now the sphere filled, through means of radiation,[f] with
atoms equably diffused. The two necessary conditions—those of
radiation[g] and of equable diffusion—are satisfied; and by the *sole*
process in which the possibility of their simultaneous satisfaction is

---

*[*]Here describe the whole process as one instantaneous flash. [Poe's handwritten
memorandum, HW. We provide asterisks to indicate what Poe's inscription refers to. He
drew a line from the end of ¶96 to the memorandum at the bottom of the page.]

---

a. P irradiation / NM, HW *radiation*
b. P particle / HW *Particle*
c. P irradiation / NM, HW *radiation*
d. P irradiation / NM, HW *radiation*
e. P exhausted. / HW *exhausted.** [Poe added the note; we supply the asterisk.]
f. P irradiation / NM, HW *radiation*
g. P irradiation / NM, HW *radiation*

conceivable. For this reason, I confidently expect to find, lurking in the present condition of the atoms as distributed throughout the sphere, the secret of which I am in search—the all-important principle of the *modus operandi* of the Newtonian law. Let us examine, then, the actual condition of the atoms.

98   They lie in a series of concentric strata. They are equably diffused throughout the sphere.[a]

99   The atoms being *equably* distributed, the greater the superficial extent of any of these concentric strata, or spheres, the more atoms will lie upon it. In other words, the number of atoms lying upon the surface of any one of the concentric spheres, is directly proportional with the extent of that surface.

100   *But, in any series of concentric spheres, the surfaces are directly proportional with the squares of the distances from the centre.*[*]

101   Therefore the number of atoms in any stratum is directly proportional with the square of that stratum's distance from the centre.

102   But the number of atoms in any stratum is the measure of the force which emitted that stratum—that is to say, is *directly proportional* with the force.

103   Therefore the force which radiated[b] any stratum is directly proportional with the square of that stratum's distance from the centre:— or, generally,

104   *The force of the radiation[c] has been directly proportional with the squares of the distances:*—or, particularly,

105   The force by which any individual atom was sent to its position in the sphere, was directly proportional with the square of that atom's distance, while in that position, from the centre of the sphere.[d]

106   Now, Rëaction, as far as we know anything of it, is Action conversed. The *general* principle of Gravity being, in the first place, understood as the rëaction of an act—as the expression of a desire on

* Succinctly—The surfaces of spheres are as the squares of their radii.

a. P sphere. They have been irradiated into these states. / NM radiated [The rest of the sentence is unchanged.] / HW *sphere.* [Sentence is omitted.]

b. P irradiated / NM, HW *radiated*

c. P *irradiation* [italics] / NM, HW *radiation* [italics] [We follow HW.]

d. P *distances.* [italics] / HW *distances* [italics]:—*or, particularly,*

The force by which any individual atom was sent to its position in the sphere, was directly proportional with the square of that atom's distance, while in that position, from the center of the sphere. [Nelson's entry does not show the italics on *distances,* the capital T on The, or the new paragraph that Poe indicates in H.W.]

the part of Matter, while existing in a state of diffusion, to return into the Unity whence it was diffused; and, in the second place, the mind being called on[a] to determine the *character* of the desire—the manner in which it would, naturally, be manifested; in other words, being called on[b] to conceive a probable law, or *modus operandi,* for the return; could not well help arriving at the conclusion that this law of return would be precisely the converse of the law of departure. That such would be the case, any one, at least, would be abundantly justified in taking for granted, until such time as some person should suggest something like a plausible reason why it should *not* be the case—until such period as a law of return shall be imagined which the intellect can consider as preferable.

107   Matter, then, radiated[c] into space with a force varying as the squares of the distances, might, *à priori* be supposed to return towards its centre of radiation[d] with a force varying *inversely* as the squares of the distances: and I have already shown[*] that any principle which will explain why the atoms should tend, according to any law, to the general centre, must be admitted as satisfactorily explaining, at the same time, why, according to the same law, they should tend each to each. For, in fact, the tendency to the general centre is not to a centre as such, but because of its being a point in tending towards which each atom tends most directly to its real and essential centre, *Unity*—the absolute and final Union of all.

108   The consideration here involved presents to my own mind no embarrassment whatever—but this fact does not blind me to the possibility of its being obscure to those who may have been less in the habit of dealing with abstractions:—and, on[e] the whole, it may be as well to look at the matter from one or two other points of view.

109   The absolute, irrelative particle primarily created by the Volition of God, must have been in a condition of positive *normality,* or rightfulness—for wrongfulness implies *relation.* Right is positive; wrong is negative—is merely the negation of right; as cold is the negation of heat—darkness of light. That a thing may be wrong, it is necessary

---

*Page[s 33–34.] [Poe's note, referring to the pagination of P, reads, *Page 44.]

a. P upon / HW *on*
b. P upon / HW *on*
c. P irradiated / NM, HW *radiated*
d P irradiation / NM, HW *radiation*
e. P upon / HW *on*

that there be some other thing in *relation* to which it *is* wrong—some condition which it fails to satisfy; some law which it violates; some being whom it aggrieves. If there be no such being, law, or condition, in respect to which the thing is wrong—and, still more especially, if no beings, laws, or conditions exist at all—then the thing can*not* be wrong and consequently must be *right.*

110   Any[a] deviation from normality involves a tendency to return into it. A difference from the normal—from the right—from the just— can be understood as effected only by the overcoming a difficulty; and if the force which overcomes the difficulty be not infinitely continued, the ineradicable tendency to return will at length be permitted to act for its own satisfaction. On[b] withdrawal of the force, the tendency acts. This is the principle of rëaction as the inevitable consequence of finite action. Employing a phraseology of which the seeming affectation will be pardoned for its expressiveness, we may say that Rëaction is the return from the condition of *as it is and ought not to be* into the condition of *as it was, originally, and therefore ought to be:*—and let me add here that the *absolute* force of Rëaction would no doubt be always found in direct proportion with the reality—the truth—the absoluteness—of the *originality*—if ever it were possible to measure this latter:—and, consequently, the greatest of all conceivable rëactions must be that manifested in[c] the tendency which we now discuss—the tendency to return into the *absolutely* original[d]— into the *supremely* primitive. Gravity, then, *must be the strongest of forces*— an idea reached *à priori* and abundantly confirmed by induction. What use I make of the idea, will be seen in the sequel.

111   The atoms, now, having been diffused from their normal condition of Unity, seek to return to——what? Not to any particular *point,* certainly; for it is clear that if, on[e] the diffusion, the whole Universe of matter had been projected, collectively, to a distance from the point of radiation,[f] the atomic tendency to the general centre of the sphere would not have been disturbed in the least:—the atoms would not have sought the point *in absolute space* from which they

a. P [no paragraph] Any / HW [paragraph] *Any*
b. P Upon / HW *On*
c. P produced by / HW *manifested in*
d. P *original* [italics] / HW *original* [Rom. See ¶31, note a.]
e. P upon / HW *on*
f. P irradiation / NM, HW *radiation*

were originally impelled. It is merely the *condition,* and not the point or locality at which this condition took its rise, that these atoms seek to re-establish;—it is merely *that condition which is their normality,* that they desire. "But they seek a centre," it will be said, "and a centre is a point." True; but they seek this point not in its character of point—(for, were the whole sphere moved from its position, they would seek, equally, the centre; and the centre *then* would be a *new* point)—but because it so happens, on account of the form in which they collectively exist—(that of the sphere)—that only *through* the point in question—the sphere's centre—they can attain their true object, Unity. In the direction of the centre each atom perceives more atoms than in any other direction. Each atom is impelled towards the centre because along the straight line joining it and the centre and passing on to the surface[a] beyond, there lie a greater number of atoms than along any other straight line—joining it, the atom, with any point of the sphere—[b] a greater number of objects that seek it, the individual atom—a greater number of tendencies to Unity—a greater number of satisfactions for its own tendency to Unity—in a word, because in the direction of the centre lies the utmost possibility of satisfaction, generally, for its own individual appetite. To be brief, the *condition,* Unity, is all that is really sought; and if the atoms *seem* to seek the centre of the sphere, it is only impliedly—[c] through implication—because such centre happens to imply, to include, or to involve, the only essential centre, Unity. But *on account of* this implication or involution, there is no possibility of practically separating the tendency to Unity in the abstract, from the tendency to the concrete centre. Thus the tendency of the atoms to the general centre *is,* to all practical intents and for all logical purposes, the tendency each to each; and the tendency each to each *is* the tendency to the centre; and the one tendency may be assumed *as* the other; whatever will apply to the one must be thoroughly applicable to the other; and, in conclusion, whatever principle will satisfactorily explain the one, cannot be questioned as an explanation of the other.

112   In looking carefully around me for rational objection to what I

a. P circumference / HW *surface*
b. P line— / NM line—joining it, the atom, and any point within the sphere [Nelson rejects this reading.] / HW *line—joining it, the atom, with any point of the sphere—*
c. P impliedly, / HW *impliedly—*

have advanced, I am able to discover nothing;[a]—but of that class of objections usually urged by the doubters for Doubt's sake, I very readily perceive *three;* and proceed to dispose of them in order.

113   It may be said, first: "The proof that the force of radiation[b] (in the case described) is directly proportional with[c] the squares of the distances, depends on[d] an unwarranted assumption—that of the number of atoms in each stratum being the measure of the force with which they are emitted."

114   I reply, not only that I am warranted in such assumption, but that I should be utterly *un*warranted in any other. What I assume is, simply, that an effect is the measure of its cause—that every exercise of the Divine Will will be proportional with[e] that which demands the exertion—that the means of Omnipotence, or of Omniscience, will be exactly adapted to its purposes. Neither can a deficiency nor an excess of cause bring to pass any effect. Had the force which radiated[f] any stratum to its position, been either more or less than was needed for the purpose—that is to say, not *directly proportional* with[g] the purpose—then to its position that stratum could not have been radiated.[h] Had the force which, with a view to general equability of distribution, emitted the proper number of atoms for each stratum, been not *directly proportional* with[i] the number, then the number would *not* have been the number demanded for the equable distribution.

115   The second supposable objection is somewhat better entitled to an answer.

116   It is an admitted principle in Dynamics that every body, on receiving an impulse, or disposition to move, will move onward in a straight line, in the direction imparted by the impelling force, until deflected, or stopped, by some other force. How then, it may be asked, is my first or external stratum of atoms to be understood as discontinuing their movement at the surface[j] of the imaginary glass sphere,

a. P *nothing;* [italics] / HW *nothing;* [Rom. See ¶31, note a.]
b. P irradiation / NM, HW *radiation*
c. P to / NM, HW *with*
d. P upon / HW *on*
e. P to / NM, HW *with*
f. P irradiated / NM, HW *radiated*
g. P to / NM, HW *with*
h. P irradiated / NM, HW *radiated*
i. P to / NM, HW *with*
j. P circumference / NM, HW *surface* [See ¶116n.]

when no second force, of more than an imaginary character, appears, to account for the discontinuance?

117   I reply that the objection, in this case, actually does arise out of "an unwarranted assumption"—on the part of the objector—the assumption of a principle, in Dynamics, at an epoch when *no* "principles," in *anything,* exist:—I use the word "principle," of course, in the objector's understanding of the word.

118   "In the beginning" we can admit—indeed we can comprehend—but one *First Cause*—the truly ultimate *Principle*—the Volition of God. The primary *act*—that of Radiation[a] from Unity—must have been independent of all that which the world now calls "principle"—because all that we so designate is but a consequence of the rëaction of that primary act:—I say *"primary"* act; for the creation of the absolute material Particle[b] is more properly to be regarded as a *conception* than as an *"act"* in the ordinary meaning of the term. Thus, we must regard the primary act as an act for the establishment of what we now call "principles." But this primary act itself is to be considered as *continuous Volition.* The Thought of God is to be understood as originating the Diffusion—as proceeding with it—as regulating it—and, finally, as being withdrawn from it on[c] its completion. *Then* commences Rëaction, and through Rëaction, "Principle," as we employ the word. It will be advisable, however, to limit the application of this word to the two *immediate* results of the discontinuance of the Divine Volition—that is, to the two agents, *Attraction* and *Repulsion.* Every other Natural agent depends, either more or less immediately, on[d] these two, and therefore would be more conveniently designated as *sub*-principle.

119   It may be objected, thirdly, that, in general, the peculiar mode of distribution which I have suggested for the atoms, is "an hypothesis and nothing more."

120   Now, I am aware that the word "hypothesis"[e] is a ponderous sledge-hammer, grasped immediately, if not lifted, by all very diminutive thinkers, on[f] the first appearance of any proposition wearing, in any particular, the garb of *a theory*. But "hypothesis" cannot be

a. P Irradiation / NM, HW *Radiation*
b. P particle / HW *Particle*
c. P upon / HW *on*
d. P upon / HW *on*
e. P hypothesis / HW *"hypothesis"*
f. P upon / HW *on*

wielded *here* to any good purpose, even by those who succeed in lifting it—little men or great.

121   I maintain, first, that *only* in the mode described is it conceivable that Matter could have been diffused so as to fulfil at once the conditions of radiation[a] and of generally equable distribution. I maintain, secondly, that these conditions themselves have been imposed upon me, as necessities, in a train of ratiocination as rigorously logical as that which establishes any demonstration in Euclid;[b] and I maintain, thirdly, that even if the charge of "hypothesis" were as fully sustained as it is, in fact, unsustained and untenable, still the validity and indisputability of my result would not, even in the slightest particular, be disturbed.

122   To explain:—The Newtonian Gravity—a law of Nature—a law whose existence as such no one out of Bedlam questions—a law whose admission as such enables us to account for nine-tenths of the Universal phænomena—a law which, merely because it does so enable us to account for these phænomena, we are perfectly willing, without reference to any other considerations, to admit, and cannot help admitting, as a law—a law, nevertheless, of which neither the principle nor the *modus operandi* of the principle, has ever yet been traced by the human analysis—a law, in short, which, neither in its detail nor in its generality, has been found susceptible of explanation *at all*—is at length seen to be at every point thoroughly explicable, provided only we yield our assent to——what? To an hypothesis? Why,[c] *if* an hypothesis—if the merest hypothesis—if an hypothesis for whose assumption—as in the case of that *pure* hypothesis the Newtonian law itself—no shadow of *à priori* reason could be assigned—if an hypothesis, even so absolute as all this implies, would enable us to perceive a principle for the Newtonian law—would enable us to understand as satisfied, conditions so miraculously—so ineffably complex and seemingly irreconcileable as those involved in the relations of which Gravity tells us,—what rational being *could* so expose his fatuity as to call even this absolute hypothesis an hypothesis any longer—unless, indeed, he were to persist in so calling it, with the understanding that he did so, simply for the sake of consistency *in words?*

a. P irradiation / NM, HW *radiation*
b. P *as rigorously logical as that which establishes any demonstration in Euclid;* [italics] / HW *as rigorously logical as that which establishes any demonstration in Euclid;* [Rom. See ¶31, note a.]
c. P Why / HW *Why,*

123   But what is the true state of our present case? What is *the fact?* Not only that it is *not* an hypothesis which we are required *to adopt,* in order to admit the principle at issue explained, but that it *is* a logical conclusion which we are requested *not* to adopt if we can avoid it—which we are simply invited to *deny if we can:*—a conclusion of so accurate a logicality that to dispute it would be the effort—to doubt its validity beyond our power:—a conclusion from which we see no mode of escape, turn as we will; a result which confronts us either at the end of an *in*ductive journey from the phænomena of the very Law discussed, or at the close of a *de*ductive career from the most rigorously simple of all conceivable assumptions—*the assumption, in a word, of Simplicity itself.*

124   And if here,[a] it be urged, that although my starting-point is, as I assert, the assumption of absolute Simplicity, yet Simplicity, considered merely in itself, is no axiom; and that only deductions from axioms are indisputable—it is thus that I reply:[b]

125   Every other science than Logic is the science of certain concrete relations. Arithmetic, for example, is the science of the relations of number—Geometry, of the relations of form—Mathematics in general, of the relations of quantity in general—of whatever can be increased or diminished. Logic, however, is the science of Relation in the abstract—of absolute Relation—of Relation considered solely in itself. An axiom in any particular science other than Logic is, thus, merely a proposition announcing certain concrete relations which seem to be too obvious for dispute—as when we say, for instance, that the whole is greater than its part:—and, thus again, the principle of the *Logical* axiom—in other words, of an axiom in the abstract—is, simply, *obviousness of relation.* Now, it is clear, not only that what is obvious to one mind may not be obvious to another, but that what is obvious to one mind at one epoch, may be anything but obvious, at another epoch, to the same mind. It is clear, moreover, that what, to-day, is obvious even to the majority of mankind, may to-morrow be, to either majority, more or less obvious, or in no respect obvious at all. It is seen, then, that the *axiomatic principle* itself is susceptible of variation, and of course that axioms are susceptible of similar change. Being mutable, the "truths" which grow out of them are

a. P here, for the mere sake of cavilling, / HW *here,*
b. P reply:— / HW *reply:*

necessarily mutable too; or, in other words, are never to be positively depended on[a] as truths at all—since Truth and Immutability are one.

126 It will now be readily understood that no axiomatic idea—no idea founded in the fluctuating principle, obviousness of relation—can possibly be so secure—so reliable a basis for any structure erected by the Reason, as *that* idea—(whatever it is, wherever we can find it, or *if* it be practicable to find it anywhere)—which is *ir*relative altogether— which not only presents to the understanding *no obviousness* of rela- tion, either greater or less, to be considered, but subjects the intellect, not in the slightest degree, to the necessity of even looking at *any re- lation at all.* If such an idea be not what we too heedlessly term "an axiom," it is at least preferable, as a logical[b] basis, to any axiom ever propounded, or to all imaginable axioms combined:—and such, pre- cisely, is the idea with which my deductive process, so thoroughly corroborated by induction, commences. My *Particle[c] Proper[d]* is but *Absolute[e] Irrelation.*

127 To[f] sum up what has been here advanced:—As a starting point I have taken it for granted, simply, that the Beginning had nothing behind it or before it—that it was a Beginning in fact—that it was a Beginning[g] and nothing different from a Beginning[h]—in short that this Beginning was——*that which it was.* If this be a "mere assump- tion" then a "mere assumption" let it be.

128 To conclude this branch of the subject:—I am fully warranted in announcing that *the Law which we call[i] Gravity exists on account of Mat- ter's having been radiated,[j] at its origin, atomically, into a limited[*] sphere of Space, from one, individual, unconditional, irrelative, and absolute Par-*

---

[*]A sphere is *necessarily* limited. I prefer tautology to a chance of misconception.[k]

---

a. P upon / HW *on*
b. P Logical / HW *logical*
c. P *particle* [italics] / HW *Particle* [italics] [We follow HW.]
d. P *proper* [italics] / HW *Proper* [italics] [We follow HW.]
e. P *"absolute"* [italics] / HW *"Absolute"* [italics] [We follow HW.]
f. P [no paragraph] To / HW [paragraph] *To*
g. P beginning / NM, HW *Beginning*
h. P beginning / NM, HW *Beginning*
i. P *we have been in the habit of calling* [italics] / HW *we call* [italics]
j. P *irradiated* [italics] / NM, HW *radiated* [italics] [We follow HW.]
k. P "*Limited sphere*"—A sphere is *necessarily* limited. I prefer tautology to a chance of mis- conception. / NM, HW *A sphere is **necessarily** [italics] limited. I prefer tautology to a chance of mis- conception.* [In NM, Poe neglected to strike out the dash before "A sphere," a variation Nelson omits.]

ticle Proper, by the sole process in which it was possible to satisfy, at the same time, the two conditions, radiation[a] and equable[b] distribution throughout the sphere—that is to say, by a force varying in direct proportion with the squares of the distances between the radiated[c] atoms, respectively, and the Particular centre of Radiation.[d]

129   I have already given my reasons for presuming Matter to have been diffused by a determinate rather than by a continuous or infinitely continued force. Supposing a continuous force, we should be unable, in the first place, to comprehend a rëaction at all; and we should be required, in the second place, to entertain the impossible conception of an infinite extension of Matter. Not to dwell upon the impossibility of the conception, the infinite extension of Matter is an idea which, if not positively disproved, is at least not in any respect warranted by telescopic observation of the stars—a point to be explained more fully hereafter; and this empirical reason for believing in the original finity of Matter is unempirically confirmed. For example:— Admitting, for the moment, the possibility of understanding Space as *filled*[e] with the radiated[f] atoms—that is to say, admitting, as well as we can, for argument's sake, that the succession of the atoms[g] had absolutely *no end*—then it is clear[h] that, even when the Volition of God had been withdrawn from them, and thus the tendency to return into Unity permitted (abstractly) to be satisfied, this permission would have been nugatory and invalid—practically valueless and of no effect whatever. No Rëaction could have taken place; no movement toward Unity could have been made; no Law of Gravity could have obtained.

130   To explain:—Grant the *abstract* tendency of any one atom to any one other as the inevitable result of diffusion from the normal Unity:— or, what is the same thing, admit any given atom as *proposing* to move in any given direction—it is clear that, since there is an *infinity* of atoms on all sides of the atom proposing to move, it never can actually move toward the satisfaction of its tendency in the direction giv-

a. P *irradiation,* [italics] / NM. *radiation,* / HW *radiation* [italics] [We follow HW.]
b. P *and generally-equable* [italics] / HW *and equable* [italics] [We follow HW.]
c. P *irradiated* [italics] / NM, HW *radiated* [italics] [We follow HW.]
d. P *Irradiation* [italics] / NM, HW *Radiation* [italics] [We follow HW.]
e. P Space *filled* [italics] / HW *Space* as *filled* [*filled* italicized] [We follow HW.]
f. P irradiated / NM, HW *radiated*
g. P the irradiated atoms / HW *the atoms*
h. P is abundantly clear / HW *is clear*

en, on account of a precisely equal and counter-balancing tendency in the direction diametrically opposite. In other words, exactly as many tendencies to Unity are behind the hesitating atom as before it; for it is mere[a] folly[b] to say that one infinite line is longer or shorter than another infinite line, or that one infinite number is greater or less than another number that is infinite. Thus the atom in question must remain stationary forever. Under the impossible circumstances which we have been merely endeavoring to conceive for argument's sake, there could have been no aggregation of Matter—no stars—no worlds—nothing but a perpetually atomic and inconsequential Universe. In fact, view it as we will, the whole idea of unlimited Matter is not only untenable, but impossible and preposterous.

131   With the understanding of a *sphere* of atoms, however, we perceive, at once, a *satisfiable* tendency to union. The general result of the tendency each to each, being a tendency of all to the centre, the *general* process of condensation, or approximation, commences immediately, by a common and simultaneous movement, on withdrawal of the Divine Volition; the *individual* approximations, or coalescences of atom with atom,[c] being subject to almost infinite variations of time, degree, and condition, on account of the excessive multiplicity of relation, arising from the differences of form assumed as characterizing the atoms at the moment of their quitting the Particle Proper; as well as from the subsequent particular inequidistance, each from each.

132   What I wish to impress upon the reader is the certainty of there arising, at once, (on withdrawal of the diffusive force, or Divine Volition,) out of the condition of the atoms as described, at innumerable points throughout the Universal sphere, innumerable agglomerations, characterized by innumerable specific differences of form, size, essential nature, and distance each from each. The development of Repulsion (Electricity) must have commenced, of course, with the very earliest particular efforts at Unity, and must have proceeded constantly in the ratio of coalescence[d]—that is to say, *in that of Condensation,* or, again, of Heterogeneity.

a. P a mere / HW *mere*
b. P sotticism / HW *folly*
c. P or coalescences—not cöalitions / HW *or cöalescences* [Nelson's list makes it seem that Poe struck out "of atom" in HW. Poe did not.]
d. P Cöalescence / HW *cöalescence*

133   Thus the two Principles Proper, *Attraction* and *Repulsion*—the Material and the Spiritual—accompany each other, in the strictest fellowship, forever. Thus *The Body and The Soul walk hand in hand.*

134   If now, in fancy, we select any one[a] of the agglomerations considered as in their primary stages throughout the Universal sphere, and suppose this incipient agglomeration to be taking place at that point where the centre of our Sun exists—or rather where it *did* exist originally; for the Sun is perpetually shifting his position—we shall find ourselves met, and borne onward for a time at least, by the most magnificent of theories—by the Nebular Cosmogony of Laplace:—although "Cosmogony" is far too comprehensive a term for what he really discusses—which is the constitution of our solar system alone—of one among the myriad of similar systems which make up the Universe of Stars.[b]

135   Confining himself to an *obviously limited* region—that of our solar system with its comparatively immediate vicinity—and *merely* assuming—that is to say, assuming without any basis whatever,—[c]*much* of what I have been just endeavoring to place upon a more stable basis than assumption; assuming, for example, matter as diffused (without pretending to account for the diffusion) throughout, and somewhat beyond, the space occupied by our system—diffused in a state of heterogeneous nebulosity and obedient to that omniprevalent law of Gravity at whose principle he ventured to make no guess;—assuming all this (which is quite true, although he had no logical right to its assumption) Laplace has shown, dynamically and mathematically, that the results in such case necessarily ensuing, are those and those alone which we find manifested in the actually existing condition of the system itself.

136   To explain:—Let us conceive *that* particular agglomeration of which we have just spoken—the one at the point designated by our Sun's centre—to have so far proceeded that a vast quantity of nebulous matter has here assumed a roughly globular form; its centre being, of course, coincident with what is now, or rather was originally, the centre of our Sun; and its surface[d] extending out beyond

a. P *any one* [italics] / HW *any one* [Rom.] See ¶31, note a. [We follow HW.]
b. P the Universe Proper—that Universal sphere—that all-inclusive and absolute *Kosmos* which forms the subject of my present Discourse / HW *the Universe of Stars.*
c. P whatever, either deductive or inductive / HW *whatever,*
d. P periphery / HW *surface*

the orbit of Neptune, the most remote of our planets:—in other words, let us suppose the diameter of this rough sphere to be some 6000 millions of miles. For ages, this mass of matter has been undergoing condensation, until at length it has become reduced into the bulk we imagine; having proceeded gradually, of course, from its atomic and imperceptible state, into what we understand of appreciable[a] nebulosity.

137   Now, the condition of this mass implies a rotation about an imaginary axis—a rotation which, commencing with the absolute incipiency of the aggregation, has been ever since acquiring velocity. The very first two atoms which met, approaching each other from points not diametrically opposite, would, in rushing partially past each other, form a nucleus for the rotary movement described. How this would increase in velocity, is readily seen. The two atoms are joined by others:—an aggregation is formed. The mass continues to rotate while condensing. But any atom at the surface[b] has, of course, a more rapid motion than one nearer the centre. The outer atom, however, with its superior velocity, approaches the centre; carrying this superior velocity with it as it goes. Thus every atom, proceeding inwardly, and finally attaching itself to the condensed centre, adds something to the original velocity of that centre—that is to say, increases the rotary movement of the mass.

138   Let us now suppose this mass so far condensed that it occupies *precisely* the space circumscribed by the orbit of Neptune, and that the velocity with which the surface of the mass moves, in the general rotation, is precisely that velocity with which Neptune now revolves about the Sun. At this epoch, then, we are to understand that the constantly increasing centrifugal force, having gotten the better of the non-increasing centripetal, loosened and separated the exterior and least condensed stratum, or a few of the exterior and least condensed strata, at the equator of the sphere, where the tangential velocity predominated; so that these strata formed about the main body an independent ring encircling the equatorial regions:— just as the exterior portion thrown off, by excessive velocity of rotation, from a grindstone, would form a ring about the grindstone, but for the solidity of the superficial material: were this caoutchouc, or

a. P of visible, palpable, or otherwise appreciable / HW *of appreciable*
b. P circumference / HW *surface*

anything similar in consistency, precisely the phænomenon I describe would be presented.

139 The ring thus whirled from the nebulous mass, *revolved,* of course, *as* a separate ring, with just that velocity with which, while the surface of the mass, it *rotated.* In the meantime, condensation still proceeding, the interval between the discharged ring and the main body continued to increase, until the former was left at a vast distance from the latter.

140 Now, admitting the ring to have possessed, by some seemingly accidental arrangement of its heterogeneous materials, a constitution nearly uniform, then this ring, *as* such, would never have ceased revolving about its primary; but, as might have been anticipated, there appears to have been enough irregularity in the disposition of the materials, to make them cluster about centres of superior solidity; and thus the annular form was destroyed.* No doubt, the band was soon broken up into several portions, and one of these portions, predominating in mass, absorbed the others into itself; the whole settling, spherically, into a planet. That this latter, *as* a planet, continued the revolutionary movement which characterized it while a ring, is sufficiently clear; and that it took upon itself, also, an additional movement in its new condition of sphere, is readily explained. The ring being understood as yet unbroken, we see that its exterior, while the whole revolves about the parent body, moves more rapidly than its interior. When the rupture occurred, then, some portion in each fragment must have been moving with greater velocity than the others. The superior movement prevailing, must have whirled each fragment round—that is to say, have caused it to rotate; and the direction of the rotation must, of course, have been the direction of the revolution whence it arose. *All* the fragments having become subject to the rotation described, must, in cöalescing,[a] have imparted it to the one planet constituted by their cöalescence.[b]—This planet was Neptune. Its material continuing to undergo condensation,

---

*Laplace assumed his nebulosity heterogeneous, merely that he might be thus enabled to account for the breaking up of the rings; for had the nebulosity been homogeneous, they would not have broken. I reach the same result—heterogeneity of the secondary masses immediately resulting from the atoms—purely from an *à priori* consideration of their general design—*Relation.*

---

a. P coalescing / HW *cöalescing*
b. P coalescence / HW *cöalescence*

and the centrifugal force generated in its rotation getting, at length, the better of the centripetal, as before in the case of the parent orb, a ring was whirled also from the equatorial surface of this planet: this ring, having been ununiform in its constitution, was broken up, and its several fragments, being absorbed by the most massive, were collectively spherified into a moon. Subsequently, the operation was repeated, and a second moon was the result. We thus account for the planet Neptune, with the two satellites which accompany him.[*][a]

141   In throwing off a ring from its equator, the Sun re-established that equilibrium between its centripetal and centrifugal forces which had been disturbed in the process of condensation; but, as this condensation still proceeded, the equilibrium was again immediately disturbed, through the increase of rotation. By the time the mass had so far shrunk that it occupied a spherical space just that circumscribed by the orbit of Uranus, we are to understand that the centrifugal force had so far obtained the ascendency that new relief was needed: a second equatorial band was, consequently, thrown off, which, proving ununiform, was broken up, as before in the case of Neptune; the fragments settling into the planet Uranus; the velocity of whose actual revolution about the Sun indicates, of course, the rotary speed of that Sun's equatorial surface at the moment of the separation. Uranus, adopting a rotation from the collective rotations of the fragments composing it, as previously explained, now threw off ring after ring; each of which, becoming broken up, settled into a moon:—three moons, at different epochs, having been formed, in this manner, by the rupture and general spherification of as many distinct ununiform rings.

142   By the time the Sun had shrunk until it occupied a space just that circumscribed by the orbit of Saturn, the balance, we are to suppose, between its centripetal and centrifugal forces had again become so far disturbed, through increase of rotary velocity, the result of condensation, that a third effort at equilibrium became necessary; and an annular band was therefore whirled off, as twice before; which,

---

*When this book went to press the *ring* of Neptune had not been positively determined. [New footnote inscribed in pencil, HW.]

---

a. P accompany him. / NM *When this work went to press it was not definitely ascertained that Neptune had a ring. / HW *When this book went to press the ring of Neptune had not been positively determined. [Poe added the asterisk and note. He also italicized the word *ring* in this sentence in NM and in HW. Nelson gives "previously" instead of "positively" for HW.]

on rupture through ununiformity, became consolidated into the planet Saturn. This latter threw off, in the first place, seven ununiform[a] bands, which on rupture, were spherified respectively into as many moons; but, subsequently, it appears to have discharged, at three distinct but not very distant epochs, three rings whose equability of constitution was, by apparent accident, so considerable as to present no occasion for their rupture; thus they continue to revolve as rings. I use the phrase "*apparent* accident;" for of accident in the ordinary sense there was, of course, nothing:—the term is properly applied only to the result of indistinguishable or not immediately traceable *law*.

143   Shrinking still farther, until it occupied just the space circumscribed by the orbit of Jupiter, the Sun now found need of farther effort to restore the counterbalance of its two forces, continually disarranged in the still continued increase of rotation. Jupiter, accordingly, was now thrown off; passing from the annular to the planetary condition; and, on attaining this latter, threw off in its turn, at four different epochs, four rings, which finally resolved themselves into so many moons.

144   Still shrinking, until its sphere occupied just the space defined by the orbit of the Asteroids, the Sun now discarded a ring which appears to have had *nine*[b] centres of superior solidity, and, on breaking up, to have separated into nine[c] fragments no one of which so far predominated in mass as to absorb the others.[*d] All therefore, as distinct although comparatively small planets, proceeded to revolve in orbits whose distances, each from each, may be considered as in some degree the measure of the force which drove them asunder:—all the orbits, nevertheless, being so closely cöincident[e] as to admit of our calling them *one,* in view of the other planetary orbits.

NM *An additional asteroid has been discovered since the work went to press /
HW *Another asteroid discovered since this work went to press. [Poe's handwritten memorandum, HW. Because of the informal wording, we agree with Nelson ("An Apparatus for a Definitive Edition") that this is Poe's memorandum to himself and not a finished footnote.] [No asterisk, note, or memo in P. Poe's handwritten comment in NM reads more like a finished footnote than does his memo in HW.]

a. P seven uniform / W, NM, HW, *seven ununiform*
b. P *eight* [italics] / NM, HW *nine* [italics] [We follow HW.]
c. P eight / NM, HW *nine*
d. P the others.
e. P coincident / HW *cöincident*

145   Continuing to shrink, the Sun, on becoming so small as just to fill the orbit of Mars, now discharged this planet—of course by the process repeatedly described. Since he has[a] no moon, however, Mars could have thrown off no ring. In fact, an epoch had now arrived in the career of the parent body, the centre of the system. The *de*crease of its nebulosity, which is the *in*crease of its density, and which again is the *de*crease of its condensation, out of which latter arose the constant disturbance of equilibrium—must, by this period, have attained a point at which the efforts for restoration would have been more and more ineffectual just in proportion as they were less frequently needed. Thus the processes of which we have been speaking would everywhere show signs of exhaustion—in the planets, first, and secondly, in the original mass. We must not fall into the error of supposing the decrease of interval observed among the planets as we approach the Sun, to be in any respect indicative of an increase of frequency in the periods at which they were discarded. Exactly the converse is to be understood. The longest interval of time must have occurred between the discharges of the two interior; the shortest between those of the two exterior, planets. The decrease of the interval of space is, nevertheless, the measure of the density, and thus inversely of the condensation, of the Sun, throughout the processes detailed.

146   Having shrunk, however, so far as to fill only the orbit of our Earth, the parent sphere whirled from itself still one other body—the Earth— in a condition so nebulous as to admit of this body's discarding, in its turn, yet another, which is our Moon;—but here terminated the lunar formations.

147   Finally, subsiding to the orbits first of Venus and then of Mercury, the Sun discarded these two interior planets; neither of which has given birth to any moon.

148   Thus from his original bulk—or, to speak more accurately, from the condition in which we first considered him—from a partially spherified nebular mass, *certainly* much more than 5,600 millions of miles in diameter—the great central orb and origin of our solar-planetary-lunar system, has gradually descended, by condensation, in obedience to the law of Gravity, to a globe only 882,000 miles in diameter; but it by no means follows, either that its condensation is

a. P Having no / HW *Since he has no*

yet complete, or that it may not still possess the capacity of whirling from itself another planet.

149   I have here given—in outline of course, but still with all the detail necessary for distinctness—a view of the Nebular Theory as its author himself conceived it. From whatever point we regard it, we shall find it *beautifully true*. It is by far too beautiful, indeed, *not* to possess Truth as its essentiality—and here I am very profoundly serious in what I say. In the revolution of the satellites of Uranus, there does appear something seemingly inconsistent with the assumptions of Laplace; but that *one* inconsistency can invalidate a theory constructed from a million of intricate consistencies, is a fancy fit only for the fantastic. In prophesying,[a] confidently, that the apparent anomaly to which I refer, will, sooner or later, be found one of the strongest possible corroborations of the general hypothesis, I pretend to no especial spirit of divination. It is a matter which the only difficulty seems *not* to foresee.[*]

150   The bodies whirled off in the processes described, would exchange, it has been seen, the superficial *rotation* of the orbs whence they originated, for a *revolution* of equal velocity about these orbs as distant centres; and the revolution thus engendered must proceed, so long as the centripetal force, or that with which the discarded body gravitates toward its parent, is neither greater nor less than that by which it was discarded; that is, than the centrifugal, or, far more properly, than the tangential, velocity. From the unity, however, of the origin of these two forces, we might have expected to find them as they are found—the one accurately counterbalancing the other. It has been shown, indeed, that the act of whirling-off is, in every case, merely an act for the preservation of the counterbalance.

151   After referring, however, the centripetal force to the omniprevalent law of Gravity, it has been the fashion with astronomical treatises, to seek beyond the limits of mere Nature—that is to say, of *Secondary* Cause—a solution of the phænomenon of tangential velocity. This latter they attribute directly to a *First* Cause—to God. The force which

*I am prepared to show that the anomalous revolution of the satellites of Uranus is a simply perspective anomaly arising from the *bouleversement*[b] of the axis of the planet.

a. P, HW prophecying / NM *prophesying* [We assume Poe overlooked the spelling error in HW. The word *prophesy* does not appear in Pollin's *Word Index to Poe's Fiction*, and so there was no convenient way to check for other instances of Poe's practice.]
b. P inclination / HW *bouleversement* [italics]

carries a stellar body around its primary they assert to have originat-
ed in an impulse given immediately by the finger—this is the child-
ish phraseology employed—by the finger of Deity itself. In this view,
the planets, fully formed, are conceived to have been hurled from the
Divine hand, to a position in the vicinity of the suns, with an impetus
mathematically adapted to the masses, or attractive capacities, of the
suns themselves. An idea so grossly unphilosophical, although so su-
pinely adopted, could have arisen only from the difficulty of other-
wise accounting for the absolutely accurate adaptation, each to each,
of two forces so seemingly independent, one of the other, as are the
gravitating and tangential. But it should be remembered that, for a
long time, the coincidence between the moon's rotation and her si-
dereal revolution—two matters seemingly far more independent than
those now considered—was looked upon as positively miraculous; and
there was a strong disposition, even among astronomers, to attribute
the marvel to the direct and continual agency of God—who, in this
case, it was said, had found it necessary to interpose, specially, among
his general laws, a set of subsidiary regulations, for the purpose of
forever concealing from mortal eyes the glories, or perhaps the hor-
rors, of the other side of the Moon—of that mysterious hemisphere
which has always avoided, and must perpetually avoid, the telescopic
scrutiny of mankind. The advance of Science, however, soon demon-
strated—what to the philosophical instinct needed *no* demonstra-
tion—that the one movement is but a portion—something more,
even, than a consequence—of the other.

152   For my part, I have no patience with fantasies at once so timorous,
so idle, and so awkward. They belong to the veriest cowardice[a] of
thought. That Nature and the God of Nature are distinct, no think-
ing being can long doubt. By the former we imply merely the laws
of the latter. But with the very idea of God, omnipotent, omniscient,
we entertain, also, the idea of *the infallibility* of his laws. With Him
there being neither Past nor Future—with Him all being *Now*—do
we not insult him in supposing his laws so contrived as not to pro-
vide for every possible contingency?—or, rather, what idea *can* we
have of *any* possible contingency, except that it is at once a result and
a manifestation of his laws? He who, divesting himself of prejudice,
shall have the rare courage to think absolutely for himself, cannot

a. P *cowardice* [italics] / HW *cowardice* [Rom.] See ¶31, note a.

fail to arrive, in the end, at the condensation of *laws* into *Law*—cannot fail of reaching the conclusion that *each law of Nature is dependent at all points upon all other laws,* and that all are but consequences of one primary exercise of the Divine Volition. Such is the principle of the Cosmogony which, with all necessary deference, I here venture to suggest and to maintain.

153 In this view, it will be seen that, dismissing as frivolous, and even impious, the fancy of the tangential force having been imparted to the planets immediately by "the finger of God," I consider this force as originating in the rotation of the stars:—this rotation as brought about by the in-rushing of the primary atoms, towards their respective centres of aggregation:—this in-rushing as the consequence of the law of Gravity:—this law as but the mode in which is necessarily manifested the tendency of the atoms to return into imparticularity:—this tendency[a] as but the inevitable rëaction of the first and most sublime of Acts—that act by which a God, self-existing and alone existing, became all things at once, through dint of his volition, while all things were thus constituted a portion of God.

154 The radical assumptions of this Discourse suggest to me, and in fact imply, certain important *modifications* of the Nebular Theory as given by Laplace. The efforts of the repulsive power I have considered as made for the purpose of preventing contact among the atoms, and thus as made in the ratio of the approach to contact—that is to say, in the ratio of condensation.* In other words, *Electricity,* with its involute phænomena, heat, light and magnetism, is to be understood as proceeding as condensation proceeds, and, of course, inversely as density proceeds, or the *cessation to condense.* Thus the Sun, in the process of its consolidation,[b] must soon, in developing repulsion, have become excessively heated—incandescent:[c] and we can perceive how the operation of discarding its rings must have been materially assisted by the slight encrustation[d] of its surface consequent on cooling. Any common experiment shows us how readily a crust of the character suggested, is separated, through heterogeneity, from the interior mass. But, on every successive rejection of the crust, the new

*See page 53 / [Poe's note in P., referring to the pagination of P., reads "*See page 70."].

a. P tendency to return / HW *tendency*
b. P aggregation / HW *consolidation*
c. P heated—perhaps incandescent / HW *heated—incandescent*
d. P incrustation / HW *encrustation*

surface would appear incandescent as before; and the period at which it would again become so far encrusted as to be readily loosened and discharged, may well be imagined as exactly cöincident[a] with that at which a new effort would be needed, by the whole mass, to restore the equilibrium of its two forces, disarranged through condensation. In other words:—by the time the electric influence (Repulsion) has prepared the surface for rejection, we are to understand that the gravitating influence (Attraction) is precisely ready to reject it. Here, then, as everywhere, *the Body and the Soul walk hand in hand.*

155   These ideas are empirically confirmed at all points. Since condensation can never, in any body, be considered as absolutely at an end, we are warranted in anticipating that, whenever we have an opportunity of testing the matter, we shall find indications of resident luminosity in *all* the stellar bodies—moons and planets as well as suns. That our Moon is self-luminous,[b] we see at her every total eclipse, when, if not so, she would disappear. On the dark part of the satellite, too, during her phases, we often observe flashes like our own Auroras; and that these latter, with our various other so-called electrical phænomena, without reference to any more steady radiance, must give our Earth a certain appearance of luminosity to an inhabitant of the Moon, is quite evident. In fact, we should regard all the phænomena referred to, as mere manifestations, in different moods and degrees, of the Earth's feebly-continued condensation.

156   If my views are tenable, we should be prepared to find the newer planets—that is to say, those nearer the Sun—more luminous than those older and more remote:—and the extreme brilliancy of Venus (on whose dark portions, during her phases, the Auroras are frequently visible) does not seem to be altogether accounted for by her mere proximity to the central orb. She is no doubt vividly self-luminous, although less so than Mercury: while the luminosity of Neptune may be comparatively nothing.

157   Admitting what I have urged, it is clear that, from the moment of the Sun's discarding a ring, there must be a continuous diminution both of his heat and light, on account of the continuous encrustation of his surface; and that a period would arrive—the period immediately previous to a new discharge—when a *very material* decrease of both

a. P coincident / HW *cöincident*
b. P Moon is strongly self-luminous / W *Moon is self-luminous*

light and heat, must become apparent. Now, we know that tokens of such changes are distinctly recognizable. On the Melville islands—to adduce merely one out of a hundred examples—we find traces of *ultra-tropical* vegetation—of plants that never could have flourished without immensely more light and heat than are at present afforded by our Sun to any portion of the surface of the Earth. Is such vegetation referable to an epoch immediately subsequent to the whirling-off of Venus? At this epoch must have occurred to us our greatest access of solar influence; and, in fact, this influence must then have attained its maximum:—leaving out of view, of course, the period when the Earth itself was discarded—the period of its mere organization.

158   Again:—we know that there exist *non-luminous suns*—that is to say, suns whose existence we determine through the movements of others, but whose luminosity is not sufficient to impress us. Are these suns invisible merely on account of the length of time elapsed since their discharge of a planet? And yet again:—may we not—at least in certain cases—account for the sudden appearances of suns where none had been previously suspected, by the hypothesis that, having rolled with encrusted surfaces throughout the few thousand years of our astronomical history, each of these suns, in whirling off a new secondary, has at length been enabled to display the glories of its still incandescent interior?—To the well-ascertained fact of the proportional increase of heat as we descend into the Earth, I need of course, do nothing more than refer:—it comes in the strongest possible corroboration of all that I have said on the topic now at issue.

159   In speaking, not long ago, of the repulsive or electrical influence, I remarked that "the important phænomena of vitality, consciousness, and thought, whether we observe them generally or in detail, seem to proceed *at least in the ratio of the heterogeneous.* "* I mentioned, too, that I would recur to the suggestion:—and this is the proper point at which to do so. Looking at the matter, first, in detail, we perceive that not merely the *manifestation* of vitality, but its importance, consequence, and elevation of character, keep pace, very closely, with the heterogeneity, or complexity, of the animal structure. Looking at the question, now, in its generality, and referring to the first movements of the atoms towards mass-constitution, we find that

*Page 28[a].

---

a. P *Page 36 / O, NM, HW *Page 37 [Poe corrected an error in P; the words quoted are on page 37 of the 1848 edition.] For the present edition, the note should read, * *Page 28.*

heterogeneousness, brought about directly through condensation, is proportional with it forever. We thus reach the proposition that *the importance of the development of the terrestrial vitality proceeds as*[a] *the terrestrial condensation.*

160   Now this is in[b] accordance with what we know of the succession of animals on the Earth. As it has proceeded in its condensation, superior and still superior races have appeared. Is it impossible that the successive geological revolutions which have attended, at least, if not immediately caused, these successive elevations of vitalic character— is it improbable that these revolutions have themselves been produced by the successive planetary discharges from the Sun—in other words, by the successive variations in the solar influence on the Earth? Were this idea tenable, we should not be unwarranted in the fancy that the discharge of yet a new planet, interior to Mercury, may give rise to yet a new modification of the terrestrial surface—a modification from which may spring a race both materially and spiritually superior to Man. These thoughts impress me with all the force of truth—but I throw them out, of course, merely in their obvious character of suggestion.

161   The Nebular Theory of Laplace has lately received far more confirmation than it needed, at the hands of the philosopher, Comte.[c] These two have thus together shown—*not,* to be sure, that Matter at any period actually existed as described, in a state of nebular diffusion, but that, admitting it so to have existed throughout the space and much beyond the space now occupied by our solar system, *and to have commenced a movement towards a centre*—it must gradually have assumed the various forms and motions which are now seen, in that system, to obtain. A demonstration such as this—a dynamical and mathematical demonstration, as far as demonstration can be—and one empirically confirmed—a demonstration[d]—unquestionable and unquestioned—unless, indeed, by that unprofitable and disreputable tribe, the professional questioners—the mere madmen who deny the Newtonian law of Gravity on which the results of the French mathemati-

a. P, HW *proceeds equably with* [italics] / NM *proceeds as* [italics] [The NM seems clearer. Poe's sense is *"proceeds as a function of the terrestrial condensation."*]
b. P in precise accordance / HW *in accordance*
c. P Compte. / HW *Comte.*
d. P can be— / HW *can be—and one empirically confirmed—a demonstration*— [Nelson omits the word *"one."*]

cians are based—a demonstration, I say, such as this, would to most intellects be conclusive—and I confess that it is so to mine—of the validity of the nebular hypothesis upon which the demonstration depends.

162   That the demonstration does not *prove* the hypothesis, according to the common understanding of the word "proof," I admit, of course. To show that certain existing results—that certain established facts— may be, even mathematically, accounted for by the assumption of a certain hypothesis, is by no means to establish the hypothesis itself. In other words:—to show that, certain data being given, a certain existing result might, or even *must*, have ensued, will fail to prove that this result *did* ensue, *from the data,* until such time as it shall be also shown that there are, *and can be,* no other data from which the result in question might *equally* have ensued. But, in the case now discussed, although all must admit the deficiency of what we are in the habit of terming "proof," still there are many intellects, and those of the loftiest order, to which *no* proof could bring one iota of additional *conviction*. Without going into details which might impinge upon the Cloud-Land of Metaphysics, I may as well here observe that the force of conviction, in cases such as this will always, with the right-thinking, be proportional with[a] the amount of *complexity* intervening between the hypothesis and the result. To be less abstract:—The greatness of the complexity found existing among cosmical conditions, by rendering great in the same proportion the difficulty of accounting for all these conditions *at once,* strengthens, also in the same proportion, our faith in that hypothesis which does, in such manner, satisfactorily account for them:—and as *no* complexity can well be conceived greater than that of the astronomical conditions, so no conviction can be stronger—to *my* mind at least—than that with which I am impressed by an hypothesis that not only reconciles these conditions, with mathematical accuracy, and reduces them into a consistent and intelligible whole, but is, at the same time, the *sole* hypothesis by means of which the human intellect has been ever enabled to account for them *at all.*

163   A most unfounded opinion has become latterly current in gossiping and even in scientific circles—the opinion that the so-called Nebular Cosmogony has been overthrown. This fancy has arisen from the

a. P to / HW *with*

report of late observations made, among what hitherto have been termed the "nebulæ," through the large telescope of Cincinnati, and the world-renowned instrument of Lord Rosse. Certain spots in the firmament which presented, even to the most powerful of the old telescopes, the appearance of nebulosity, or haze, had been regarded for a long time as confirming the theory of Laplace. They were looked upon as stars in that very process of condensation which I have been attempting to describe. Thus it was supposed that we "had ocular evidence"—an evidence, by the way, which has always been found very questionable—of the truth of the hypothesis; and, although certain telescopic improvements, every now and then, enabled us to perceive that a spot, here and there, which we had been classing among the nebulae, was, in fact, but a cluster of stars deriving its nebular character only from its immensity of distance—still it was throught that no doubt could exist as to the actual nebulosity of numerous other masses, the strong-holds of the nebulists, bidding defiance to every effort at segregation. Of these latter the most interesting was the great "nebula"[a] in the constellation Orion:—but this, with innumerable other miscalled "nebulæ," when viewed through the magnificent modern telescopes, has become resolved into a simple collection of stars. Now this fact has been very generally understood as conclusive against the Nebular Hypothesis of Laplace; and, on announcement of the discoveries in question, the most enthusiastic defender and most eloquent popularizer of the theory, Dr. Nichol, went so far as to "admit the necessity of abandoning" an idea which had formed the material of his most praiseworthy book.[*]

164   Many of my readers will no doubt be inclined to say that the result of these new investigations *has* at least a strong *tendency* to overthrow the hypothesis; while some of them, more thoughtful, will

---

[*] *"Views of the Architecture of the Heavens."* A letter, purporting to be from Dr. Nichol to a friend in America, went the rounds of our newspapers, about two years ago, I think, admitting "the necessity" to which I refer. In a subsequent Lecture, however, Dr. N. appears in some manner to have gotten the better of the necessity, and does not quite *renounce* the theory, although he seems to wish that he could sneer at it as "a purely hypothetical one." What else was the Law of Gravity before the Maskelyne experiments? and who questioned the Law of Gravity, even then? The late experiments of Comte, however, are to the Laplacian theory what those of Maskelyne were to the Newtonian.[b] [Last sentence inscribed in pencil, HW.]

---

a. P "nebulae" / O, NM, HW *"nebula"*
b. P then? / HW *then? The late experiments of Comte, however, are to the Laplacian theory what those of Maskelyne were to the Newtonian.*

suggest that, although the theory is by no means disproved through the segregation of the particular "nebulæ" alluded to, still a *failure* to segregate them, with such telescopes, might well have been understood as a triumphant *corroboration* of the theory:—and this latter class will be surprised, perhaps, to hear me say that even with *them* I disagree. If the propositions of this Discourse have been comprehended, it will be seen that, in my view, a failure to segregate the "nebulæ" would have tended to the refutation, rather than to the confirmation, of the Nebular Hypothesis.

165   Let me explain:—The Newtonian Law of Gravity we may, of course, assume as demonstrated. This law, it will be remembered, I have referred to the rëaction of the first Divine Act—to the rëaction of an exercise of the Divine Volition temporarily overcoming a difficulty. This difficulty is that of forcing the normal into the abnormal— of impelling that whose originality, and therefore whose rightful condition, was *One,* to take upon itself the wrongful condition of *Many.* It is only by conceiving this difficulty as *temporarily* overcome, that we can comprehend a rëaction. There could have been no rëaction had the act been infinitely continued. So long as the act *lasted,* no rëaction, of course, could commence; in other words, no *gravitation* could take place—for we have considered the one as but the manifestation of the other. But gravitation *has* taken place; therefore the act of Creation has ceased: and gravitation has long ago taken place; therefore the act of Creation has long ago ceased. We can no more expect, then, to observe *the primary processes* of Creation; and to these primary processes the condition of nebulosity has already been explained to belong.

166   Through what we know of the propagation of light, we have direct proof that the more remote of the stars have existed, under the forms in which we now see them, for an inconceivable number of years. So far back *at least,* then, as the period when these stars underwent condensation, must have been the epoch at which the mass-constitutive processes began. That we may conceive these processes, then, as still going on in the case of certain "nebulæ," while in all other cases we find them thoroughly at an end, we are forced into assumptions for which we have really *no* basis whatever—we have to thrust in, again, upon the revolting Reason, the blasphemous idea of special interposition—we have to suppose that, in the particular instances of these "nebulæ," an unerring God found it necessary to

introduce certain supplementary regulations—certain improvements of the general law—certain retouchings and emendations, in a word, which had the effect of deferring the completion of these individual stars for centuries of centuries beyond the æra during which all the other stellar bodies had time, not only to be fully constituted, but to grow hoary with an unspeakable old age.

167 Of course, it will be immediately objected that since the light by which we recognize the nebulæ now, must be merely that which left their surfaces a vast number of years ago, the processes at present observed, or supposed to be observed, are, in fact, *not* processes now actually going on, but the phantoms of processes completed long in the Past—just as I maintain all these mass-constitutive processes *must* have been.

168 To this I reply that neither is the now-observed condition of the condensed stars their actual condition, but a condition completed long in the Past; so that my argument drawn from the *relative* condition of the stars and the "nebulæ," is in no manner disturbed. Moreover, those who maintain the existence of nebulæ, do *not* refer the nebulosity to extreme distance; they declare it a real and not merely a perspective nebulosity. That we may conceive, indeed, a nebular mass as visible at all, we must conceive it as *very near us* in comparison with the condensed stars brought into view by the modern telescopes. In maintaining the appearances in question, then, to be really nebulous, we maintain their comparative vicinity to our point of view. Thus, their condition, as we see them now, must be referred to an epoch *far less remote* than that to which we may refer the now-observed condition of at least the majority of the stars.—In a word, should Astronomy ever demonstrate a "nebula," in the sense at present intended, I should consider the Nebular Cosmogony—*not*, indeed, as corroborated by the demonstration—but as thereby irretrievably overthrown.

169 By way, however, of rendering unto Cæsar *no more* than the things that are Cæsar's, let me here remark that the assumption of the hypothesis which led him to so glorious a result, seems to have been suggested to Laplace in great measure by a misconception—by the very misconception of which we have just been speaking—by the generally prevalent misunderstanding of the character of the nebulæ, so mis-named. These he supposed to be, in reality, what their designation implies. The fact is, this great man had, very properly, an inferior faith in his own merely *perceptive* powers. In respect, there-

fore, to the actual existence of nebulæ—an existence so confident-
ly maintained by his telescopic contemporaries—he depended less
upon what he saw than upon what he heard.

170   It will be seen that the only valid objections to his theory, are those
made to its hypothesis *as* such—to what suggested it—not to what it
suggests; to its propositions rather than to its results. His most unwar-
ranted assumption was that of giving the atoms a movement towards
a centre, in the very face of his evident understanding that these at-
oms, in unlimited succession, extended throughout the Univeral
space. I have already shown that, under such circumstances, there
could have occurred no movement at all; and Laplace, consequent-
ly, assumed one on no more philosophical ground than that some-
thing of the kind was necessary for the establishment of what he in-
tended to establish.

171   His original idea seems to have been a compound of the true Epi-
curean atoms with the false nebulæ of his contemporaries; and thus
his theory presents us with the singular anomaly of absolute truth
deduced, as a mathematical result, from a hybrid datum of ancient
imagination intertangled with modern inacumen. Laplace's real
strength lay, in fact, in an almost miraculous mathematical instinct:—
on this he relied; and in no instance did it fail or deceive him:—in
the case of the Nebular Cosmogony, it led him, blindfolded, through
a labyrinth of Error, into one of the most luminous and stupendous
temples of Truth.

172   Let us now fancy,—merely fancy—[a] for the moment, that the ring
first thrown off by the Sun—that is to say, the ring whose breaking-
up constituted Neptune—did not, in fact, break up until the throw-
ing-off of the ring out of which Uranus arose; that this latter ring,
again, remained perfect until the discharge of that out of which
sprang Saturn; that this latter, again, remained entire until the dis-
charge of that from which originated Jupiter—and so on. Let us
imagine, in a word, that no dissolution occurred among the rings
until the final rejection of that which gave birth to Mercury. We thus
paint to the eye of the mind a series of cöexistent concentric circles;
and looking as well at *them* as at the processes by which, according
to Laplace's hypothesis, they were constructed, we perceive at once
a very singular analogy with the atomic strata and the process of the

a. P fancy, / HW *fancy,—merely fancy—*

original radiation[a] as I have described it. Is it impossible that, on measuring the *forces*, respectively, by which each successive planetary circle was thrown off—that is to say, on measuring the successive excesses of rotation over gravitation which occasioned the successive discharges—we should find the analogy in question more decidedly confirmed? *Is it improbable that we should discover these forces to have varied—as in the original radiation—proportionally with[b] the squares of the distances?*

173   Our solar system, consisting, in chief, of one sun, with seventeen[c] planets certainly, and possibly a few more, revolving about it at various distances, and attended by seventeen moons assuredly, but *very* probably by several others—is now to be considered as *an example* of the innumerable agglomerations which proceeded to take place throughout the Universal Sphere of atoms on withdrawal of the Divine Volition. I mean to say that our solar system is to be understood as affording a *generic instance* of these agglomerations, or, more correctly, of the ulterior conditions at which they arrived. If we keep our attention fixed on the idea of *the utmost possible Relation* as the Omnipotent design, and on the precautions taken to accomplish it through difference of form, among the original atoms, and particular inequidistance, we shall find it impossible to suppose for a moment that even any two of the incipient agglomerations reached precisely the same result in the end. We shall rather be inclined to think that *no two* stellar bodies in the Universe—whether suns, planets or moons—are particularly, while *all* are generally, similar. Still less, then, can we imagine any two *assemblages* of such bodies—any two "systems"—as having more than a general resemblance.* Our telescopes, at this point, thoroughly confirm our deductions. Taking our own solar system, then, as merely a loose or general type of all, we have so far proceeded in our subject as to survey the Universe of Stars[d] under the aspect of a spherical space, throughout which, dispersed with merely general equability, exist a number of but generally similar *sytems*.

---

*It is not *impossible* that some unlooked-for optical improvement may disclose to us, among innumerable varieties of systems, a luminous sun, encircled by luminous and non-luminous rings, within and without and between which, revolve luminous and non-luminous planets, attended by moons having moons—and even these latter again having moons.

a. P irradiation / NM, HW *radiation*
b. P *to* [italics] / NM, HW *with* [italics] [We follow HW.]
c. P sixteen / NM, HW *seventeen*
d. P Universe / HW *Universe of Stars*

174 Let us now, expanding our conceptions, look upon each of these systems as in itself an atom; which in fact it is, when we consider it as but one of the countless myriads of systems which constitute the Universe. Regarding all, then, as but colossal atoms, each with the same ineradicable tendency to Unity which characterizes the actual atoms of which it consists—we enter at once a[a] new order of aggregations. The smaller systems, in the vicinity of a larger one, would, inevitably, be drawn into still closer vicinity. A thousand would assemble here; a million there—perhaps here, again, even a billion—leaving, thus, immeasurable vacancies in space. And if, now, it be demanded why, in the case of these systems—of these merely Titanic atoms—I speak, simply, of an "assemblage," and not, as in the case of the actual atoms, of a more or less consolidated agglomeration:—if it be asked, for instance, why I do not carry what I suggest to its legitimate conclusion, and describe, at once, these assemblages of system-atoms as rushing to consolidation in spheres—as each becoming condensed into one magnificent sun—my reply is that μελλοντα ταυτα—I am but pausing, for a moment, on the awful threshold of *the Future.* For the present, calling these assemblages "clusters," we see them in the incipient stages of their consolidation. Their *absolute* consolidation is *to come.*

175 We have now reached a point from which we behold the Universe of Stars[b] as a spherical space, interspersed, *unequably,* with *clusters.* It will be noticed that I here prefer the adverb "unequably" to the phrase "with a merely general equability," employed before. It is evident, in fact, that the equability of distribution will diminish in the ratio of the agglomerative processes—that is to say, as the things distributed diminish in number. Thus the increase of *in*equability— an increase which must continue until, sooner or later, an epoch will arrive at which the largest agglomeration will absorb all the others— should be viewed as, simply, a corroborative indication of the *tendency to One.*

176 And here, at length, it seems proper to inquire whether the ascertained *facts* of Astronomy confirm the general arrangement which I have thus, deductively, assigned to the Heavens. Thoroughly, they *do.* Telescopic observation, guided by the laws of perspective, enables

a. P once upon a / HW *once a*
b. P Universe / HW *Universe of Stars*

us to understand that the perceptible Universe exists as *a roughly spherical*[a] *cluster of clusters, irregularly disposed.*

177   The "clusters" of which this Universal *"cluster of clusters"* consists, are merely what we have been in the practice of designating "nebulæ"—and, of these "nebulæ," *one* is of paramount interest to mankind. I allude to the Galaxy, or Milky Way. This interests us, first and most obviously, on account of its great superiority in apparent size, not only to any one other cluster in the firmament, but to all the other clusters taken together. The largest of these latter occupies a mere point, comparatively, and is distinctly seen only with the aid of a telescope. The Galaxy sweeps throughout the Heaven and is brilliantly visible to the naked eye. But it interests man chiefly, although less immediately, on account of its being his home; the home of the Earth on which he exists; the home of the Sun about which this Earth revolves; the home of that "system" of orbs of which the Sun is the centre and primary—the Earth one of seventeen[b] secondaries, or planets—the Moon one of seventeen tertiaries, or satellites. The Galaxy, let me repeat, is but one of the *clusters* which I have been describing—but one of the mis-called "nebulæ" revealed to us—by the telescope alone, sometimes—as faint hazy spots in various quarters of the sky. We have no reason to suppose the Milky Way *really* more extensive than the least of these "nebulæ." Its vast superiority in size is but an apparent superiority arising from our position in regard to it—that is to say, from our position in its midst. However strange the assertion may at first appear to those unversed in Astronomy, still the astronomer himself has no hesitation in asserting that we are *in the midst* of that inconceivable host of stars—of suns—of systems—which constitute the Galaxy. Moreover, not only have *we*—not only has *our* Sun a right to claim the Galaxy as its own especial cluster, but, with slight reservation, it may be said that all the distinctly visible stars of the firmament—all the stars visible to the naked eye—have equally a right to claim it as *their* own.

178   There has been a great deal of misconception in respect to the *shape* of the Galaxy; which, in nearly all our astronomical treatises, is said to resemble that of a capital Y. The cluster in question has, in reality, a certain general—*very* general resemblance to the planet Saturn, with its encompassing triple ring. Instead of the solid orb

a. P *a cluster* [italics] / HW *a roughly spherical cluster* [italics] [We follow HW.]
b. P sixteen / NM, HW *seventeen*

of that planet, however, we must picture to ourselves a lenticular star-island, or collection of stars; our Sun lying excentrically—near the shore of the island—on that side of it which is nearest the constellation of the Cross and farthest from that of Cassiopeia. The surrounding ring, where it approaches our position, has in it a longitudinal gash, which does, in fact, cause *the ring, in our vicinity,* to assume, loosely, the appearance of a capital Y.

179   We must not fall into the error, however, of conceiving the somewhat indefinite girdle as at all *remote,* comparatively speaking, from the also indefinite lenticular cluster which it surrounds; and thus, for mere purpose of explanation, we may speak of our Sun as actually situated at that point of the Y where its three component lines unite; and, conceiving this letter to be of a certain solidity—of a certain thickness, very trivial in comparison with its length—we may even speak of our position as *in the middle* of this thickness. Fancying ourselves thus placed, we shall no longer find difficulty in accounting for the phænomena presented—which are perspective altogether. When we look upward or downward—that is to say, when we cast our eyes in the direction of the letter's *thickness*—we look through fewer stars than when we cast them in the direction of its *length,* or *along* either of the three component lines. Of course, in the former case, the stars appear scattered—in the latter, crowded.— To reverse this explanation:—An inhabitant of the Earth, when looking, as we commonly express ourselves, *at* the Galaxy, is then beholding it in some of the directions of its length—is looking *along* the lines of the Y—but when, looking out into the general Heaven, he turns his eyes *from* the Galaxy, he is then surveying it in the direction of the letter's thickness; and on this account the stars seem to him scattered; while, in fact, they are as close together, on an average, as in the mass of the cluster. *No* consideration could be better adapted to convey an idea of this cluster's stupendous extent.

180   If, with a telescope of high space-pentrating power, we carefully inspect the firmament, we shall become aware of *a belt of clusters*— of what we have hitherto called "nebulæ"—a *band,* of varying breadth, stretching from horizon to horizon, at right angles to the general course of the Milky Way. This band is the ultimate *cluster of clusters.* This belt is *The Universe of Stars.*[a] Our Galaxy is but one, and perhaps

---

a. P *The Universe* [italics] / HW *The Universe of Stars* [italics] [We follow HW.]

one of the most inconsiderable, of the clusters which go to the con-stitution of this ultimate, Universal *belt* or *band*. The appearance of this cluster of clusters, to our eyes, *as* a belt or band, is altogether a perspective phænomenon of the same character as that which causes us to behold our own individual and roughly-spherical cluster, the Galaxy, under guise also of a belt, traversing the Heavens at right angles to the Universal one. The shape of the all-inclusive cluster is, of course *generally,* that of each individual cluster which it includes. Just as the scattered stars which, on looking *from* the Galaxy, we see in the general sky, are, in fact, but a portion of that Galaxy itself, and as closely intermingled with it as any of the telescopic points in what seems the densest portion of its mass—so are the scattered "nebulæ" which, on casting our eyes *from* the Universal *belt,* we perceive at all points of the firmament—so, I say, are these scattered "nebulæ" to be understood as only perspectively scattered, and as but a portion[a] of the one supreme and Universal *sphere.*

181 No astronomical fallacy is more untenable, and none has been more pertinaciously adhered to, than that of the absolute *illimitation* of the Universe of Stars. The reasons for limitation, as I have already assigned them, *à priori,* seem to me unanswerable; but, not to speak of these, *observation* assures us that there is, in numerous directions around us, certainly, if not in all, a positive limit—or, at the very least, affords us no basis whatever for thinking otherwise. Were the succes-sion of stars endless, then the background of the sky would present us an uniform luminosity, like that displayed by the Galaxy—since there could be absolutely no point, in all that background, at which would not exist a star.[b] The only mode, therefore, in which, under such a state of affairs, we could comprehend the *voids* which our tele-scopes find in innumerable directions, would be by supposing the distance of the invisible background so immense that no ray from it has yet been able to reach us at all. That this *may* be so, who shall venture to deny? I maintain, simply, that we have not even the shad-ow of a reason for believing that it *is* so.

182 When speaking of the vulgar propensity to regard all bodies on the Earth as tending merely to the Earth's centre, I observed that,

a. P part and parcel / HW *but a portion*
b. P *since there could be absolutely no point, in all that background, at which would not exist a star.* [ital-ics] / HW *since there could be absolutely no point, in all that background, at which would not exist a star.* [Rom. See ¶31, note a. We follow HW.]

"with certain exceptions to be specified hereafter, every body on the Earth tends[a] not only to the Earth's centre, but in every conceivable direction besides."[*] The "exceptions" refer to those frequent gaps in the Heavens, where our utmost scrutiny can detect not only no stellar bodies, but no indications of their existence:—where yawning chasms, blacker than Erebus, seem to afford us glimpses, through the boundary walls of the Universe of Stars, into the illimitable Universe of Vacancy, beyond. Now as any body, existing on the Earth, chances to pass, either through its own movement or the Earth's, into a line with any one of these voids, or cosmical abysses, it clearly is no longer attracted *in the direction of that void,* and for the moment, consequently, is "heavier" than at any period, either after or before. Independently of the consideration of these voids, however, and looking only at the generally unequable distribution of the stars, we see that the absolute tendency of bodies on the Earth to the Earth's centre, is in a state of perpetual variation.

183   We comprehend, then, the insulation of our Universe. We perceive the isolation of *that*—of *all* that which we grasp with the senses. We know that there exists one cluster of clusters[c]—a collection around which, on all sides, extend the immeasurable wildernesses of a Space *to all human perception* untenanted. But *because* on[d] the confines of this Universe of Stars we are compelled to pause, through want of farther evidence from the senses, is it right to conclude that, in fact, there *is* no material point beyond that which we have thus been permitted to attain? Have we, or have we not, an analogical right to the inference that this perceptible Universe—that this cluster of clusters—is but one of *a series* of clusters of clusters, the rest of which are invisible through distance—through the diffusion of their light being so excessive, ere it reaches us, as not to produce upon our reti-

---

*Page 31[b].

---

a. P tended / NM, HW *tends*

b. P*Page 62 / O, NM, HW *Page 40 [Poe's numbers refer to the pages on which related material appears. Page 62 of P contains paragraphs 116, 117, and part of 118, which deal with material similar to what he argues in ¶182. But Poe realized that that reference was not the one he had been looking for and corrected himself in O, NM, and HW because on page 40, in ¶64, the *same* passage appears, together with a promise to say more about it later. Our edition refers to the page in our book on which ¶64 appears.]

c. P *cluster of clusters* [italics] / HW *cluster of clusters* [Rom. See ¶31, note a. We follow HW.]

d. P upon / HW *on*

nae[a] a light-impression—or from there being no such emanation as light at all, in those[b] unspeakably distant worlds—or, lastly, from the mere interval being so vast, that the electric tidings of their presence in Space, have not yet—through the lapsing myriads of years—been enabled to traverse that interval?

184   Have we any right to inferences—have we any ground whatever for visions such as these? If we have a right to them in *any* degree, we have a right to their infinite extension.

185   The human brain has obviously a leaning to the *"Infinite,"* and fondles the phantom of the idea. It seems to long with a passionate fervor for this impossible conception, with the hope of intellectually believing it when conceived. What is general among the whole race of Man, of course no individual of that race can be warranted in considering abnormal; nevertheless, there *may* be a class of superior intelligences, to whom the human bias alluded to may wear all the character of monomania.

186   My question, however, remains unanswered:—Have we any right to infer—let us say, rather, to imagine—an interminable succession of the "clusters of clusters," or of "Universes" more or less similar?

187   I reply that the "right," in a case such as this, depends absolutely on[c] the hardihood of that imagination which ventures to claim the right. Let me declare, only, that, as an individual, I myself feel impelled to the *fancy*—without daring to call it more—that there *does* exist a *limitless* succession of Universes, more or less similar to that of which we have cognizance—to that of which *alone* we shall ever have cognizance—at the very least until the return of our own particular Universe into Unity. *If* such clusters of clusters exist, however—*and they do*—it is abundantly clear that, having had no part in our origin, they have no portion in our laws. They neither attract us, nor we them. Their material—their spirit is not ours—is not that which obtains in any part of our Universe. They can[d] not impress our senses or our souls. Among them and us—considering all, for the moment, collectively—there are no influences in common. Each exists apart and independently, *in the bosom of its proper and particular God.*

a. P retinas / NM, / HW retinae [The Putnam *Eureka* always prints æ as a digraph. In this handwritten correction, Poe did not write the "a" and "e" together.]
b. P these / HW *those*
c. P upon / HW *on*
d. P could / HW *can*

188   In the conduct of this Discourse, I am aiming less at physical than at metaphysical order. The clearness with which even material phæ-nomena are presented to the understanding, depends very little, I have long since learned to perceive, upon a merely natural, and al-most altogether upon a moral, arrangement. If then I seem to step somewhat too discursively from point to point of my topic, let me suggest that I do so in the hope of thus the better keeping unbro-ken that chain of *graduated impression* by which alone the intellect of Man can expect to encompass the grandeurs of which I speak, and, in their majestic totality, to comprehend them.

189   So far, our attention has been directed, almost exclusively, to a gen-eral and relative grouping of the stellar bodies in space. Of specifica-tion there has been little; and whatever ideas of *quantity* have been conveyed—that is to say, of number, magnitude, and distance—have been conveyed incidentally and by way of preparation for more defini-tive conceptions. These latter let us now attempt to entertain.

190   Our solar system, as has been already mentioned, consists, in chief, of one sun and seventeen[a] planets certainly, but in all probability a few others, revolving around it as a centre, and attended by seven-teen moons of which we know, with possibly several more of which as yet we know nothing. These various bodies are not true spheres, but oblate spheroids—spheres flattened at the poles of the imaginary axes about which they rotate:—the flattening being a consequence of the rotation. Neither is the Sun absolutely the centre of the sys-tem; for this Sun itself, with all the planets, revolves about a perpetu-ally shifting point of space, which is the system's general centre of gravity. Neither are we to consider the paths through which these different spheroids move—the moons about the planets, the plan-ets about the Sun, or the Sun about the common centre—as circles in an accurate sense. They are, in fact, *ellipses—one of the foci being the point about which the revolution is made.* An ellipse is a curve, returning into itself, one of whose diameters is longer than the other. In the longer diameter are two points, equidistant from the middle of the line, and so situated otherwise that if, from each of them a straight line be drawn to any one point of the curve, the two lines, taken to-gether, will be equal to the longer diameter itself. Now let us conceive such an ellipse. At one of the points mentioned, which are the *foci*,

a. P sixteen / NM, HW *seventeen*

let us fasten an orange. By an elastic thread let us connect this orange with a pea; and let us place this latter on the circumference of the ellipse. Let us now move the pea continuously around the orange—keeping always on the circumference of the ellipse. The elastic thread, which, of course, varies in length as we move the pea, will form what in geometry is called a *radius vector*. Now, if the orange be understood as the Sun, and the pea as a planet revolving about it, then the revolution should be made at such a rate—with a velocity so varying—that the *radius vector* may pass over *equal areas of space in equal times*. The progress of the pea *should be*—in other words the progress of the planet *is*, of course,—slow in proportion to its distance from the Sun—swift in proportion to its proximity. Those planets, moreover, move the more slowly which are the farther from the Sun; *the squares of their periods of revolution having the same proportion to each other, as have to each other the cubes of their mean distances from the Sun.*

191   The wonderfully complex laws of revolution here described, however, are not to be understood as obtaining in our system alone. They *everywhere* prevail where Attraction prevails. They control the *Universe of Stars*.[a] Every shining speck in the firmament is, no doubt, a luminous sun, resembling our own, at least in its general features, and having in attendance upon it a greater or less number of planets, greater or less, whose still lingering luminosity is not sufficient to render them visible to us at so vast a distance, but which, nevertheless, revolve, moon-attended, about their starry centres, in obedience to the principles just detailed—in obedience to the three omniprevalent laws of revolution—the three immortal laws *guessed* by the imaginative Kepler, and but subsequently demonstrated and accounted for by the patient and mathematical Newton. Among a tribe of philosophers who pride themselves excessively upon matter-of-fact, it is far too fashionable to sneer at all speculation under the comprehensive *sobriquet,* "guess-work." The point to be considered is, *who* guesses. In guessing with Plato, we spend our time to better purpose, now and then, than in hearkening to a demonstration by Alcmæon.

192   In many works on Astronomy I find it distinctly stated that the laws of Kepler are *the basis* of the great principle, Gravitation. This idea must have arisen from the fact that the suggestion of these laws by Kepler, and his proving them *à posteriori* to have an actual existence,

a. P *Universe* [italics] / HW *Universe of Stars* [italics] [We follow HW.]

led Newton to account for them by the hypothesis of Gravitation, and, finally, to demonstrate them *à priori*, as necessary consequences of the hypothetical principle. Thus so far from the laws of Kepler being the basis of Gravity, Gravity is the basis of these laws—as it is, indeed, of all the laws of the material Universe which are not referable to Repulsion alone.

193   The mean distance of the Earth from the Moon—that is to say, from the heavenly body in our closest vicinity—is 237,000 miles. Mercury, the planet nearest the Sun, is distant from him 37 millions of miles. Venus, the next, revolves at a distance of 68 millions:—the Earth, which comes next, at a distance of 95 millions:—Mars, then, at a distance of 144 millions. Now come the nine[a] Asteroids (Ceres, Juno, Vesta, Pallas, Astræa, Flora, Iris, Hebe and . . .)[b] at an average distance of about 250 millions. Then we have Jupiter, distant 490 millions; then Saturn, 900 millions; then Uranus, 19 hundred millions; finally Neptune, lately discovered, and revolving at a distance, say of 28[*] hundred millions. Leaving Neptune out of the account—of which as yet we know little accurately and which is, possibly, one of a system of Asteroids—it will be seen that, within certain limits, there exists an *order of interval* among the planets. Speaking loosely, we may say that each outer planet is twice as far from the Sun as is the next inner one. May not the *order* here mentioned—*may not the law of Bode*—*be deduced from consideration of the analogy suggested by me as having place between the solar discharge of rings and the mode of the atomic radiation?*[c]

194   The numbers hurriedly mentioned in this summary of distance, it is folly to attempt comprehending, unless in the light of abstract arithmetical facts. They are not practically tangible ones. They convey no precise ideas. I have stated that Neptune, the planet farthest from the Sun, revolves about him at a distance of 28 hundred millions of miles. So far good:—I have stated a mathematical fact; and, without

[*] O Another just discovered. [This memo to Poe himself appears at the bottom of page 106 in the O copy, so we put the note after the last word on the page. But it obviously refers to the list of asteroids earlier in the paragraph; see variant a above, where Poe changed "eight" to "nine."]

a. P eight / NM, HW *nine*
b. P and Hebe) / HW actually reads: "Iris, and Hebe) and" [Poe deleted the first "and" then added the second. He seems to have left his correction incomplete, because "Iris, Hebe) and" makes no sense; it is Poe's error. Other editors give *"Hebe and . . .)"* meaning "and a new asteroid yet to be named." That makes sense and is likely what Poe intended.]
c. P *irradiation* [italics] / NM, HW *radiation* [italics] [We follow HW.]

comprehending it in the least, we may put it to use—mathematically. But in mentioning, even, that the Moon revolves about the Earth at the comparatively trifling distance of 237,000 miles, I entertained no expectation of giving any one to understand—to know—to feel—how far from the Earth the Moon actually *is*. 237,000 *miles!* There are, perhaps, few of my readers who have not crossed the Atlantic ocean; yet how many of them have a distinct idea of even the 3,000 miles intervening between shore and shore? I doubt, indeed, whether the man lives who can force into his brain the most remote conception of the interval between one milestone and its next neighbor upon the turnpike. We are in some measure aided, however, in our consideration of distance, by combining this consideration with the kindred one of velocity. Sound passes through 1100 feet of space in a second of time. Now were it possible for an inhabitant of the Earth to see the flash of a cannon discharged in the Moon, and to hear the report, he would have to wait, after perceiving the former, more than 13 entire days and nights before getting any intimation of the latter.

195   However feeble be the impression, even thus conveyed, of the Moon's real distance from the Earth, it will, nevertheless, effect a good object in enabling us more clearly to see the futility of attempting to grasp such intervals as that of the 28 hundred millions of miles between our Sun and Neptune; or even that of the 95 millions between the Sun and the Earth we inhabit. A cannon-ball, flying at the greatest velocity with which such a ball has ever been known to fly, could not traverse the latter interval in less than 20 years; while for the former it would require 590.

196   Our Moon's real diameter is 2160 miles; yet she is comparatively so trifling an object that it would take nearly 50 such orbs to compose one as great as the Earth.

197   The diameter of our own globe is 7912 miles—but from the enunciation of these numbers what positive idea do we derive?

198   If we ascend an ordinary mountain and look around us from its summit, we behold a landscape stretching, say 40 miles, in every direction; forming a circle 250 miles in circumference; and including an area of 5000 square miles. The extent of such a prospect, on account of the *successiveness* with which its portions necessarily present themselves to view, can be only very feebly and very partially appreciated:—yet the entire panorama would comprehend no more than

one 40,000th part of the mere *surface* of our globe. Were this panorama, then, to be succeeded, after the lapse of an hour, by another of equal extent; this again by a third, after the lapse of another hour; this again by a fourth after lapse of another hour—and so on, until the scenery of the whole Earth were exhausted; and were we to be engaged in examining these various panoramas for twelve hours of every day; we should nevertheless, be 9 years and 48 days in completing the general survey.

199   But if the mere surface of the Earth eludes the grasp of the imagination, what are we to think of its cubical contents? It embraces a mass of matter equal in weight to at least 2 sextillions, 200 quintillions of tons. Let us suppose it in a state of quiescence; and now let us endeavor to conceive a mechanical force sufficient to set it in motion! Not the strength of all the myriads of beings whom we may conclude to inhabit the planetary worlds of our system—not the combined physical strength of *all* these beings—even admitting all to be more powerful than man—would avail to stir the ponderous mass *a single inch* from its position.

200   What are we to understand, then, of the force, which under similar circumstances, would be required to move the *largest* of our planets, Jupiter? This is 86,000 miles in diameter, and would include within its surface[a] more than a thousand orbs of the magnitude of our own. Yet this stupendous body is actually flying around the Sun at the rate of 29,000 miles an hour—that is to say, with a velocity 40 times greater than that of a cannon-ball! The thought of such a phænomenon cannot well be said to *startle* the mind:—it palsies and appals it. Not unfrequently we task our imagination in picturing the capacities of an angel. Let us fancy such a being at a distance of some hundred miles from Jupiter—a close eye-witness of this planet as it speeds on its annual revolution. Now *can* we, I demand, fashion for ourselves any conception so distinct of this ideal being's spiritual exaltation, as *that* involved in the supposition that, even by this immeasurable mass of matter, whirled immediately before his eyes, with a velocity so unutterable, he—an angel—angelic though he be—is not at once struck into nothingness and overwhelmed?

201   At this point, however, it seems proper to suggest that, in fact, we have been speaking of comparative trifles. Our Sun, the central and

a. P periphery / HW *surface*

controlling orb of the system to which Jupiter belongs, is not only greater than Jupiter, but greater by far than all the planets of the system taken together. This fact is an essential condition, indeed, of the stability of the system itself. The diameter of Jupiter has been mentioned:—it is 86,000 miles:—that of the Sun is 882,000 miles. An inhabitant of the latter, travelling 90 miles a day, would be more than 80 years in going round its[a] circumference. It occupies a cubical space of 681 quadrillions, 472 trillions of miles. The Moon, as has been stated, revolves about the Earth at a distance of 237,000 miles—in an orbit, consequently, of nearly a million and a half. Now, were the Sun placed upon the Earth, centre over centre, the body of the former would extend, in every direction, not only to the line of the Moon's orbit, buy beyond it, a distance of 200,000 miles.

202   And here, once again, let me suggest that, in fact, we have *still* been speaking of comparative trifles. The distance of the planet Neptune from the Sun has been stated:—it is 28 hundred millions of miles; its[b] orbit, therefore, is about 17 billions. Let this be borne in mind while we glance at some one of the brightest stars. Between this and the star of *our* system, (the Sun,) there is a gulf of space, to convey any idea of which we should need the tongue of an archangel. From *our* system, then, and from *our* Sun, or star, the star at which we suppose ourselves glancing is a thing altogether apart:—still, for the moment, let us imagine it placed upon our Sun, centre over centre, as we just now imagined this Sun itself placed upon the Earth. Let us now conceive the particular star we have in mind, extending, in every direction, beyond the orbit of Mercury—of Venus—of the Earth:—still *on,* beyond the orbit of Mars—of the Asteroids—of Jupiter—of Saturn[c]—of Uranus—until, finally, we fancy it filling the circle—17 *billions of miles in circumference*—which is described by the revolution of Leverrier's planet. When we have conceived all this, we shall have entertained no extravagant conception. There is the very best reason for believing that many of the stars are even far larger than the one we have imagined. I mean to say that we have the very best *empirical* basis for such belief:—and, in looking back at the original, atomic arrangements for *diversity,* which have been assumed as a part of the Divine plan in the constitution of the Universe, we shall

a. P round a great circle of its / NM, HW *round its*
b. P miles; the circumference of its / HW *miles; its*
c. P Mars—of Jupiter— / HW *Mars—of the Asteroids—of Jupiter—of Saturn—*

be enabled easily to understand, and to credit, the existence of even far vaster disproportions in stellar size than any to which I have hitherto alluded. The largest orbs, of course, we must expect to find rolling through the widest vacancies of Space.

203   I remarked, just now, that to convey an idea of the interval between our Sun and any one of the other stars, we should require the eloquence of an archangel. In so saying, I should not be accused of exaggeration; for, in simple truth, these are topics on which it is scarcely possible to exaggerate. But let us bring the matter more distinctly before the eye of the mind.

204   In the first place, we may get a general, *relative* conception of the interval referred to, by comparing it with the inter-planetary spaces. If, for example, we suppose the Earth, which is, in reality, 95 millions of miles from the Sun, to be only *one foot* from that luminary; then Neptune would be 40 feet distant; *and the star Alpha Lyræ, at the very least, 159.*

205   Now I presume that, in the termination of my last sentence, few of my readers have noticed anything especially objectionable— particularly wrong. I said that the distance of the Earth from the Sun being taken at *one foot,* the distance of Neptune would be 40 feet, and that of Alpha Lyræ, 159. The proportion between one foot and 159 has appeared, perhaps, to convey a sufficiently definite impression of the proportion between the two intervals—that of the Earth from the Sun and that of Alpha Lyræ from the same luminary. But my account of the matter should, in reality, have run thus:—The distance of the Earth from the Sun being taken at one foot, the distance of Neptune would be 40 feet, and that of Alpha Lyræ, 159——*miles:*—that is to say, I had assigned to Alpha Lyrae, in my first statement of the case, only the 5280*th part* of that distance which is the *least distance possible* at which it can actually lie.

206   To proceed:—However distant a mere *planet* is, yet when we look at it through a telescope, we see it under a certain form—of a certain appreciable size. Now I have already hinted at the probable bulk of many of the stars; nevertheless, when we view any one of them, even through the most powerful telescope, it is found to present us with *no form,* and consequently with *no magnitude* whatever. We see it as a point and nothing more.

207   Again;—Let us suppose ourselves walking, at night, on a highway. In a field on one side of the road, is a line of tall objects, say trees,

the figures of which are distinctly defined against the background of the sky. This line of objects extends at right angles to the road, and from the road to the horizon. Now, as we proceed along the road, we see these objects changing their positions, respectively, in relation to a certain fixed point in that portion of the firmament which forms the background of the view. Let us suppose this fixed point—sufficiently fixed for our purpose—to be the rising moon. We become aware, at once, that while the tree nearest us so far alters its position in respect to the moon, as to seem flying behind us, the tree in the extreme distance has scarcely changed at all its relative position with the satellite. We then go on to perceive that the farther the objects are from us, the less they alter their positions; and the converse. Then we begin, unwittingly, to estimate the distances of individual trees by the degrees in which they evince the relative alteration. Finally, we come to understand how it might be possible to ascertain the actual distance of any given tree in the line, by using the amount of relative alteration as a basis in a simple geometrical problem. Now this relative alteration is what we call "parallax;" and by parallax we calculate the distances of the heavenly bodies. Applying the principle to the trees in question, we should, of course, be very much at a loss to comprehend the distance of *that* tree, which, however far we proceeded along the road, should evince *no* parallax at all. This, in the case described, is a thing impossible; but impossible only because all distances on our Earth are trivial indeed:— in comparison with the vast cosmical quantities, we may speak of them as absolutely nothing.

208   Now, let us suppose the star Alpha Lyræ directly overhead; and let us imagine that, instead of standing on the Earth, we stand at one end of a straight road stretching through Space to a distance equalling the diameter of the Earth's orbit—that is to say, to a distance of 190 *millions of miles*. Having observed, by means of the most delicate micrometrical instruments, the exact position of the star, let us now pass along this inconceivable road, until we reach its other extremity. Now, once again, let us look at the star. It is *precisely* where we left it. Our instruments, however delicate, assure us that its relative position is absolutely—is identically the same as at the commencement of our unutterable journey. *No* parallax—none whatever—has been found.

209   The fact is, that, in regard to the distance of the fixed stars—of

any one of the myriads of suns glistening on the farther side of that awful chasm which separates our system from its brothers in the cluster to which it belongs—astronomical science, until very lately, could speak only with a negative certainty. Assuming the brightest as the nearest, we could say, even of *them,* only that there is a certain incomprehensible distance on the *hither* side of which they cannot be:—how far they are beyond it we had in no case been able to ascertain. We perceived, for example, that Alpha Lyræ cannot be nearer to us than 19 trillions, 200 billions of miles; but, for all we knew, and indeed for all we now know, it may be distant from us the square, or the cube, or any other power of the number mentioned. By dint, however, of wonderfully minute and cautious observations, continued, with novel instruments, for many laborious years, *Bessel,* not long ago deceased, has lately succeeded in determining the distance of six or seven stars; among others, that of the star numbered 61 in the constellation of the Swan. The distance in this latter instance ascertained, is 670,000 times that of the Sun; which last it will be remembered, is 95 millions of miles. The star 61 Cygni, then, is nearly 61 trillions of miles from us—or more than three times the distance assigned, *as the least possible,* for Alpha Lyræ.

210   In attempting to appreciate this interval by the aid of any considerations of *velocity,* as we did in endeavoring to estimate the distance of the moon, we must leave out of sight, altogether, such nothings as the speed of a cannon-ball, or of sound. Light, however, according to the latest calculations of Struve, proceeds at the rate of 167,000 miles in a second. Thought itself cannot pass through this interval more speedily—if, indeed, thought can traverse it at all. Yet, in coming from 61 Cygni to us, even at this inconceivable rate, light occupies more than *ten years;* and, consequently, were the star this moment blotted out from the Universe, still, *for ten years,* would it continue to sparkle on, undimmed in its paradoxical glory.

211   Keeping now in mind whatever feeble conception we may have attained of the interval between our Sun and 61 Cygni, let us remember that this interval, however unutterably vast, we are permitted to consider as but the *average* interval among the countless host of stars composing that cluster, or "nebula," to which our system, as well as that of 61 Cygni, belongs. I have, in fact, stated the case with great moderation:—we have excellent reason for believing 61 Cygni to be one of the *nearest* stars, and thus for concluding, at least for the present,

that its distance from us is *less* than the average distance between star and star in the magnificent cluster of the Milky Way.

212   And here, once again and finally, it seems proper to suggest that even as yet we have been speaking of trifles. Ceasing to wonder at the space between star and star in our own or in any particular cluster, let us rather turn our thoughts to the intervals between cluster and cluster, in the all comprehensive cluster of the Universe.

213   I have already said that light proceeds at the rate of 167,000 miles in a second—that is, about 10 millions of miles in a minute, or about 600 millions of miles in an hour:—yet so far removed from us are some of the "nebulæ" that even light, speeding with this velocity, could not and does not reach us, from those mysterious regions, in less than 3 *millions of years*. This calculation, moreover, is made by the elder Herschell [*sic*], and in reference merely to those comparatively proximate clusters within the scope of his own telescope. There *are* "nebulæ," however, which, through the magical tube of Lord Rosse, are this instant whispering in our ears the secrets of *a million of ages* by-gone. In a word, the events which we behold now—at this moment—in those worlds—are the identical events which interested their inhabitants *ten hundred thousand centuries ago*. In intervals—in distances such as this suggestion forces upon the *soul*—rather than upon the mind—we find, at length, a fitting climax to all hitherto frivolous considerations of *quantity*.

214   Our fancies thus occupied with the cosmical distances, let us take the opportunity of referring to the difficulty which we have so often experienced, while pursuing *the beaten path* of astronomical reflection, *in accounting* for the immeasurable voids alluded to—in comprehending why chasms so totally unoccupied and therefore apparently so needless, have been made to intervene between star and star—between cluster and cluster—in understanding, to be brief, a sufficient reason for the Titanic scale, in respect of mere *Space,* on which the Universe of Stars[a] is seen to be constructed. A rational cause for the phænomenon, I maintain that Astronomy has palpably failed to assign:—but the considerations through which, in this Essay, we have proceeded step by step, enable us clearly and immediately to perceive that *Space and Duration are one.* That the Universe of Stars[b] might *endure* throughout an æra at all commensurate with

a. P Universe / HW *Universe of Stars*
b. P Universe / HW *Universe of Stars*

the grandeur of its component material portions and with the high majesty of its spiritual purposes, it was necessary that the original atomic diffusion be made to so inconceivable an extent as to be only not infinite. It was required, in a word, that the stars should be gathered into visibility from invisible nebulosity—proceed from visibility[a] to consolidation—and so grow grey in giving birth and death to unspeakably numerous and complex variations of vitalic development:—it was required that the stars should do all this—should have time thoroughly to accomplish all these Divine purposes—*during the period* in which all things were effecting their return into Unity with a velocity accumulating in the inverse proportion of the squares of the distances at which lay the inevitable End.

215   Throughout all this we have no difficulty in understanding the absolute accuracy of the Divine *adaptation.* The density of the stars, respectively, proceeds, of course, as their condensation diminishes; condensation and heterogeneity keep pace with each other; through the latter, which is the index of the former, we estimate the vitalic and spiritual development. Thus, in the density of the globes, we have the measure in which their purposes are fulfilled. *As* density proceeds—*as* the divine intentions *are* accomplished—*as* less and still less remains *to be* accomplished—so—in the same ratio—should we expect to find an acceleration of *the End:*—and thus the philosophical mind will easily comprehend that the Divine designs in constituting the stars, advance *mathematically* to their fulfilment:—and more; it will readily give the advance a mathematical expression; it will decide that this advance is inversely proportional with the squares of the distances of all created things from the starting-point and goal of their creation.

216   Not only is this Divine adaptation, however, mathematically accurate, but there is that about it which stamps it *as divine,* in distinction from that which is merely the work of human constructiveness. I allude to the complete *mutuality* of adaptation. For example; in human constructions a particular cause has a particular effect; a particular intention brings to pass a particular object; but this is all; we see no reciprocity. The effect does not re-act upon the cause; the intention does not change relations with the object. In Divine constructions the object is either design or object as we choose to regard it—and we

a. P nebulosity / NM, HW *visibility*

may take at any time a cause for an effect, or the converse—so that we can never absolutely decide which is which.

217   To give an instance:—In polar climates the human frame, to maintain its animal heat, requires, for combustion in the capillary system, an abundant supply of highly azotized food, such as train-oil. But again:—in polar climates nearly the sole food afforded man is the oil of abundant seals and whales. Now, whether is oil at hand because imperatively demanded, or the only thing demanded because the only thing to be obtained? It is impossible to decide. There is an absolute *reciprocity of adaptation.*

218   The pleasure which we derive from any display of human ingenuity is in the ratio of *the approach* to this species of reciprocity. In the construction of *plot,* for example, in fictitious literature, we should aim at so arranging the incidents that we shall not be able to determine, of any one of them, whether it depends from any one other or upholds it. In this sense, of course, *perfection* of plot[a] is really, or practically, unattainable—but only because it is a finite intelligence that constructs. The plots of God are perfect. The Universe is a plot of God.

219   And now we have reached a point at which the intellect is forced, again, to struggle against its propensity for analogical inference— against its monomaniac grasping at the infinite. Moons have been seen *revolving* about planets; planets about stars; and the poetical instinct of humanity—its instinct of the symmetrical, even if[b] the symmetry be but a symmetry of surface:—this *instinct,* which the Soul, not only of Man but of all created beings, took up, in the beginning, from the *geometrical* basis of the Universal radiation[c]—impels us to the fancy of an endless extension of this system of *cycles.* Closing our eyes equally to *de*duction and *in*duction, we insist upon imagining a *revolution* of all the orbs of the Galaxy about some gigantic globe which we take to be the central pivot of the whole. Each cluster in the great cluster of clusters is imagined, of course, to be similarly supplied and constructed; while, that the "analogy" may be wanting at no point, we go on to conceive these clusters themselves, again, as *revolving* about some still more august sphere;—this latter, still again, *with* its encircling clusters, as but one of a yet more magnificent series of agglom-

a. P *plot* [italics] / HW *plot* [Rom. See ¶31, note a. We follow HW.]
b. P if / HW *even if*
c. P irradiation / NM, HW *radiation*

erations, *gyrating* about yet another orb central *to them*—some orb still more unspeakably sublime—some orb, let us rather say, of infinite sublimity endlessly multiplied by the infinitely sublime. Such are the conditions, continued in perpetuity, which the voice of what some people term "analogy" calls upon the Fancy to depict and the Reason to contemplate, if possible, without becoming dissatisfied with the picture. Such, *in general,* are the interminable gyrations beyond gyration which we have been instructed by Philosophy to comprehend and to account for—at[a] least in the best manner we can. Now and then, however, a philosopher proper—one whose phrenzy takes a very determinate turn—whose genius, to speak more reverentially, has a strongly-pronounced washer-womanish bias, doing every thing up by the dozen—enables us to see *precisely* that point out of sight, at which the revolutionary processes in question do, and of right ought to, come to an end.

220   It is hardly worth while, perhaps, even to sneer at the reveries of Fourier:[b]—but much has been said, latterly, of the hypothesis of Mädler—that there exists, in the centre of the Galaxy, a stupendous globe about which all the systems of the cluster revolve. The *period* of our own, indeed, has been stated—117 million of years.

221   That our Sun has a motion in space, independently of its rotation, and revolution about the system's centre of gravity, has long been suspected. This motion, granting it to exist, would be manifested perspectively. The stars in that firmamental region which we were leaving behind us, would, in a very long series of years, become crowded; those in the opposite quarter, scattered. Now, by means of astronomical History, we ascertain, cloudily, that some such phænomena have occurred. On this ground it has been declared that our system is moving to a point in the heavens diametrically opposite the star Zeta Herculis:—but this inference is, perhaps, the maximum to which we have any logical right. Mädler, however, has gone so far as to designate a particular star, Alcyone in the Pleiades, as being at or about the very spot around which a general *revolution* is performed.

222   Now, since by "analogy" we are led, in the first instance, to these dreams, it is no more than proper that we should abide by analogy, at least in some measure, during their development; and *that*[c] anal-

a. P for, / HW *for—*
b. P Fourrier / W, HW *Fourier*
c. P that / HW *that* [italics]

ogy which suggests the revolution, suggests at the same time a central orb about which it should be performed:—so far the astronomer was consistent. This central orb, however, should, dynamically, be greater than all the orbs, taken together, which surround it. Of these there are about 100 millions. "Why, then," it was of course demanded, "do we not *see* this vast central sun—*at least equal* in mass to 100 millions of such suns as ours—why do we not *see* it—*we*, especially, who occupy the mid region of the cluster—the very locality *near* which, at all events, must be situated this incomparable star?" The reply was ready—"It must be non-luminous, as are our planets." Here, then, to suit a purpose, analogy is suddenly let fall. "Not so," it may be said—"we know that non-luminous suns actually exist." It is true that we have reason at least for supposing so; but we have certainly no reason whatever for supposing that the non-luminous suns in question are encircled by *luminous* suns, while these again are surrounded by non-luminous planets:—and it is precisely all this with which Mädler is called upon to find any thing analogous in the heavens—for it is precisely all this which he imagines in the case of the Galaxy. Admitting the thing to be so, we cannot help here picturing to ourselves how sad a puzzle the *why it is so* must prove to all *à priori* philosophers.

223   But granting, in the very teeth of analogy and of every thing else, the non-luminosity of the vast central orb, we may still inquire how this orb, so enormous, could fail of being rendered visible by the flood of light thrown upon it from the 100 millions of glorious suns glaring in all directions about it. On[a] the urging of this question, the idea of an actually solid central sun appears, in some measure, to have been abandoned; and speculation proceeded to assert that the systems of the cluster perform their revolutions merely about an immaterial centre of gravity common to all. Here again then, to suit a purpose, analogy is let fall. The planets of our system revolve, it is true, about a common centre of gravity; but they do this in connexion with, and in consequence of, a material sun whose mass more than counterbalances the rest of the system.

224   The mathematical circle is a curve composed of an infinity of straight lines. But this idea of the circle—an idea which, in view of all ordinary geometry, is merely the mathematical, as contradistin-

a. P Upon / HW *On*

guished from the practical, idea—is, in sober fact, the *practical* conception which alone we have any right to entertain in regard to the majestic circle with which we have to deal, at least in fancy, when we suppose our system revolving about a point in the centre of the Galaxy. Let the most vigorous of human imaginations attempt but to take a single step towards the comprehension of a sweep so ineffable! It would scarcely be paradoxical to say that a flash of lightning itself, travelling *forever* on[a] the circumference of this unutterable circle, would still, *forever,* be travelling in a straight line. That the path of our Sun in such an orbit would, to any human perception, deviate in the slightest degree from a straight line, even in a million of years, is a proposition not to be entertained:—yet we are required to believe that a curvature has become apparent during the brief period of our astronomical history—during the[b] mere point—during the utter nothingness of two or three thousand years.

225   It may be said that Mädler *has* really ascertained a curvature in the direction of our system's now well-established progress through Space. Admitting, if necessary, this fact to be in reality such, I maintain that nothing is thereby shown except the reality of this fact—the fact of a curvature. For its *thorough* determination, ages will be required; and, when determined, it will be found indicative of some binary or other multiple relation between our Sun and some one or more of the proximate stars. I hazard nothing,[c] however, in predicting, that, after the lapse of many centuries, all efforts at determining the path of our Sun through Space, will be abandoned as fruitless. This is easily conceivable when we look at the infinity of perturbation it must experience, from its perpetually-shifting relations with other orbs, in the common approach of all to the nucleus of the Galaxy.

226   But in examining other "nebulæ" than that of the Milky Way—in surveying, generally, the clusters which overspread the heavens—do we or do we not find confirmation of Mädler's hypothesis? We do not. The forms of the clusters are exceedingly diverse when casually viewed; but on close inspection, through powerful telescopes, we recognize the sphere, very distinctly, as at least the proximate form of all:—their constitution, in general, being at variance with the idea of revolution about a common centre.

a. P upon / HW *on*
b. P a / HW *the*
c. P nothing / HW *nothing,*

227   "It is difficult," says Sir John Herschell [*sic*], "to form any conception of the dynamical state of such systems. On one hand, without a rotary motion and a centrifugal force, it is hardly possible not to regard them as in a state of *progressive collapse*. On the other, granting such a motion and such a force, we find it no less difficult to reconcile their forms with the rotation of the whole system [meaning cluster] around any single axis, without which internal collision would appear to be inevitable."

228   Some remarks lately made about the "nebulæ" by Dr. Nichol, in taking quite a different view of the cosmical conditions from any taken in this Discourse—have a very peculiar applicability to the point now at issue. He says:

229   "When our greatest telescopes are brought to bear upon them, we find that those which were thought to be irregular, are not so; they approach nearer to a globe. Here is one that looked oval; but Lord Rosse's telescope brought it into a circle. . . . . Now there occurs a very remarkable circumstance in reference to these comparatively sweeping circular masses of nebulæ. We find they are not entirely circular, but the reverse; and that all around them, on every side, there are volumes of stars, *stretching out apparently as if they were rushing towards a great central mass in consequence of the action of some great power.*"[*]

230   Were I to describe, in my own words, what must necessarily be the existing condition of each nebula,[a] on the hypothesis that all matter is, as I suggest, now returning to its original Unity, I should simply be going over, nearly verbatim, the language here employed by Dr. Nichol, without the faintest suspicion of that stupendous truth which is the key to these nebular phænomena.

231   And here let me fortify my position still farther, by the voice of a greater than Mädler—of one, moreover, to whom all the data of Mädler have long been familiar things, carefully and thoroughly considered. Referring to the elaborate calculations of Argelander— the very researches which form Mädler's basis—*Humboldt,* whose generalizing powers have never, perhaps,[b] been equalled, has the following observation:

*I must be understood as denying, *especially,* only the *revolutionary* portion of Mädler's hypothesis. Of course, if no great central orb exists *now* in our cluster, such will exist hereafter. Whenever existing, it will be merely the *nucleus* of the consolidation.

a. P nebula / HW *nebula,*
b. P perhaps / NM, HW *perhaps,*

232   "When we regard the real, proper, or non-perspective motions of the stars, we find *many groups of them moving in opposite directions;* and the data as yet in hand render it not necessary, at least, to conceive that the systems composing the Milky Way, or the clusters, generally, composing the Universe, are revolving about any particular centre unknown, whether luminous or non-luminous. It is but Man's longing for a fundamental First Cause, that impels both his intellect and his fancy to the adoption of such an hypothesis."[*]

233   The phænomenon here alluded to—that of "many groups moving in opposite directions"—is quite inexplicable by Mädler's idea; but arises, as a necessary consequence, from that which forms the basis of this Discourse. While the *merely general direction* of each atom—of each moon, planet, star, or cluster—would, on my hypothesis, be, of course, absolutely rectilinear; while the *general* path of all bodies would be a right line leading to the centre of all; it is clear, nevertheless, that this general rectilinearity would be compounded of what, with scarcely any exaggeration, we may term an infinity of particular curves—an infinity of local deviations from rectilinearity—the result of continuous differences of relative position among the multitudinous[a] masses, as each proceeds[b] on its own proper journey to the End.

234   I quoted, just now, from Sir John Herschell [*sic*], the following words, used in reference to the clusters:—"On one hand, without a rotary motion and a centrifugal force, it is hardly possible not to regard them as in a state of *progressive collapse.*" The fact is, that, in surveying the "nebulæ" with a telescope of high power, we shall find it quite impossible, having once conceived this idea of "collapse," not to gather, at all points, corroboration of the idea. A nucleus is always apparent, in the direction of which the stars seem to be precipitating themselves; nor can these nuclei be mistaken for merely perspective phænomena:—the clusters are *really* denser near the centre—sparser in the regions more remote from it. In a word, we see every

---

[*]Betrachtet man die nicht perspectivischen eigenen Bewegungen der Sterne, so scheinen viele gruppenweise in ihrer Richtung entgegengesetzt; und die bisher gesaminelten Thatsachen machen es auf's wenigste nicht nothwendig, anzunehmen, dass alle Theile unserer Sternenschicht oder gar der gesammten Sterneninseln, welche den Weltraum fullen, sich um einen grossen, unbekannten, leuchtenden oder dunkeln Centralkörper bewegen. Das Streben nach den letzten und höchsten Grundursachen macht freilich die reflectirende Thätigkeit des Menschen, wie seine Phantasie, zu einer solchen Annahme geneigt.

---

a. P multudinous / NM, HW *multitudinous*
b. P proceeded / HW *proceeds*

thing as we *should* see it were a collapse taking place; but, in general, it may be said of these clusters, that we can fairly entertain, while looking at them, the idea of *orbital movement about a centre,* only by admitting the *possible* existence, in the distant domains of space, of dynamical laws with which *we* are unacquainted.

235   On the part of Herschell [*sic*], however, there is evidently *a reluctance* to regard the nebulæ as in "a state of progressive collapse." But if facts—if even appearances justify the supposition of their being in this state, *why,* it may well be demanded, is he disinclined to admit it? Simply on account of a prejudice;—merely because the supposition is at war with a preconceived and utterly baseless notion—that of the endlessness—that of the eternal stability of the Universe.

236   If the propositions of this Discourse are tenable, the "state of progressive collapse" is *precisely* that state in which alone we are warranted in considering All Things; and, with due humility, let me here confess that, for my part, I am at a loss to conceive how any *other* understanding of the existing condition of affairs, could ever have made its way into the human brain. "The tendency to collapse" and "the attraction of gravitation" are convertible phrases. In using either, we speak of the rëaction of the First Act. Never was necessity less obvious than that of supposing Matter imbued with an ineradicable *quality* forming part of its material nature—a quality, or instinct, *forever* inseparable from it, and by dint of which inalienable principle every atom is *perpetually* impelled to seek its fellow.[a] Never was necessity less obvious than that of entertaining this unphilosophical idea. Going boldly behind the vulgar thought, we have to conceive, metaphysically, that the gravitating principle appertains to Matter *temporarily*—only while diffused—only while existing as Many instead of as One—appertains to it by virtue of its state of radiation[b] alone—appertains, in a word, altogether to its *condition,* and not in the slightest degree to *itself.* In this view, when the radiation[c] shall have returned into its source—when the rëaction shall be completed—the gravitating principle will no longer exist. And, in fact, astronomers, without at any time reaching the idea here suggested, seem to have been approximating it, in the assertion that "if there were but one body in the Universe, it would be impossible to understand how the principle,

a. P fellow-atom. / NM *fellow.*
b. P irradiation / NM, HW *radiation*
c. P irradiation / NM, HW *radiation*

Gravity, could obtain:"—that is to say, from a consideration of Matter as they find it, they reach a conclusion at which I deductively arrive. That so pregnant a suggestion as the one just quoted should have been permitted to remain so long unfruitful, is, nevertheless, a mystery which I find it difficult to fathom.

237   It is, perhaps, in no little degree, however, our propensity for the continuous—for the analogical—in the present case more particularly for the symmetrical—which has been leading us astray. And, in fact, the sense of the symmetrical is an instinct which may be depended on[a] with an almost blindfold reliance. It is the poetical essence of the Universe—*of the Universe* which, in the supremeness of its symmetry, is but the most sublime of poems. Now symmetry and consistency are convertible terms:—thus Poetry and Truth are one. A thing is consistent in the ratio of its truth—true in the ratio of its consistency. *A perfect consistency, I repeat, can be nothing but an absolute truth.* We may take it for granted, then, that Man cannot long or widely err, if he suffer himself to be guided by his poetical, which I have maintained to be his truthful, in being his symmetrical, instinct. He must have a care, however, lest, in pursuing too heedlessly the superficial symmetry of forms and motions, he leave out of sight the really essential symmetry of the principles which determine and control them.

238   That the stellar bodies would finally be merged in one—that, at last, all would be drawn into the substance of *one stupendous central orb already existing*—is an idea which, for some time past, seems, vaguely and indeterminately, to have held possession of the fancy of mankind. It is an idea, in fact, which belongs to the class of the *excessively obvious*. It springs, instantly, from a superficial observation of the cyclic and seemingly *gyrating,* or *vortical* movements of those individual portions of the Universe which come most immediately and most closely under our observation. There is not, perhaps, a human being, of ordinary education and of average reflective capacity, to whom, at some period, the fancy in question[b] has not occurred, as if spontaneously, or intuitively, and wearing all the character of a very profound and very original conception. This conception, however, so commonly entertained, has never, within my knowledge, arisen out of any abstract considerations. Being, on the contrary, always suggested, as I say, by the vortical movements about centres,

a. P upon / HW *on*
b. P inquestion / NM, HW *in question*

a reason for it, also,—a *cause* for the ingathering of all the orbs into one, *imagined to be already existing,* was naturally sought in the same direction—among these cyclic movements themselves.[a]

239   Thus it happened that, on announcement of the gradual and perfectly regular decrease observed in the orbit of Encke's[b] comet, at every successive revolution about our Sun, astronomers were nearly unanimous in the opinion that the cause in question was found—that a principle was discovered sufficient to account, physically, for that final, universal agglomeration which, I repeat, the analogical, symmetrical or poetical instinct of Man had predetermined to understand as something more than a simple hypothesis.

240   This cause—this sufficient reason for the final ingathering—was declared to exist in an exceedingly rare but still material medium pervading space; which medium, by retarding, in some degree, the progress of the comet, perpetually weakened its tangential force; thus giving a predominance to the centripetal; which, of course, drew the comet nearer and nearer at each revolution, and would eventually precipitate it upon the Sun.

241   All this was strictly logical—admitting the medium or ether; but this ether was assumed, most illogically, on the ground that no *other* mode than the one mentioned[c] could be discovered, of accounting for the observed decrease in the orbit of the comet:—as if from the fact that we could *discover* no other mode of accounting for it, it followed, in any respect, that no other mode of accounting for it existed. It is clear that innumerable causes might operate, in combination, to diminish the orbit, without even a possibility of our ever becoming acquainted with even[d] one of them. In the meantime, it has never been fairly shown, perhaps, why the retardation occasioned by the skirts of the Sun's atmosphere, through which the comet passes at perihelion, is not enough to account for the phænomenon. That Encke's[e] comet will be absorbed into the Sun, is probable; that all the comets of the system will be absorbed, is more than merely possible; but, in such case, the principle of absorption must be re-

a. P them selves / NM, HW *them-selves* [The word appeared at a line break in the 1848 edition, and the printer omitted the hyphen. Poe penciled it in. We treat "themselves" as one word.]
b. P Enck's / O, W, NM, HW *Encke's*
c. P spoken of / HW *mentioned*
d. P with one / HW *with even one*
e. P Enck's / O, W, NM, HW *Encke's*

ferred to eccentricity of orbit—to the close approximation to the Sun, of the comets at their perihelia; and is a principle not affecting, in any degree, the ponderous *spheres,* which are to be regarded as the true material constituents of the Universe.—Touching comets, in general, let me here suggest, in passing, that we cannot be far wrong in looking upon them as the *lightning-flashes of the cosmical Heaven.*

242   The idea of a retarding ether and, through it, of a final agglomeration of all things, seemed at one time, however, to be confirmed by the observation of a positive decrease in the orbit of the solid moon. By reference to eclipses recorded 2500 years ago, it was found that the velocity of the satellite's revolution *then* was considerably less than it is *now;* that on the hypothesis that its motion[a] in its orbit is uniformly in accordance with Kepler's law, and was accurately determined *then*—2500 years ago—it is now in advance of the position it *should* occupy, by nearly 9000 miles. The increase of velocity proved, of course, a diminution of orbit; and astronomers were fast yielding to a belief in an ether, as the sole mode of accounting for the phaenomenon, when Lagrange came to the rescue. He showed that, owing to the configurations of the spheroids, the shorter axes of their ellipses are subject to variation in length; the longer axes being permanent; and that this variation is continuous and vibratory—so that every orbit is in a state of transition, either from circle to ellipse, or from ellipse to circle. In the case of the moon, where the shorter axis is *de*creasing, the orbit is passing from circle to ellipse and, consequently, is *de*creasing too; but, after a long series of ages, the ultimate eccentricity will be attained; then the shorter axis will proceed to *in*crease, until the orbit becomes a circle; when the process of shortening will again take place;—and so on forever. In the case of the Earth, the orbit is passing from ellipse to circle. The facts thus demonstrated do away, of course, with all necessity for supposing an ether, and with all apprehension of the system's instability—*on the ether's account.*[b]

243   It will be remembered that I have myself assumed what we may term *an ether.* I have spoken of a subtle *influence* which we know to be ever in attendance on[c] matter, although becoming manifest only through matter's heterogeneity. To this *influence*—without daring to

a. P motions / NM, HW *motion*
b. P on the ether's account / HW *on the ether's account* [italics]
c. P upon / HW *on*

touch it at all in any effort at explaining its awful *nature*—I have referred the various phænomena of electricity, heat, light, magnetism; and more—of vitality, consciousness, and thought—in a word, of spirituality. It will be seen, at once, then, that the ether thus conceived is radically distinct from the ether of the astronomers; inasmuch as theirs is *matter* and mine *not*.

244   With the idea of a material ether, seems, thus, to have departed altogether the thought of that universal agglomeration so long predetermined by the poetical fancy of mankind:—an agglomeration in which a sound Philosophy might have been warranted in putting faith, at least to a certain extent, if for no other reason than that by this poetical fancy it *had* been so predetermined. But so far as Astronomy—so far as mere Physics have yet spoken, the cycles of the Universe are perpetual—the Universe has no conceivable end. Had an end been demonstrated, however, from so purely collateral a cause as an ether, Man's instinct of the Divine *capacity to adapt,* would have rebelled against the demonstration. We should have been forced to regard the Universe with some such sense of dissatisfaction as we experience in contemplating an unnecessarily complex work of human art. Creation would have affected us as an imperfect *plot* in a romance, where the *dénoûment* is awkwardly brought about by interposed incidents external and foreign to the main subject; instead of springing out of the bosom of the thesis—out of the heart of the ruling idea—instead of arising as a result of the primary proposition—as inseparable and inevitable part and parcel of the fundamental conception of the book.

245   What I mean by the symmetry of mere surface will now be more clearly understood. It is simply by the blandishment of this symmetry that we have been beguiled into the general idea of which Mädler's hypothesis is but a part—the idea of the vorticial indrawing of the orbs. Dismissing this nakedly physical conception, the symmetry of *principle*[a] sees the end of all things metaphysically involved in the thought of a beginning; seeks and finds,[b] in this origin of all things,[c] the *rudiment* of this end; and perceives the impiety of supposing this end likely to be brought about less simply—less directly—less obviously—less artistically—than through *the rëaction of the originating Act.*

a. P principle / HW *principle* [italics]
b. P finds / HW *finds,*
c. P things / HW *things,*

246   Recurring, then, to a previous suggestion, let us understand the systems—let us understand each star, with its attendant planets—as but a Titanic atom existing in space with precisely the same inclination for Unity which characterized, in the beginning, the actual atoms after their radiation[a] throughout the Universal sphere. As these original atoms rushed towards each other in generally straight lines, so let us conceive as at least generally rectilinear, the paths of the system-atoms towards their respective centres of aggregation:—and in this direct drawing together of the systems into clusters, with a similar and simultaneous drawing together of the clusters themselves while undergoing consolidation, we have at length attained the great *Now*—the awful Present—the Existing Condition of the Universe.

247   Of the still more awful Future a not irrational analogy may guide us in framing an hypothesis. The equilibrium between the centripetal and centrifugal forces of each system, being necessarily destroyed on[b] attainment of a certain proximity to the nucleus of the cluster to which it belongs, there must occur, at once, a chaotic or seemingly chaotic precipitation, of the moons upon the planets, of the planets upon the suns, and of the suns upon the nuclei; and the general result of this precipitation must be the gathering of the myriad now-existing stars of the firmament into an almost infinitely less number of almost infinitely superior spheres. In being immeasurably fewer, the worlds of that day will be immeasurably greater than our own. Then, indeed, amid unfathomable abysses, will be glaring unimaginable suns. But all this will be merely a climacic magnificence foreboding the great End. Of this End the new genesis described[c] can be but a very partial postponement. While undergoing consolidation, the clusters themselves, with a speed prodigiously accumulative, have been rushing towards their own general centre—and now, with a million-fold[d] electric velocity, commensurate only with their material grandeur and with their[e] spiritual passion[f] for oneness, the majestic remnants of the tribe of Stars flash, at length, into a common embrace. The inevitable catastrophe is at hand.

a. P irradiation / NM, HW *radiation*
b. P upon / HW *on*
c. P described, / HW *described*
d. P thousand-fold / HW *million-fold*
e. P the spiritual / HW *their spiritual*
f. P passion of their appetite / HW *passion*

248   But this catastrophe—what is it? We have seen accomplished the ingathering of the orbs. Henceforward, are we not to understand *one material globe of globes* as comprehending and constituting[a] the Universe? Such a fancy would be altogether at war with every assumption and consideration of this Discourse.

249   I have already alluded to that absolute *reciprocity of adaptation* which is the idiosyncrasy of the Divine[b] Art—stamping it divine. Up to this point of our reflections, we have been regarding the electrical influence as a something by dint of whose repulsion alone Matter is enabled to exist in that state of diffusion demanded for the fulfilment of its purposes:—so far, in a word, we have been considering the influence in question as ordained for Matter's sake—to subserve the objects of matter. With a perfectly legitimate reciprocity, we are now permitted to look at Matter, as created *solely for the sake of this influence*—solely to serve the objects of this spiritual Ether. Through the aid—by the means—through the agency of Matter, and by dint of its heterogeneity—is this Ether manifested—is *Spirit individualized*. It is merely in the development of this Ether, through heterogeneity, that particular masses of Matter become animate—sensitive—and in the ratio of their heterogeneity;—some reaching a degree of sensitiveness involving what we call *Thought* and thus attaining obviously[c] Conscious Intelligence.

250   In this view, we are enabled to perceive Matter as a Means—not as an End. Its purposes are thus seen to have been comprehended in its diffusion; and with the return into Unity these purposes cease. The absolutely consolidated globe of globes would be *objectless:*— therefore not for a moment could it continue to exist. Matter, created for an end, would unquestionably, on fulfilment of that end, be Matter no longer. Let us endeavor to understand that it would disappear, and that God would remain all in all.

251   That every work of Divine conception must cöexist and cöexpire with its particular design, seems to me especially obvious; and I make no doubt that, on perceiving the final globe of globes to be *objectless,* the majority of my readers will be satisfied with my *"therefore* it cannot continue to exist." Nevertheless, as the startling thought of its instantaneous disappearance is one which the most powerful in-

a. P constituting and comprehending / HW *comprehending and constituting*
b. P divine Art / HW *Divine Art*
c. P thus attaining / HW *thus attaining obviously*

tellect cannot be expected readily to entertain on grounds so decid-
edly abstract, let us endeavor to look at the idea from some other
and more ordinary point of view:—let us see how thoroughly and
beautifully it is corroborated in an *à posteriori* consideration of Mat-
ter as we actually find it.

252   I have before said that "Attraction and Repulsion being undeni-
ably the sole properties by which Matter is manifested to Mind, we
are justified in assuming that Matter *exists* only as Attraction and
Repulsion—in other words that Attraction and Repulsion *are* Mat-
ter; there being no conceivable case in which we may not employ
the term 'Matter'[a] and the terms 'Attraction' and 'Repulsion' tak-
en together, as equivalent, and therefore convertible, expressions
in Logic."*

253   Now the very definition of Attraction implies particularity—the
existence of parts, particles, or atoms; for we define it as the tendency
of "each atom &c. to every other atom" &c. according to a certain
law. Of course where there are *no* parts—where there is absolute
Unity—where the tendency to oneness is satisfied—there can be no
Attraction:—this has been fully shown, and all Philosophy admits it.
When, on fulfilment of its purposes, then, Matter shall have returned
into its original condition of *One*—a condition which presupposes
the expulsion of the separative Ether,[b] whose province and whose
capacity are limited to keeping the atoms apart until that great day
when, this Ether[c] being no longer needed, the overwhelming pres-
sure of the finally collective Attraction shall at length just sufficient-
ly predominate** and expel it:—when, I say, Matter, finally, expelling
the Ether, shall have returned into absolute Unity,—it will then (to
speak paradoxically for the moment) be Matter without Attraction

---

*Page 28–29.[d]
**"Gravity, therefore, must be the strongest of forces."—See page 45. [P 39.][e]

---

a. P Matter / HW *'Matter'*
b. P ether / HW *Ether*
c. P ether / HW *Ether*
d. P *Page 37. / O, NM *Page 38 / HW *Page 57. [Nelson, "Apparatus for a Definitive Edition"
198, notes that it is likely that Poe made an error in the annotation in HW. We have changed
the page number to match this volume: *Page 28–29.]
e. P See page 39. / O, NM, HW *See page 59. [We have changed the page number to match
our text: *(*)See page 45. P contains no example of two footnotes on the same page. Ours are
the result of an accident of pagination. P uses one asterisk to indicate a footnote; we provide a
second for clarity. The original read, *"Gravity, therefore, must be the strongest of forces."—
See page 39.]

and without Repulsion—in other words, Matter without Matter—in other words, again, *Matter no more*. In sinking into Unity, it will sink at once into that Nothingness which, to all finite[a] perception,[b] Unity must be—into that Material Nihility from which alone we can conceive it to have been evoked—to have been *created* by the Volition of God.

254   I repeat then—Let us endeavor to comprehend that the final globe of globes will instantaneously disappear, and that God will remain all in all.

255   But are we here to pause? Not so. On the Universal agglomeration and dissolution, we can readily conceive that a new and perhaps totally different series of conditions may ensue—another creation and radiation,[c] returning into itself—another action and rëaction of the Divine Will. Guiding our imaginations by that omniprevalent law of laws, the law of periodicity, are we not, indeed, more than justified in entertaining a belief—let us say, rather, in indulging a hope—that the processes we have here ventured to contemplate will be renewed forever, and forever, and forever; a novel Universe swelling into existence, and then subsiding into nothingness, at every throb of the Heart Divine?

256   And now—this Heart Divine—what is it? *It is our own.*

257   Let not the merely seeming irreverence of this idea frighten our souls from that cool exercise of consciousness—from that deep tranquility[d] of self-inspection—through which alone we can hope to attain the presence of this, the most sublime of truths, and look it leisurely in the face.

258   The *phænomena* on which our conclusions must at this point depend, are merely spiritual shadows, but not the less thoroughly substantial.

259   We walk about, amid the destinies of our world-existence, encompassed by dim but ever present *Memories* of a Destiny more vast—very distant in the by-gone time, and infinitely awful.

260   We live out a Youth peculiarly haunted by such shadows;[e] yet never mistaking them for dreams. As Memories we *know* them. *During our Youth* the distinction is too clear to deceive us even for a moment.

a. P Finite / HW *finite*
b. P Perception / HW *perception*
c. P irradiation / NM, HW *radiation*
d. P tranquillity / HW *tranquility*
e. P such dreams / NM such thoughts / HW *such shadows*

261   So long as this Youth endures, the feeling *that we exist,* is the most natural of all feelings. We understand it *thoroughly*. That there was a period at which we did *not* exist—or, that it might so have happened that we never had existed at all—are the considerations, indeed, which *during this Youth,*[a] we find difficulty in understanding. Why we should *not* exist, is, *up to the epoch of our Manhood,* of all queries the most unanswerable. Existence—self-existence—existence from all Time and to all Eternity—seems, up to the epoch of Manhood, a normal and unquestionable condition:—*seems, because it is.*

262   But now comes the period at which a conventional World-Reason awakens us from the truth of our dream. Doubt, Surprise and Incomprehensibility arrive at the same moment. They say:—"You live and the time was when you lived not. You have been created. An Intelligence exists greater than your own; and it is only through this Intelligence you live at all." These things we struggle to comprehend and cannot:—*cannot,* because these things, being untrue, are thus, of necessity, incomprehensible.

263   No thinking being lives who, at some luminous point of his life of thought, has not felt himself lost amid the surges of futile efforts at understanding, or believing, that anything exists *greater than his own soul.* The utter impossibility of any one's soul feeling itself inferior to another; the intense, overwhelming dissatisfaction and rebellion at the thought;—these, with the omniprevalent aspirations at perfection, are but the spiritual, coincident with the material, struggles towards the original Unity—are, to my mind at least, a species of proof far surpassing what Man terms demonstration, that no one soul *is* inferior to another—that nothing is, or can be, superior to any one soul—that each soul is, in part, its own God—its own Creator:—in a word, that God—the material *and* spiritual God—*now* exists solely in the diffused Matter and Spirit of the Universe; and that the regathering of this diffused Matter and Spirit will be but the re-constitution of the *purely Spiritual*[b] and Individual God.

264   In this view, and in this view alone, we comprehend the riddles of Divine Injustice—of Inexorable Fate. In this view alone the existence of Evil becomes intelligible; but in this view it becomes more—it becomes endurable. Our souls no longer rebel at a *Sorrow* which we ourselves have imposed upon ourselves, in furtherance of our own

a. P *youth* [italics] / NM, HW *Youth* [italics] [We follow HW.]
b. P Spiritual / HW *Spiritual* [italics]

purposes—with a view—if even with a futile view—to the extension of our own *Joy.*

265   I have spoken of *Memories* that haunt us during our Youth.[a] They sometimes pursue us even into[b] our Manhood:—assume gradually less and less indefinite shapes:—now and then speak to us with low voices, saying:

266   "There was an epoch in the Night of Time, when a still-existent Being existed—one of an absolutely infinite number of similar Beings that people the absolutely infinite domains of the absolutely infinite space.[*] It was not and is not in the power of this Being—any more than it is in your own—to extend, by actual increase, the joy of his Existence; but just as it *is* in your power to expand or to concentrate your pleasures (the absolute amount of happiness remaining always the same) so did and does a similar capability appertain to this Divine Being, who thus passes his Eternity in perpetual variation of Concentrated Self and almost Infinite Self-Diffusion. What you call The Universe of Stars[c] is but his present expansive existence. He now feels his life through an infinity of imperfect pleasures—the partial and pain-intertangled pleasures of those inconceivably numerous things which you designate as his creatures, but which are really but infinite individualizations of Himself. All these creatures—*all*—those whom[d] you term animate, as well as those to which[e] you deny life for no better reason than that you do not behold it in operation—*all* these creatures have, in a greater or less degree, a capacity for pleasure and for pain:—*but the general sum of their sensations is precisely that amount of Happiness which appertains by right to the Divine Being when concentrated within Himself.* These creatures are all, too, more or less, and more or less obviously[f] conscious Intelligences; conscious, first, of a proper identity; conscious, secondly and by faint indeterminate glimpses, of an identity with the Divine Being of whom we speak—

[*]See page 77[g]—Paragraph commencing "I reply that the right," and ending "proper and particular God."

a. P youth / NM HW *Youth*
b. P even in / HW *even into*
c. P Universe / HW *Universe of Stars*
d. P those which / HW *those whom*
e. P to whom / HW *to which*
f. P or less / HW *or less, and more or less obviously*
g. P, O, NM, HW. See page 102–103. [We have changed the page number to match our text, added the asterisk omitted in P, O, NM, HW, and allowed the agreement error—"page 102–103"—to stand in this variant note.]

of an identity with God. Of the two classes of consciousness, fancy that the former will grow weaker, the latter stronger, during the long succession of ages which must elapse before these myriads of individual Intelligences become blended—when the bright stars become blended—into One. Think that the sense of individual identity will be gradually merged in the general consciousness—that Man, for example, ceasing imperceptibly to feel himself Man, will at length attain that awfully triumphant epoch when he shall recognize his existence as that of Jehovah. In the meantime bear in mind that all is Life—Life—Life within Life—the less within the greater, and all within the *Spirit Divine.* "[a]

THE END

Note—The pain of the consideration that we shall lose our individual identity, ceases at once when we further reflect that the process, as above described, is, neither more nor less than that of the absorption, by each individual intelligence, of all other intelligences (that is, of the Universe) into its own. That God may be all in all, *each* must become God.[b]

a. P *Divine.* [italics] / O, NM, HW *Divine.* " [italics] [We follow HW.]
b. HW contains an endnote that Poe wrote in pencil. We include it at the end of the text.

APPENDIX

Poe's Postscript to a Letter about
the Lecture "Eureka"

Because Poe's letter of February 29, 1848, to his Maine correspondent George W. Eveleth was largely about his lecture "Eureka" and contains a very long postscript that Poe called "a few addenda," some commentators, following Woodberry, have treated the postscript as though Poe intended it as an addition to the text. We see no evidence for this conclusion. Poe seems to mean "some additional ideas on Laplace"; these are "addenda" to the long letter, some other thoughts on the matter, but not intended for incorporation into *Eureka*. Indeed, Poe said in the first paragraph of the postscript that he wrote them earlier. Poe four times annotated copies of *Eureka* and never added these ideas. Moreover, while in *Eureka* the scientific speculation is usually based on sound synthesis of current knowledge, in the postscript it is not. One guesses that it was written before Poe briefed himself on the science he so ably summarizes in *Eureka*.

Since Poe's manuscript has disappeared (see "A Note on the Text" under "Editorial Method" and *Collected Works*, ed. Mabbott, 3:1320) and some quite uncharacteristic locutions appear in this postscript, it is perfectly possible that at least portions are inauthentic. Poe writes "votical" here instead of the "vorticial" which he coined in *Eureka* (Pollin, *Poe, Creator of Words*). That might be because he wrote this earlier. Much odder is "as I have shown, back" (¶13), which, as BRP notes, is not Poe's style at all. BRP wonders also at a passage in paragraph 17—"dividing by the breadth to its own periphery that to the periphery of the other." It does not sound like Poe (indeed, it is not very well written). Speculation is possible: careless transcription (or willful distortion?) by Eveleth, careless writing (or "mystification" ?) by Poe, even a forgery by some third party, perhaps after 1896, when the manuscript was last seen.

Of the mathematics in this postscript, Bruce Twarog observes that "it is just numerology" and "all nonsense"; there is nothing in it on which he can comment. Note that unlike Woodberry's consultant Irving Stringham, Twarog reports that the summary of scientific data and theory in the body of *Eureka* is generally very competent and, sometimes, even contains good original observations and plausible speculation. (But see ¶172 of *Eureka* and our note to it for an exception which, significantly, is related to this "Postscript.") Why then would Poe have recommended the material in the postscript to Eveleth? Perhaps—if Poe wrote the letter *after* writing *Eureka*—because he had forgotten much of what he had learned in writing *Eureka;* perhaps, if the letter came first, because he had not yet mastered the scientific information; perhaps because some authors hate to allow anything they have written to go to waste, especially if it involves extra labor, as the fanciful mathematics did. Perhaps it was to show off a bit, too, before a correspondent who might not catch the unsoundness of the calculations.

Probably Poe wrote the postscript for a combination of reasons. Certainly the possibility that he had forgotten the sound science might trouble readers who would rather find evidence of Poe's fervent belief in the lofty arguments of *Eureka*.

A Note on the Text

We reprint the postscript here in a copy made by Eveleth and kindly provided by the rare book department of the Alderman Library at the University of Virginia. This version is more complete than any we know. T. O. Mabbott included it among Poe's works of fiction (*Collected Works,* 3:1319–23) but stopped at the end of paragraph 5; Woodberry's text (293–301, 295) lacks the final sentence of that paragraph. Ostrom (*Letters of Edgar Allan Poe,* 2:360–62) prints the body of the letter, not the postscript. *Collected Works* contains a list of extant versions of the material and variants through paragraph 5. Our introductory note contains observations on some peculiarities in this document.

The Postscript

1   By the bye, lest you infer that my views, in detail, are the same with those advanced in the *Nebular Hypothesis,* I venture to offer a few addenda, the substance of which was penned, though never printed, several years ago, under the head of—A Prediction.

2   As soon as the next century it will be entered in *the books,* that the

Sun was originally condensed *at once* (not gradually, according to the supposition of Laplace) into his smallest size; that, thus condensed, he rotated on an axis; that this axis of rotation was not the centre of his figure, so that he not only rotated, but revolved in an elliptical orbit (the rotation and revolution are one; but I separate them for convenience of illustration); that, thus formed and thus revolving, he was on fire (in the same way that a volcano and an ignited meteoric stone are on fire) and sent into space his substance in the form of vapor, this vapor reaching farthest on the side of the larger hemisphere, partly on account of the largeness, but principally because the force of the fire was greater here; that, in due time, this vapor, not necessarily carried then to the place now occupied by Neptune, condensed into Neptune; that the planet took, as a matter of necessity, the same figure that the Sun had, which figure made his rotation a revolution in an elliptical orbit; that, in consequence of such revolution—in consequence of his being *carried backward* at each of the *daily* revolutions—the velocity of his *annual* revolution is not so great as it would be, if it depended solely upon the Sun's velocity of rotation (Kepler's Third Law); that his figure, by influencing his rotation—the heavier half, as it turns downward toward the Sun, gains an impetus sufficient to carry it by the direct line of attraction, and thus to *throw outward* the centre of gravity—gave him power to save himself from falling to the Sun (and, perhaps, to work himself gradually outward to the position he now holds); that he received, through a series of ages, the Sun's heat, which penetrated to his centre, causing volcanic eruptions eventually, and thus throwing off vapor; and which evaporated substances upon his surface, till finally his moons and his gaseous ring (if it is true that he has a ring) were produced; that these moons took elliptical forms, rotated and revolved "both under one", were kept in their *monthly* orbits by the centrifugal force acquired in their *daily* orbits, and required a longer time to make their monthly revolutions than they would have required if they had had no daily revolutions.

3   I have said enough, without referring to the other planets, to give you an inkling of my hypothesis, which is all I intended to do. I did not design to offer any evidence of its reasonableness; since I have not, in fact, any collected, excepting as it is flitting, in the shape of a shadow, to and fro within my brain.

4   You perceived that I hold to the idea that our Moon must rotate upon her axis oftener than she revolves round her primary, the same being the case with the satellites accompanying Jupiter, Saturn and Uranus.

5   Since the penning, a closer analysis of the matter contained has led me to modify somewhat my opinion as to the origin of the satellites—that is, I think now that these came, not from vapor sent off in volcanic burnings and by simple diffusion under the solar rays, but from rings of it which were left in the inter-planetary spaces, after the precipitation of the primaries. There is no insuperable obstacle in the way of the conception that aerolites and "shooting-stars" have their source in matter which has gone off from the Earth's surface and from out her bowels; but it is hardly supposable that a sufficient quantity could be produced thus to make a body so large as, by centrifugal force resulting from rotation, to withstand the absorptive power of its parent's rotation. The event implied may take place not until the planets have become flaming suns—*from an accumulation of their own Sun's caloric, reaching from centre to circumference, which shall, in the lonesome latter days, melt all the elements and dissipate the solid foundations out as a scroll!* (Please substitute the idea for that in "Conversation of Eiros and Charmion").

----

6   The Sun forms, in rotating, a vortex in the ether surrounding him. The planets have their orbits lying within this vortex at different distances from its centre; so that their liabilities to be absorbed by it are, other things being equal, inversely just according to those distances, since length, not surface, is the measure of the absorptive power along the lines marking the orbits. Each planet overcomes its liability—i.e., keeps in its orbit—through a counter-vortex generated by its own rotation. The force of such counter-vortex is measured by multiplying together the producing planet's density and rotary velocity; which velocity depends, not upon the length of the planet's equatorial circumference, but upon the distance through which a given point of the equator is carried during a rotary period. Then *if* Venus and Mercury, for example, have now the orbits in which they commenced their revolutions—the orbit of the former 68 million miles, and that of the latter 37 million miles, from the centre of the Sun's vortex; if the diameter of Venus is $2\frac{2}{3}$ times the diameter, and

her density is the same with the density, of Mercury; and if the rotary velocity of the equator of Venus is 1000 miles per hour, that of Mercury's equator is 1900 miles per hour, making the diameter of his *orbit of rotation* 1450 miles—nearly 5 times that of himself. But I pass this point without farther examination. Whether there is or is not a difference in the relative conditions of the different planets, sufficient to cause such diversity in the extents of their peripheries of rotation as is indicated, still each planet is to be considered to have, other things being equal, a vortical resistence bearing the same proportion, inversely, to that of every other planet which its distance from the centre of the solar vortex bears to the distance of every other from the same; so that, if it be removed inward or outward from its position, it will increase or diminish that resistence, accordingly, by adding to or subtracting from its speed of rotation. As the rotary period must be the same in the two cases, the greater or less speed can be produced only by the lengthening or the shortening of the circumference described by the rotation.

7   Then Mercury, at the distance of Venus, would rotate in an orbit only $37/68$ as broad as the one in which he does rotate; so his centrifugal force, in that position, would be only $37/68$ as great as it is in his own position; so his capability, while there, of resisting the *forward pressure* of the Sun's vortex, which (pressure) prevents him from passing his full (*circle*) distance behind his centre of rotation and thus adds to his velocity in his *annual orbit,* would be but $37/68$ what it is in his own place. But this forward pressure is only $37/68$ as great at the distance of Venus as it is at that of Mercury. Then Mercury, with his own rotary speed in the annual orbit of Venus, would move in this orbit but $37/68$ as fast as Venus moves in it; while Venus, with her rotary speed in Mercury's annual orbit, would move $68/37$ as fast as she moves in her own—that is, $68/37$ of $68/37$ as fast as Mercury would move in the same (annual orbit of Venus); it follows that the square root of $68/37$ is the measure of the velocity of Mercury in his own annual orbit with his own rotary speed, compared with that of Venus in her annual orbit with her own rotary speed—in accordance with fact.

8   Such is my explanation of Kepler's first and third laws, which laws *cannot* be explained upon the principle of Newton's Theory.

---

9   Two planets, gathered from portions of the Sun's vapor into one orbit, would rotate through the same ellipse with velocities proportional to their densities—that is, the denser planet would rotate the more swiftly; since, in condensing, it would have descended farther toward the Sun. For example, suppose the Earth and Jupiter to be the two planets in one orbit. The diameter of the former is 8000 miles; period of rotation, 24 hours. The diameter of the latter is 88000 miles; period, 9 ½ hours. The ring of vapor out of which the Earth was formed, was of a certain (perpendicular) width; that out of which Jupiter was formed, was of a certain greater width. In condensing, the springs of ether lying among the particles (these springs having been latent before the condensation began) were let out, the number of them along any given radial line being the number of spaces between all the couples of the particles constituting the line. If the two condensations had gone on in simple diametric proportions, Jupiter would have put forth only 11 times as many springs as the Earth did, and his velocity would have been but 11 times her velocity. But the fact that the falling-downward of her particles was completed when they had got so far that 24 hours were required for her equator to make its circuit; while that of his particles continued till but about ⅖ of her period was occupied by his equator in effecting *its* revolution; shows that his springs were increased above hers in still another ratio of 2 ½, making, in the case, his velocity and his vortical force (2 ½ × 11 =) 27 times her velocity and force.

10   Thus the planets' densities are inversely as their rotary periods; and their rotary velocities and degrees of centrifugal force are, other things being equal, directly as their densities.

---

11   Two planets, revolving in one orbit, in rotating would approach the Sun, therefore enlarge their rotary ellipses, therefore accelerate their rotary velocities, therefore increase their powers of withstanding the influence of the solar vortex, inversely according to the products of their diameters into their densities—that is, the smaller and less dense planet, having to resist an amount of influence equal to that resisted by the other, would multiply the number of its resisting springs by the ratios of the other's diameter and density to the diameter and density of itself. Thus, the Earth, in Jupiter's orbit,

would have to rotate in an ellipse 27 times as broad as herself, in order to make her power correspond with his.

12   Then the breadths, in a perpendicular direction, of the rotary ellipses of the planets in their several orbits are inversely as the products obtained by multiplying together the bodies' densities, diameters and distances from the centre of the solar vortex. Thus, the product of Jupiter's density, diameter and distance being ($2\frac{1}{2}$ times 11 times $5\frac{1}{4}$ =) 140 times the product of the Earth's density, diameter and distance, the breadth of the latter's ellipse is about 1.120.000 miles; this upon the foundation, of course, that Jupiter's ellipse coincides, precisely, with his own equatorial diameter.

13   It will be observed that that process, in its last analysis, presents the point that rotary speed (hence that vortical force) is in exact inverse proportion to distance. Then, since the movement in orbit is a part of the rotary movement—being the rate at which the *centre of the rotary ellipse* is carried along the line marking the orbit—and since that centre and the planet's centre are not identical, the former being the point around which the latter revolves, causing, by the act, a relative loss of time in the inverse ratio of the square root of distance (as I have shown, back); the speed in orbit is inversely according to the square root of distance. Demonstration—The Earth's orbital period contains $365\frac{1}{4}$ of her rotary periods. During these periods, her equator passes through a distance of (1.120.000 × $\frac{22}{7}$ × $365\frac{1}{4}$ =) about 1286 million miles; and the centre of her rotary ellipse through a distance of (95.000.000 × 2 × $\frac{22}{7}$ =) about 597 million miles. Jupiter's orbital period has ($365\frac{1}{4}$ × $2\frac{1}{2}$ × 12 years =) about 10.957 of his rotary periods, during which his equator courses (88.000 × $\frac{22}{7}$ × 10.957 =) about 3.050 million miles; and the centre of his rotary ellipse, about the same number of miles (490.000.000 × 2 × $\frac{22}{7}$). Dividing this distance by 12 years ($\frac{3.050.000.000}{12}$ =) gives the length of Jupiter's *double* journey during one of the Earth's orbital periods = 254 million miles—Relative velocities in ellipse ($\frac{1286}{254}$ =), 5 to 1, which is inversely as the distances; and relative velocities in orbit ($\frac{597}{254}$ =), 2 to 1, inversely as the square roots of the distances.

---

14   The Sun's period of rotation being 25 days, his density is only $\frac{1}{25}$ of that of a planet having a period of 24 hours—that of Mercury, for

instance. Hence Mercury has, for the purpose now in view, virtually, a diameter equal to a little more than $^1/_{12}$ of that of the Sun (888.000 / 25 = 35.520; 35.520 / 3000 = 11.84; 888.000 / 11.84 =)— say, 75 thousand miles.

15   Here, we have a conception of the planet in the *mid-stage*, so to speak, of its condensation—after the breaking-up of the vaporous ring which was to produce it, and just at the taking-on of the globular form. But before the arrival at this stage, the figure was that of a *truck*, the vortical diameter of which is identifiable in the periphery of the globe (75.000 × 22 / 7 =)—236 thousand miles. Half-way down this diameter, the body settled into its (original) orbit—*would have* settled, had it been the only body, besides its parent, in the Solar System—an orbit distant from the Sun's equator (236.000 / 2 =) 118 thousand miles; and from the centre of the solar vortex (118.000 + 888.000 / 2 =), 562 thousand miles. To this last are to be added, successively, the lengths of the semi-diameters of the *trucks* of Venus, of the Earth—and so on outward.

16   There, the planets' *original* distances—rather, speaking strictly, the widths from the common centre to the outer limits of their rings of vapor—are pointed at. From them, as foundations, the present distances may be deduced. A simple outline of the process to the deduction is this:—Neptune took his orbit first; then Uranus took his. The effect of the coming into close conjunction of the two bodies was such as would have been produced by bringing each so much nearer the centre of the solar vortex. Each enlarged its rotary ellipse and increased its rotary velocity in the ratio of the decrease of distance. A secondary result—the *final* consequence—of the enlargement and of the increase was the propulsion of each outward, the square root of the relative decrease being the measure of the length through which each was sent. The *primary* result of course was the drawing of each inward; and it is fairly presumable that there were oscillations inward and outward, outward and inward, during several successive periods of rotation. It is probable—at any rate, not glaringly improbable—that, in the oscillations across the remnants of the rings of vapor (the natural inference is that these were not *completely* gathered into the composition of the bodies), portions of the vapor were *whirled* into satellites, which followed in the last passage outward.

17   Saturn's ring (I have no allusion to the rings now existing), as well

as that of each of the other planets after him, while it was gradually being cast off from the Sun's equator, was carried along in the track of its next predecessor, the distance, here, being the full quotient (not the square root of the quotient) found in dividing by the breadth to its own periphery that to the periphery of the other. Thus, reckoning for Uranus a breadth of 17 million miles, and for Saturn one of 14 million miles, the latter (still in his vaporous state) was conducted outward (through a sort of capillary attraction) $^{14}/_{17}$ as far as the former (after condensation) was driven by means of the vortical influence of Neptune. The new body and the two older bodies *interchanged forces,* and another advance outward (of all three) was made. Combining all of the asteroids into one of the *Nine Great Powers* (assuming that there is no planet inside of Mercury), there were eight stages of the general movement away from the centre; and, granting that we have, exact, the diameters and the rotary periods (i.e., the densities) of all of the participants in the movement, the measurement of each stage, by itself, and of all the stages together can be calculated exactly.

18 How will *that* do for a postscript?

NOTES

Eureka

Title: "I have found [it]," a famous remark attributed to Archimedes (ca. 287–212 B.C.E.), who supposedly so exclaimed on finding a way through displacement to determine the amount of gold in an alloy.

Dedication: Humboldt: Friedrich Heinrich Alexander von Humboldt (1769–1850). See notes to paragraphs 9, 231, and 232.

Preface: In his story "Loss of Breath" (1835), Poe wrote, "William Godwin . . . says in his 'Mandeville,' that 'invisible things are the only realities.'" Poe used a modified version of the phrase from Godwin in the tale "Berenice" (1835) as well. The phrase probably connects also to a passage in the *Memories of the Life of Sir Humphry Davy, Bart* by Davy's brother, John, a book Poe used elsewhere; the passage speaks of "the universal mind" in which man's intellect at its strongest is no more than "a mere image in a dream" (Pollin, *Discoveries in Poe*, 109, 177–78).

rise again . . . Everlasting: Poe echoes John 5:24: "He that heareth my word, and believeth on him that sent me, hath everlasting life, and shall not come into condemnation; but is passed from death into life." Burton R. Pollin (BRP) suggests that the association came via William Cullen Bryant's poem "The Battle-Field," stanza 9 of which includes, "Truth, crushed to earth, shall rise again; / Th' eternal years of God are hers." The poem was first published in the *Democratic Review* in October 1837; the stanza in question became famous because of a widely reported incident. Benjamin F. Butler, attorney general under presidents Jackson and Van Buren, quoted it to loud applause in a speech in Tammany Hall. A voice from the crowd called for a cheer for Shakespeare. Butler said it was not by Shakespeare but by an American contemporary, Bryant, and the crowd went wild (Godwin, *A Biography*, 1:337n).

1 solemn—. . . august: BRP asks of this opening paragraph, "Is Poe serious or aiming to be breathless?" He notes that "august" usually applies to persons and wonders about Poe's "humility." Certainly, the heavy use of dashes is often in Poe a sign of less than serious intention (see note to paragraph 122).

7 Ætna: Mt. Aetna (or Etna) was very active, and explorers, "as Poe probably knew," had found it to be "a truncated cone without a top." Thus nobody could whirl

on his heel on "the top" of Etna (Holman, "Splitting Poe's 'Epicurean Atoms'"). On the other hand, Etna was the universal symbol of a big, high, dominant peak in that era; it was "ready to hand" for numerous writers. Poe used it himself in an important aesthetic fantasy philosophically close to *Eureka,* "The Domain of Arnheim" (a briefer version, "The Landscape Garden," appeared in 1842 and 1845, the longer in 1847). Ellison, an ideally gifted and inspired poetic visionary landscape architect, searches for years for a perfect site for his masterpiece: "We came at length to an elevated table-land of wonderful fertility and beauty, affording a panoramic prospect very little less in extent than that of Ætna" (*Collected Works,* 3:1278; *Short Fiction,* 11; *Thirty-Two Stories,* 212). The volcano in Sicily, the idea of panoramic sweep, and the notion of cosmic unity are common to both pieces. Holman also detects a submerged allusion here to Lord Rosse (see ¶163ff.), Etna being part of the Rossi Mountains. Ketterer also sees humor in Poe's locating his viewer on "top" of a volcano. But, loosely, one does reach the top; the spinning on the heel to get a sense of oneness strikes us as funnier.

The idea of viewing the earth from the height of Etna appears, along with a wide range of other ideas that also recur in various places in Poe, in chapter 1, paragraphs 32 and 33 of the Philadelphia 1834 edition (and a large number of subsequent editions) of John Herschel's *A Treatise on Astronomy,* a work Poe used in *Eureka* and quoted from (see ¶227 and note). The ideas include the "insufficient supply of *air*" at high altitudes, seeing a great portion of the surface of the earth, famous balloon ascensions, whether the earth would look concave or convex from that height, Cotopaxi, and the process of compressing air. Because the range of associations occurs in other writers, one does not want to make firm claims about influence, but the concentration of common referents here and in Poe is striking. See especially Poe's "The Balloon-Hoax" (1844), "Hans Pfaall" (1835), and "Mellonta Tauta," glossed in *Short Fiction,* and more fully in *Collected Writings,* vol. 1. Posey has suggested this passage in Herschel as a source for "Hans Pfaall." A review of the scholarship is in *Collected Writings,* 1:487.

9 Humboldt: See note to dedication. Holman ("Hog, Bacon, Ram"), who believes that satire is the main intention in *Eureka,* thinks even the praise of Humboldt ironic: she finds Poe contemptuous of broad generalizers. We disagree. Poe is contemptuous of nearsighted fact-grubbing but consistently praises bold theorizing. See what Poe says about Humboldt in paragraph 231; see also the short stories about Ellison and Dupin, the "Sonnet: To Science," and his criticism. Humboldt's *Kosmos* (Stuttgart, 1845–) was promptly available in translation in the United States: *Cosmos* (New York, 1845–). In the July 12, 1845, *Broadway Journal,* Poe noted its publication in Germany; he announced the New York edition in both the August 30 and September 13 numbers of the *Broadway Journal* and noted a review of it in the issue for October 11, 1845. See *Collected Writings,* 3:169, 3:234, 3:247, 3:281, 4:127–28nn.

synœretical: Pollin reports, "Not in *OED* as adjective for any spelling" (*Poe: Creator of Words,* 38).

11 remarkable letter . . . bottle: Much of the material in the next paragraphs (11–
24) Poe used as well in "Mellonta Tauta" (1849), a witty story set in the year 2848
(*Thirty-Two Stories*, 346–60; *Short Fiction*, 547–48, 588–96, 616–19; *Collected Works*,
3:1289–309). Its text purports to be a letter written aboard the excursion bal-
loon *Skylark* on April Fool's Day by Pundita to a friend. Although Pundita's world
has learned to theorize imaginatively, Pundita is ignorant and a snob. Poe uses
her to attack nineteenth-century technology and politics, especially the U.S.
government and its leaders, but her era is shown to be as blind as Poe's in most
ways: the tale ends with the failure of the balloon. Pundita's knowledge of "an-
tiquity" is comically distorted, but she tends to use correct spellings for the names
of figures Poe admired.

Pollin ("Poe's Use of Material") establishes Poe's frequent use of ideas from
Bernardin de Saint-Pierre's *Etudes;* entrusting a manuscript to a bottle appears
there and in several places in Poe.

"Mellonta Tauta" was prefaced by a "letter" "To the Editor of the Lady's Book,"
signed by Poe, which shares language and details with paragraph 11 of *Eureka.*
In the story, the "odd-looking MS." was found "about a year ago, tightly corked
up in a jug floating in the *Mare Tenebrarum—*a sea well described" etc. It seems
evident to us that although *Eureka* was published first, the story was written be-
fore it. *Collected Works* (3:1290) details the publication history—"Mellonta Tau-
ta" had been sold to Louis Godey for use in *Godey's Lady's Book;* Godey did not
print it until after the book *Eureka* was published and was apparently angry that
Poe had used it. See ¶18n.

Mare Tenebrarum: Poe's source is a passage in Jacob Bryant's *A New System; or, An
Analysis of Ancient Mythology:* "By the Nubian Geographer the Atlantic is uniformly
called, according to the present version, Mare Tenebrarum. Aggressi sunt mare
tenebrarum quid in eo esset, exploraturi. *They ventured into the sea of darkness, in
order to explore what it might contain"* (see ¶65 and ¶65n). Bryant's *Mythology* was
one of Poe's favorite sources of ideas. *Collected Writings* (2:xxiv–xxv) lists numer-
ous items in Poe's "Pinakidia" and "Marginalia" based on that book. Bryant's
imaginative mode of showing all ancient religions as variants of the same mirac-
ulous events provided imagery to enrich several Poe stories, although Poe knew
that the learned antiquarian Bryant was as wrong as Poe's own Pundita (Levine
and Levine, "History, Myth, Fable"). Poe quotes this passage from Bryant in "Ele-
onora." He also refers to "the Nubian geographer's account of the *Mare Tene-
brarum"* in "A Descent into the Maelstrom" (*Thirty-Two Stories*, 347n2, 159–73,
esp. 161n3; *Short Fiction*, 547–48, 616–19, 588–96, esp. 616n2, 59n3; see also
Collected Works, 2:595; 2:646, 3:1305).

Ptolemy Hephestion: Although Jacob Bryant does mention "Ptolemy Hephæs-
tion," he did not call him "the Nubian geographer." Bryant refers rather to al
Idrisi, author of *Geographia nubiensis.* Poe's error seems to be deliberate; one of
the running jokes in "Mellonta Tauta" is about antiquarians getting names, facts,
and dates wrong. Poe refers to Ptolemy Hephestion in "Berenice" and elsewhere.

The Ptolemy who was a geographer was Claudius Ptolemaeus (fl. 127–148), to whom Poe also refers elsewhere (*Collected Writings*, vol. 2; Pollin, *Dictionary of Names and Titles*). "Ptolemy Hephestion" was Ptolemy Chennos, son of Hephestion, "one of the Mythographi whose works are synopsized by Photius" (*Collected Works*, 2:220n9). Poe, in short, hides one deliberate error within another. Looking through his other references to the several Ptolemys makes it clear enough that he knew one from the other.

Transcendentalists . . . crotchets: Poe's attitude toward transcendentalism is complex. Probably envious of Emerson and generally hostile to New England Transcendentalists, he nevertheless was philosophically quite close to them. *Eureka* is, after all, a treatise on the importance of artistic, intuitive, transcendental inspiration as a source of scientific cosmological truth. Poe repeatedly mocked the very ideas in which he seemed to believe most consistently. Extensive discussion of Poe and transcendentalism appears in Levine, *Edgar Poe*, esp. 33 and 151–68.

12 Aries . . . Tottle: Aristotle is "Hindoo" in "Mellonta Tauta." BRP suggests an echo of a book by Charles Dickens that Poe praised in the June 1836 *Southern Literary Messenger* (*Complete Works*, 9:45ff.): *Watkins Tottle, and other sketches, illustrative of every-day Life, and every-day People* by Boz [Dickens]. Poe singles out the title piece for mention and quotes it at length.

expel . . . nose: Mabbott writes that "Aristotle, in *Problemata*, xxxiii, 9, said that sneezing comes from the head, the 'seat of reason'" (*Collected Works*, 3:1318n3). Poe probably had the idea secondhand. Montaigne, in Book 2, chapter 27 of his *Essays*, says that "sneezing . . . because it proceeds from the head, and is without offense, we give . . . civil reception," while frowning on other bodily exhalations. "[D]o not laugh at this distinction," Montaigne continues, "for they say it is Aristotle's" (2:375). In a chapter called "[O]n Sneezing," Sir Thomas Browne says that Aristotle feels sneezing to be a sign of mental health (there is a folk belief that idiots never sneeze). Browne writes that sneezing, "being properly a motion of the brain expelling through the nostrils what is offensive to it," is therefore a good sign. For that reason, he says, Aristotle holds it sacred. We guess that Poe's source is an article ("On the Custom of Saluting after Sneezing") in Isaac Disraeli's *Curiosities of Literature* (1791, and many subsequent editions), one of his favorite idea-mines. "Aristotle," Disraeli wrote, "has delivered some considerable nonsense on this custom: he says it is an honorable acknowledgement of the seat of good sense and genius—the head—to distinguish it from two other offensive eruptions of air, which are never accompanied by a benediction from by-standers" (35). Poe used the same material in his story "Bon-Bon," a satiric tale he revised and republished repeatedly between 1832 and 1845, more evidence of how closely related *Eureka* is to the texture of Poe's fiction. "Bon-Bon" is annotated in *Collected Works* (2:83ff.) and *Short Fiction* (356, 431–35).

truths . . . *self*-evident: Poe alludes, of course, to the Declaration of Independence.

Tuclid . . . C for a K: With slight alterations, Poe used this material in "Mellonta

Tauta." Pundita's spelling for Euclid was "Neuclid." Much of the humor in that story is temporal. To a writer in 2848, Greece of the third century B.C.E. and Germany (not Holland) of 1800 do not seem significantly distant in time from one another. Poe used the "Kant/Cant" pun several times in other works. The sneer at the transcendental idealism of Immanuel Kant (1724–1804) is not isolated, yet Poe in other works as well as in *Eureka* espouses similar ideas (Pollin, *Poe: Creator of Words,* 88; and for extended discussion of Poe and Kant, see Omans, "'Intellect, Taste'"). Thomas Ollive Mabbott (TOM) adds that Kant "was *ein Deutscher,* a German, but not *ein Hollander,* a Dutchman" (*Collected Works,* 3:1318n4).

13   Hog . . . shepherd: Francis Bacon (1561–1626), the British essayist and philosopher who argued for an analytical and inductive approach to knowledge, believed that such pooled learning would in fact produce progress. Poe's letter-writer, like Pundita in "Mellonta Tauta," makes a double error. Having called Bacon "Hog," the writer then confuses him with James Hogg (1770–1835), who was called "the Ettrick Shepherd" and whose name would have been familiar to magazine readers from his work in *Blackwood's Edinburgh Magazine,* his narrative poems, and his novels. Holman ("Hog, Bacon, Ram") thinks a link is likely between these pig jokes and the references in paragraph 18 to John Stuart Mill (¶18n). Holman's conjecture seems plausible for a stronger reason: in the same chapter from Mill that Poe quotes in paragraph 17 (¶17n), Mill makes exactly that point, even including the idea of seeing Bacon as a fallacious successor to philosophers of antiquity. Mill says that Aristotle is "the consummation of this mode of speculation" (*A System of Logic,* 467) and then writes,

> From the fundamental error of the scientific inquirers of antiquity, we pass, by a natural association, to a scarcely less fundamental one of their great rival and successor, Bacon. It has excited the surprise of philosophers that the detailed system of inductive logic, which this extraordinary man labored to construct, has been turned to so little direct use by subsequent inquirers, having neither continued, except in a few of its generalities, to be recognized as a theory, nor having conducted in practice to any great scientific results. But this, though not unfrequently remarked, has scarcely received any plausible explanation; and some, indeed, have preferred to assert that all rules of induction are useless, rather than suppose that Bacon's rules are grounded upon an insufficient analysis of the inductive process. (468)

Most likely, Poe used the Harper and Brothers 1846 New York edition, to which our page numbers refer; see especially pages 468–70, which tie together numerous items in connections that one finds also in Poe. (Holman speculates also on the possibility that Poe intended to put Delia Salter Bacon [1811–59] or her brother, Dr. Leonard Bacon, on his reader's mind. Delia Bacon was a lecturer. She and her brother moved legally against a Yale University ministerial student in a juicy breach-of-promise matter.) Pollin (*Discoveries in Poe,* 180–83, 282n45) discusses the connections among "Hog-ites," Poe's correspondent George Eveleth, and John William Draper. In a letter to Eveleth of June 26, 1849, Poe calls Draper the "chief" of Hog-ites and says, "He is aware . . . that I intended *him* in 'Eureka.'" Pollin is sure that Draper was *not* aware and concludes that Hog–Ettrick Shepherd–James Hogg "seems not to allude to Draper at all." Apparently the Hog–Draper connection was real in Poe's mind, but it is less than certain that he intended it in *Eureka.* The letter to Eveleth postdates lecture and book.

instantiæ Naturæ: Latinists translate this phrase as "instances of nature" and report that it does occur, starting in Medieval Latin, with the meaning Poe gives it. We found plentiful examples of both *instantiæ* and of *naturæ,* but even our Latinist consultants could not find the two together in Bacon (see "Hog," above) or in the Latin word lists and dictionaries of Bacon's period.

noumena . . . phenomena: The letter-writer's contrast appears in Kant ("Cant"), who opposed *noumena,* objects understood through intellectual intuition, with *phenomena,* one's "precepts or experiences of objects in the world" about one.

savans: Poe consistently used the old spelling (*savans*) of this word in *Eureka* and in the *Godey's* version of "Mellonta Tauta" (BRP reports nine instances). Most editors modernize it to *savants.*

Median: Unchangeable; see Daniel 6:8, "Now, O King, establish the interdict and sign the document so that it cannot be changed, according to the law of the Medes and the Persians" (Forrest, *Biblical Allusions*).

"Baconian": Poe's coinage (Pollin, *Poe: Creator of Words,* 74).

"Hog-ian": Poe's coinage (Pollin, *Poe: Creator of Words,* 74).

14   intuitive *leaps:* In "Mellonta Tauta," Pundita phrases it, "All true knowledge . . . makes its advances almost invariably by intuitive bounds." Poe means this seriously. Knowledge progresses mainly through intuitive inspiration, not through reasoning from given premises (Aristotle) or from sorting, classifying, and analyzing (Bacon). Although Poe sometimes mocks writers who praise intuition—Emerson, for example—he generally trusts it himself. The inspired artist has a direct line to "Truth" and is an important source of knowledge, scientific as well as aesthetic. See Poe's "Sonnet—To Science," Emerson's poem "Blight," Shelley's "Defense of Poetry" (1822), and Poe's stories about the master detective Dupin (especially "The Purloined Letter") for other contemporary statements on the efficacy of artistic inspiration. Thomas Ollive Mabbott (*Collected Works,* 3:1318n5) suggests as well "The Murders in the Rue Morgue" and number 8 in "A Chapter of Suggestions."

Aries . . . ram: In astrology, Aries the Ram is the first sign of the Zodiac. Having called Aristotle "Aries Tottle," Poe now makes a bad pun by allowing his letter-writer (the sex of the letter-writer in *Eureka* is indeterminate; in "Mellonta Tauta" it is a woman) to try her hand, inaccurately, at etymology (see also ¶12n).

15   Scotch snuff of *detail:* Pollin says, "Scotch snuff seems to be an Americanism giv-

en by Craigie (DAE) [*Dictionary of American English*] as 'finely ground snuff of a characteristic strength and pungency prepared from well dried tobacco.'" It was "used for fumigation as well as an inhalant" (*Collected Writings,* 2:486).

Hog-ites: See Pollin (*Poe: Creator of Words,* 74).

inter-Tritonic minnows: Triton is, of course, a Greek sea deity. Poe seems to mean minnows among "monstrous denizens of the sea" (TOM, notes). It is likely that he is echoing a yet-unlocated source for the phrase. See also "unlettered hind" (¶16nn). Pollin (*Poe: Creator of Words,* 74) notes that the *Oxford English Dictionary* "gives an 1836 Tritonic only."

16 on the face of the earth: From Genesis 6:1.

Bacon-engendered: Poe's coinage (Pollin, *Poe: Creator of Words,* 70).

one-idead: Poe's coinage (ibid., 58).

unlettered hind: The phrase is from the first lines of the lady in John Milton's masque "Comus" (TOM):

> This way the noise was, if mine ear be true,
> My best guide now; me thought it was the sound
> Of riot, and ill manag'd merriment,
> Such as the jocond flute, or gamesom pipe
> Stirs up among the loose unleter'd hinds,
> When for their teeming flocks, and granges full,
> In wanton dance they praise the bounteous Pan,
> And thank the gods amiss. (*Oxford Anthology,* 334)

It may be that several associations in this portion of *Eureka* connect to "Comus." The masque opens with a speech by an "attendant Spirit," which is heavy in allusions to sea deities. Poe's "inter-Tritonic minnows" of paragraph 15 just might tie that passage to this.

17 *"ex nihilo nihil fit":* The idea—"out of nothing comes nothing"— is from Lucretius (ca. 95–55 B.C.E.), whose *De Rerum Natura* Poe clearly knew. The exact phrase appears in the writings of Epicurus (ca. 340–270 B.C.E.) (TOM). A list of Poe's allusions to Lucretius is in Pollin (*Word Index*). Poe planned a collection of tales, each supposedly the creation of a different author, each a member of the "Folio Club." Poe used the title of Lucretius' work as the name of one "author," writing it, "De Rerum Naturâ, Esqr." (*Collected Works,* 2:205). Poe's immediate source, however, for this and the two propositions that follow was John Stuart Mill's *A System of Logic* (1843). In the Harper and Brothers New York 1846 edition, this quotation appears on page 462 in Book 5, chapter 3, "Fallacies of Simple Inspection; Or *A Priori* Fallacies" (see ¶13n). That the propositions appear together is one of several reasons it seems quite certain Mill is Poe's source; in the next paragraph, Poe says that Pundita is looking at Mill.

"thing . . . is not": This appears on the previous page in Mill at the start of the preceding paragraph. Mill's sense is close to Pundita's; even the idea of looking back to the errors of a previous age is in both. Mill writes, "Rather more than a century and half ago it was a philosophical maxim, disputed by no one, and which no one deemed to require any proof, that 'a thing cannot act where it is not.'"

"there . . . antipodes": Mill puts it as follows on page 460 of the same passage: "It was long held that Antipodes were impossible, because of the difficulty which men found in conceiving persons with their heads in the same direction as our feet."

"darkness . . . light": This hypothetical proposition does not appear in the passage in Mill from which we have been quoting, although its logical reason for being here is the same. To illustrate another logical error, Mill on page 463 uses an example that involves whiteness. It just may have suggested the light and dark illustration to Poe.

Although Poe's source for at least three of the four axioms is Mill (or a secondary account or review of Mill, Poe being an avid reader of magazines and collections), their appearance is a fine reminder of the lineage of *Eureka,* the tradition from early antiquity of works that were at once poetic, scientific, and religious. Poe was familiar with his contemporary Mill and with Lucretius, but ideas like these axioms are in Parmenides, too, a much earlier, pre-Socratic, philosopher of the Eleatic School to which Poe elsewhere refers—see his satiric "How to Write a Blackwood Article" (1838–45). The axioms in Mill and Poe are not, according to classicists consulted, literal quotations; Mill and Poe meant them as typical axioms of classical philosophers. See our Introduction to *Eureka* for comparison of *Eureka* to the fragments that have survived of Parmenides' great account of his visit to the Goddess of Truth. Compare Mill's and Poe's examples— "a thing cannot act where it is not," "there cannot be antipodes," and "darkness cannot proceed from light"—with these utterances of the goddess: "Gaze steadfastly at things which, though far away, are yet present to the mind. For you cannot cut off being from being: it does not scatter itself into a universe and then reunify"; "Strong conviction will not let us think that anything springs from Being except itself"; and "It is indifferent to me at what point I begin, for in any case I must return again to that from which I set out" (Wheelwright, *The Presocratics,* 96–97).

18   Pundit: In Poe's "Mellonta Tauta," Pundit is the narrator's husband (see ¶11n). Because there is no special reason for introducing these characters into his lecture or book, they suggest that the story existed first and that Poe left them in to simplify the job of editing the material for incorporation into *Eureka.*

Miller, or Mill: John Stuart Mill (1806–73). His *System of Logic* (1843) is an analysis of the process of inductive logic (¶13nn; ¶17nn; ¶18nn, next item). Holman ("Hog, Bacon, Ram"), although unable to establish firm connections, thinks that it is likely that Poe, like Carlyle, meant to charge Mill with swinishness; hence, the pig jokes of ¶¶12ff. Pollin (*Collected Writings,* 2:170 and 2:227) points out that Poe seems sometimes to confuse J. S. Mill with Mill's father, James Mill (1773–1836), but the fact that Poe is quoting J. S. Mill in this portion of *Eureka* suggests that it is he whom he intends.

Poe has his letter-writer confuse "Mill" with "Miller" to put in the reader's mind the name of Joe Miller (1684–1738), the supposed author of a famous book of jokes, *Joe Miller's Jest-Book* (see *Collected Works*, 2:259–64).

Bentham: Jeremy Bentham (1748–1832), Utilitarian philosopher. Mill was deeply influenced by Bentham, particularly by the doctrine of the greatest happiness for the greatest number, but Mill's independence from Bentham is shown in his opinion of him: "he was not a great philosopher but a great reformer in philosophy:" (Atkinson, *Jeremy Bentham*, 31). The political causes for which Mill fought would not have been attractive to Poe: Negro rights, woman suffrage, workers' rights. Bentham, moreover, had an aversion to poetry (TOM, notes). For discussion of Poe's views of the connection between Bentham and Mill, see *Collected Writings*, 2:170–72, 2:107, 2:110, and cross-referenced locations.

19 "Ah!—Ability": In the same passage from Mill that Poe uses so heavily in this portion of *Eureka* (see notes to ¶13 and ¶17 especially) Mill makes precisely the point, although not in exactly the words Poe places in quotation marks. Mill writes, for example, "[W]hat we cannot think of as existing, cannot exist at all," and, "Whatever is inconceivable is false" (*A System of Logic*, 460). Mill, like Poe, says that such reasoning is fallacious; mankind, he says, assumed that "a thing cannot act where it is not" because people could not conceive that it could be untrue. But Newtonian gravity plainly involves things acting where they are not. Therefore, "inability to conceive" is not a valid argument. Poe's recurrent fits of hostility to Mill seem illogical, for what he objects to in Mill in his items on Mill in "Marginalia" (Introduction, items 63, 124, in *Collected Writings*, vol. 2) is precisely what Mill objects to in the passage Poe uses. Mill demonstrated the fallacies of à priori reasoning.

David Hume: (1711–76). The skeptical empiricist Scottish philosopher and historian. His moral theory does, in fact, anticipate Bentham and Mill.

Joe: At least three possibilities, all plausible:

1. There was a Joseph Hume (1777–1855), Poe's contemporary and famous enough to be well known in America. A leader of the Radical Party in the House of Commons, he proposed a broad slate of reforms in government and church. Poe was generally hostile to meliorists.

2. Joe Miller (see note to ¶18).

3. "Joe" in the sense of "anybody" or "everyman." Such locutions are a literary convention of the period. Compare Thoreau's "John or Jonathan" at the close of *Walden,* in which "John" probably means "all Englishmen" and "Jonathan" all Americans.

Poe may well have intended all three possibilities.

20 sotticism: Pollin (*Poe: Creator of Words*, 37) reports that this word is "derived from French and English sottise" and does not appear in the *OED*. It is Poe's coinage and seems to mean "foolishness." BRP points out that sottise has nothing to do with the English word *sot,* habitual drunk (although Poe must have been aware that the meaning would occur to readers). BRP adds that it "was a favorite word." Pollin (*Poe: Creator of Words*) lists four instances. See also *Complete Works,* 13:51, where Poe uses it to describe the speech of an egotistical character in a play, and, below, paragraph 130, where Poe used it, then altered it to "folly."

21 Soul . . . soar: Cf. Poe's poem "To Helen" (the later poem by that title): "like thine own soul, soaring" (TOM, notes). The date strengthens the connections. Poe first published the poem, then called "To— — —," in the November 1848 issue of *Union Magazine* (later *Sartain's*).

22 Kepler: Johannes Kepler (1571–1630), great German astronomer. See subsequent note. In Poe's story "Mellonta Tauta," Kepler's is one of the few names that Pundita does not misspell. See note to paragraph 11.

Laplace: Pierre Simon, Marquis de Laplace (1749–1827), was an important French astronomer, theoretician, and mathematician. See note to paragraph 77.

23 cryptographist: Poe's interest in cryptography was considerable—see his story "The Gold Bug," especially. He even made journalistic claims about his ability to solve coded passages. The word is Poe's coinage. Pollin lists points at which he used it or the word *cryptograph* (*Poe: Creator of Words,* 84–85).

Champollion: Jean François Champollion (1790–1832), using the Rosetta Stone, learned to decipher Egyptian hieroglyphics. The stone, found in 1799, bore an inscription in two different forms of hieroglyphics and in Greek. "Solving" it was a great scholarly feat. Poe indicates respect for the accomplishment by having the letter-writer spell "Champollion" correctly.

phonetical hieroglyphics: This was Champollion's phrase (TOM, notes). Irwin observes that Poe's letter-writer in *Eureka* " . . associates Champollion's intuitive deciphering of the hieroglyphics with Kepler's intuitive grasp of the laws of gravity." Irwin concludes from this association "that Poe's own 'scientific reading' of the physical shape of the universe in *Eureka* is to be understood as an imaginative decipherment of the cosmic hieroglyph" (*American Hieroglyphics,* 43–44ff.). Irwin (46ff.) also treats at length Humboldt's discussion of Aztec hieroglyphics and Poe's other references to that subject (pt. 2 passim).

Newton: Sir Isaac Newton (1642–1727), the great English scientist whose name Poe also allowed to be remembered correctly through the fictional ages.

guessed: Hodgens observes that here Poe disagrees with Nichol, who says (Lecture 3, p. 21) that "guesses are nothing, unless verified" to "the high philosopher." John Pringle Nichol, Regius Professor of Astronomy at the University of Glasgow, was the author of *Views of the Architecture of the Heavens* (1837), and Poe's competitor for a lecture audience when *Eureka* was given as a talk. See Pollin,

"Contemporary Reviews of *Eureka,*" for details. References to Nichol's lectures are to the New York 1848 edition, *Views of Astronomy. Seven Lectures Delivered before the Mercantile Library Associations of New York in the Months of January and February, 1848,* as transcribed by Oliver Dyer, "Phonographic Writer."

Poe's letter-writer's attempt to define precisely what enabled Kepler to make a great breakthrough in astronomy is somewhat inaccurate, although Poe shows some familiarity with the history of that science. Kepler had been given by the Danish astronomer Tycho Brahe (1546–1601) the task of creating a conceptual model of the solar system that would fit Tycho's highly accurate empirical data. Tycho, however, believed that the earth was at the center of the system; he also thought in terms of circular orbits for the sun, planets, and satellites. Kepler dutifully worked at the mathematics of model-building for four fruitless years, adding to the circular orbits the circular wheels-upon-wheels of cycles and epicycles that were the traditional astronomical method of handling discrepancies between model and observations. Tycho's death freed Kepler to use a new model with the sun at the center and elliptical orbits. Kepler got his model to work but had no physical understanding of why it worked. Newton would provide the basis for a theoretical account of why Kepler's model worked. So the statement in *Eureka* is not quite right. Kepler worked for years to find the laws; there was no inspired guessing of a theory because he produced no theory, although no science historian would deny that the *model*, his visualization, might well have resulted from the combination of induction, deduction, and subliminal association that Poe describes.

Poe is being perhaps excessively fussy in not calling the "route" intuition. The argument, however, occurs so often in his work that one can define what he has in mind. Neither blind data-gathering nor simple guesswork produces truth. An informed and perceptive poetic intellect can perceive truth slantingly, as—to use Poe's analogy—the eye sees a dim star best when one does not look directly at it.

Ram-ishly: Poe's coinage (Pollin, *Poe: Creator of Words,* 87).

24 *"I care not . . . fury":* Patrick Quinn calls this a "free paraphrase of the final sentences in the Proem to Book V of Kepler's *Harmonice Mundi* (1619)" (*Edgar Allan Poe,* 1399). Margaret Alterton thinks Poe read Kepler's comments in John Drinkwater Bethune's *Life of Kepler* (1830) in "The Library of Useful Knowledge" (TOM, notes; *Collected Works,* 3:1319). Alterton quotes Bethune as follows:

> What I prophesied two and twenty years ago . . . what I firmly believed long before I had seen Ptolemy's "Harmonics." . . . Great is the absolute nature of Harmonics in all its details . . . it is found among all celestial notions . . .[.]
>
> Nothing holds me. I will indulge in my sacred fury: I will triumph . . . I have stolen the golden vases of the Egyptians.
>
> If you forgive me, I rejoice; if you are angry, I can bear it; . . . the book is written, to be read either now or by posterity. I care not which—it may well wait a century for a reader, as God has waited six thousand years for an observer. (*Origins,* 142)

Mabbott observes that Poe might have seen Kepler's "rhapsodic outburst" in a wide variety of places, because it was very well known (*Collected Works*, 3:1319n11).

26 unastronomical: Poe's coinage (Pollin, *Poe: Creator of Words*, 9).

27 Solomon Seesaw: Poe alludes to John Parish Robertson's *Solomon Seesaw* (London, 1839), a humorous novel in three volumes. There are no sonnets in it, although Robertson makes a great deal of dialects, manners, and gestures. The character Solomon Seesaw courts and eventually weds the daughter of a haughty Welsh woman. Robertson concludes, "Thus I bring to a close the not long, but eventful, History of the 'Ups and Downs of Solomon Seesaw.'" Had Seesaw written sonnets, they would likely have been poor. Poe reviewed the novel in the September 1839 *Burton's*. He also coined a similar name, "Solomon Seadrift," for a member of his "Folio Club." See ¶17n and *Collected Works*, 2:205 (TOM, notes; BRP).

29 *thought of a thought:* Mabbott (TOM, notes; *Collected Works*, 1:405–9) suggests comparison to Poe's poem "To ——— (Marie Louise Shew)" (1848), which contains the line "unthought-like thoughts that are the souls of thought" in a context that is, in fact, related to the idea here. "To ———" is a gallantly flattering piece that argues at the start that the poet had recently

> denied that ever

> A thought arose within the human brain
> Beyond the utterance of the human tongue.

The name *Marie Louise*, however, proves the speaker wrong, for the words stir "from out the abysses of his heart, Unthought-like thoughts," etc. "Unthought-like" is another of Poe's coinages (Pollin, *Poe: Creator of Words*, 67).

30 Poe's "quotations" in this paragraph are probably suppositional statements. The last one ("The mind admits . . . space") plainly is.

31 jump twenty: BRP suggests that Poe was using personal experience. Two published items cite his prowess: He is said to have gone 21½ feet (*Southern Literary Messenger* 2, 9 [Aug. 1836]: 597; *Saturday Museum*, March 4, 1843). By contemporary standards, 21½ feet would be beyond the range of an untrained broadjumper but attainable by a trained high school athlete. The world record is around twenty-nine feet.

33 insupportable: See *Collected Writings*, 2:270, for a guide to Poe on puns.

35 *I cannot* conceive. . . . fancy: BRP suggests that Poe repeated here much of what he wrote elsewhere in "his attempts to define 'fancy' and 'imagination.'" Poe's source, BRP continues, was often Coleridge (*Collected Writings*, 3:16–18; Poe on Nathaniel P. Willis, *Broadway Journal*, Jan. 18, 1845, and note to it, in *Collected Writings*, 4:17n, 17/12–36; see also Omans, "'Intellect, Taste,'" 137).

37 *inessentiality:* Poe's coinage (Pollin, *Poe: Creator of Words*, 29).

thinkers-that-they-think: Poe's coinage (ibid., 66). Poe probably echoes Descartes' "I think, therefore I am."

self-cognizance: Poe's coinage (ibid., 63).

39   periphrasing: Not listed in most modern dictionaries but not a coinage. The *OED* gives a 1652 precedent where it appears in the same sentence as "paraphrasing." It means "expressing something in a roundabout way."

It is . . . nowhere: Blaise Pascal (1623–62), *Pensees* 2:72 (TOM, notes). The French reads, "C'est une sphère dont le centre est partout, la circonférence nulle part." Pascal's *Pensées* exists in numerous editions; the wording of the line varies from one to another. We follow M. León Brunschvicg because his edition includes variants we noticed in editions from Poe's era. The wording which Poe quotes is that which Brunschvicg prefers. The *Pensées*, written "in fragments" and published posthumously, "trace the universal search for God," (W. F. Trotter, xv). This particular thought has been attributed to sources as old as Empedocles and Hermes Trismegistus and was in common use by the French authors Rabelais, Gerson, St. Bonaventure, and Vincent de Beauvais. Pascal is known to have read it in Lady Gournay's preface to the *Essays* of Montaigne: "Trismégiste, y est-il dit, appelle la Déité cercle dont le centre est . . . .etc" (Pascal, *Pensées*, ed. Brunschvicg, 348; Pascal, *Pensées*, [Paris, 1876], 118n).

40   "*Nous . . .* ourselves": Book 1, ch. i, "On Theology," sec. 1 from Jacob Friedrich Bielfeld (1717–70), *Les premiers traits de l'érudition universelle, ou analyse abregée de toutes les sciences, des beaux-arts et des belles-lettres* (TOM) (Leyden, 1767, and numerous subsequent editions (*Collected Writings*, 2:6). Mabbott notes that there was a translation by W. Hooper, M.D. (*Elements of Universal Erudition*), but Poe's English translation was not copied from it. Pollin (*Collected Writings*, 2:6) shows how extensive is Poe's use of material from Bielfeld, suggests the 1770 London edition as Poe's source, and explains that Bielfeld was a Prussian who wrote in French.

41   BRP speculates about "a parallel in tone and idea with [the motto of 'Ligeia'] (Poe-created) and [the] major theme [of that story] (as in *Collected Works* 2:310; 319–320). Note the contrived dramatic 'dialoguism' here and that in the narrative." His suggestion seems apt. See also *Thirty-Two Stories*, 54–55, 55n2, 62–63n10; *Short Fiction*, 64, 79, 103nn1, 2, 104n10. The title, "Ligeia," reinforces the connection; if man were a part of the godhead, God's will and man's, God's knowledge and man's, would be identical. Poetic inspiration (Ligeia is the spirit of divine inspiration) would be a manifestation of the transcendent oneness.

44   *If . . .* Omnipotence: Poe added this sentence for stress. Summary of Poe's argument at this point appears in A. H. Quinn (*Edgar Allan Poe*, 545–46), who repeats Poe: all creation comes from an original particle; multipicity begins in unity; God's spirit ("Nihility") created matter; only intuition can guide us to such primal truths. Poe's position is close to Emerson's.

45   Imparticularity: Poe's coinage (Pollin, *Poe: Creator of Words,* 29). Used also in paragraph 153.

   The discussion in the following passage (paragraphs 45–49) should be compared, as BRP suggests, to the character Vankirk's explanation of "unparticled matter" in the 1844 tale "Mesmeric Revelation" (*Collected Works,* 3:1029–40, esp. 1033–35; *Short Fiction,* 139–45, esp. 141–42). Hypnotized at the point of death, Vankirk is able to report back on what he has learned. God is "not spirit." "Nor is he matter" as mankind understands matter, for "there are *gradations* of matter of which man knows nothing. . . . These gradations of matter increase in rarity or fineness, until we arrive at matter *unparticled,*" which "permeates" and "impels all things. . . . . This matter is God" (*Collected Works,* 1030; *Short Fiction,* 141). Vankirk explains that "the infinitude of littleness in the spaces between [atoms] . . . is an absurdity." There is a point at which matter is so rarified that the spaces "vanish" and the mass coalesces into one imparticled whole, which is at once "matter" and what is called "spirit." But "spirit" "is . . . as fully matter as before" (*Collected Works,* 1034; *Short Fiction,* 142).

   "without . . . void": Poe quotes Genesis 1:2.

49   unimaginably yet not infinitely minute atoms: Poe may have in mind here Lucretius' *De Rerum Natura* (ca. 55 B.C.E.). See, for example, Lucretius, *On the Nature of the Universe,* 37–45. Poe was familiar with the works of Lucretius and his predecessor Epicurus. For numerous references to these authors, see the listings in Pollin, *Dictionary of Names and Titles,* 32, 58; see also ¶171, ¶171n.

50   uniquity: Perhaps this is merely a more formal way of saying "uniqueness" in the sense of "original one-ness," a term Poe might have wanted to avoid. See "How to Write a Blackwood Article" (1838): "Put in something about the Supernal Oneness. Don't say a syllable about the Infernal Twoness" (*Thirty-Two Stories,* 74–75; *Short Fiction,* 360; *Collected Works,* 2:342). Poe made fun of transcendental assumptions (see *Thirty-Two Stories,* 68ff., esp. 68–69, 70n3, 74n11; *Short Fiction,* 414–17, esp. nn3,11).

   inequidistance: Poe's coinage (Pollin, *Poe: Creator of Words,* 29). "But," BRP adds, "the adjective has a 1677 instance."

   difference of form: For a discussion of the difference of form in atoms in Lucretius, see *On the Nature of the Universe* (71–78).

   rëunion: BRP notes that this word "is apparently a theological coinage of 1635, 1693 and laically in 1893, with Poe's instance ignored by the *OED;* a convenient term for the gerund 'reuniting' or the unsuitable 'reunion.' Poe's care in placing the dieresis over the first vowel (also in "reaction" in paragraph 51, and in numerous other words formed with 're') is his regular custom, q.v. in *Collected Writings,* 2:xxxviii–xl."

52   *Relation:* Poe's use of the word is very odd. He means "physical relationship" or "physical interaction," with the added implication "of utmost complexity." He

explains his ad hoc definition of "relation" in paragraph 50, where he speaks of "the utmost possible multiplicity of *relation* out of the emphatically irrelative *One.*" The original atom, in plain language, had nothing with which to react. "Divine Will" burst it into bits that could then interact. The point of *"utmost possible Relation"* is the time of maximum diffusion.

53   *Uni-tendency:* Poe's coinage (Pollin, *Poe: Creator of Words,* 39).

the impenetrability of matter: It is now understood that it is electromagnetism that keeps one from putting one's finger through a wooden table. But there is no universal "repulsive" force of the sort Poe postulates.

54   the God: An interesting locution. We think that Poe intends it to embrace "the gods" of polytheistic religions and the "God" of monotheism, the merger implying something like "world-spirit."

the knot: Poe probably has in mind the Gordian knot, through which Alexander the Great is supposed to have cut.

56   unempirically: Poe's coinage (Pollin, *Poe: Creator of Words,* 39).

no-difference: Poe's coinage (Ibid., 58).

The amount . . . composed: Poe's formula (the italicized sentence) would not work for gravity. He is trying to say that the size of the effect is in relationship to the discrepancy between the two objects. There is no formula of this sort outside of Poe (Twarog).

57   To electricity— . . . *Thought:* Writers in Poe's era were confident that science was on the verge of providing physical and logical proof of spirituality. It is for this reason, for example, that an American literary magazine, *Atkinson's Casket* (the journal that was to become *Graham's,* with Poe as editor) in 1838 ran an item describing the work of a French experimenter in applying electricity to human nerves for therapeutic purposes. Such information was of special interest because it suggested material explanation for hitherto intangible phenomena. It is for this reason that Poe in paragraphs 55ff. extrapolates physical fact (one generates electricity by moving one electrically charged unit through the field of another) to universal speculation. If the nervous system runs via electricity, then thought, spirit, or intangible spirituality are likely to be "real," based on physics; the poetic creation and the physical universe would thus be interlocked and perhaps identical. See Poe's visionary tales, especially "The Power of Words" and other angelic colloquies.

At this stage in *Eureka,* Poe does not spell out the connection: Electricity (or some other cause) accounts for light, heat, and magnetism and also for spiritual things such as thought. There is, we shall learn, a link between physical fact and intimations of the cosmic unity. Poe would have assumed that readers caught the implications before he made them explicit; educated people all supposed that something of the sort would soon be demonstrated (Levine, *Edgar Poe,* 135).

The idea had been current for some time. Richard Lovett (1692–1780), for example, had argued in his *Electrical Philosopher* (Worcester, Eng., 1774) that the "electrical fluid" is the "mechanical Cause that we breathe live and move; the efficient Cause of all motion; the physical Cause of Gravitation, Cohesion, Magnetism, the ebbing and flowing of the Sea, and of all of the other of the most abstruse Phenomena of Nature" (19). Lovett and others who try to provide materialistic explanations of the hitherto ineffable are discussed in Schofield (*Mechanism and Materialism*, esp. 163, 200, 206). A book published in 1792 in Philadelphia (William Cullen, *First Lines of the Practice of Physic*) defines the tie from human physiology to the cosmos explicitly by making analogous connections between electricity and "aether": "As electrical matter may exist in bodies . . . so the aether in the nervous system exists" (quoted in Schofield, *Mechanism and Materialsm*, 206). Twarog adds that the idea was hardy and long-lived; it was to be incorporated into spiritualism later in Poe's century. (The matter is discussed in Brandon, *The Spiritualists*.)

Poe's suggestion that there may be something more fundamental underlying "light, heat and magnetism" that we might, "for the present," call electricity (but presumably is not quite that either) is a fine example of his ability to point to areas in which future theorizers would have to work. Poe does not "predict" the current controversial attempt to explain all physical phenomena through "superstrings," for his next paragraph moves in a different direction. But he did sense the need for totally new kinds of formulations to account for the existence and nature of the universe.

58 *Attraction* and *Repulsion:* Terms introduced into molecular theory by Ruggiero Giuseppi Boscovich (1711–87), who visualized atoms as the "nuclei of attractive and repulsive forces" (Poe, *The Science Fiction of Edgar Allan Poe*, ed. Beaver, 405n18). BRP points to a prior discussion by Poe of attraction and repulsion in "Pinakidia" (item 151). The item and a meticulous explication appear in *Collected Writings*, 2:93–94, where Poe's main source is identified as Baron Jacob Bielfeld's *Elements of Universal Erudition*.

Woodberry and his scientific consultant, Irving Stringham, said of Poe's theory that Poe's "position, that matter came from nihility and consisted of centers of force, had been put forth as a scientific theory by Boscovich in 1758–59, had been widely discussed, and had found its way into American text-books" (Poe, *The Works of Edgar Allan Poe*, ed. Stedman and Woodberry, 9:309). Woodberry's treatment of *Eureka* seems uncharacteristically offhanded and abrupt; he was plainly impatient with it.

62 metaphysical schools: BRP writes, "For Poe's disdain for these 'schools,' see his scornful coinage 'metaphysicianism'" in Pollin, *Poe: Creator of Words*, 31, which guides the reader to instances in Poe's fiction, criticism, and miscellaneous writing.

famous . . . experiments: In 1774, Nevil Maskelyne (1732–1811) conducted a famous experiment at Mt. Schehallion, Perthshire, Scotland (not Wales). The idea was to measure the deflection from vertical of a pendulum caused by the proximity of the mountain, thus determining the gravitational constant—that is, G—through a formula:

$$\text{"}F = \frac{G \times M^1 M^2}{R^2}$$

in which F = force due to gravity, G = gravitational constant, M^1 and M^2 = the masses of the two objects, and R = the distance between the two objects" (Twarog).

Cavendish: Working independently, as Poe suggests, Henry Cavendish (1731–1810) did similar work with an "apparatus of movable lead balls" (TOM, notes). Cavendish's results were published in 1798.

Bailly: Poe's spelling suggests that he confused the French astronomer J. Sylvain Bailly with the British astronomer Francis Baily (1774–1844), who "laboriously repeated" the Cavendish experiments following 1838 (TOM, notes). But Poe might simply have misspelled the name.

65 Bryant . . . "Mythology": One of Poe's favorite sources was *A New System; or, An Analysis of Antient Mythology* (1774–76) by Jacob Bryant (1718–1804), a book which, on the basis of linguistic evidence—evidence that was, alas, quickly seen to be unsound—argues that intimate relationships connect a wide range of ancient myths and religions. Though Bryant's *Mythology* was unconvincing, it was immensely learned and remains fascinating. Poe loved it, although he saw through it, and borrowed from it the symbolic underpinnings of several stories, notably "Metzengerstein" (1832) and "Shadow" (1835). His ambivalence toward Bryant, who seemed to him both imaginatively intriguing and funny, is important for understanding Poe's attitude toward *Eureka*. This analogical reference to Bryant *seems* perfectly serious, yet it is plain that Poe was, to some extent, pulling our leg. "Erudite" is ironic. Poe knew exactly how "erudite" poor Bryant had been. Fuller discussion of Poe's use of Bryant, including the passage quoted here, is in Levine and Levine, "History, Myth, Fable," in which are plentiful examples of Poe's attitude—for instance, the section in "Four Beasts in One—The Homocameleopard" (written by 1833, published 1836) in which Poe concludes a passage based on material derived from Bryant, "what great fools are antiquarians." In the story "The Purloined Letter" and item 70 of "Pinakidia" Poe uses this quotation, which may be found in volume 2, page 173, of the 1807 London edition of Bryant (*Thirty-Two Stories*, 267n12; *Short Fiction*, 249n12). See also paragraph 11 note, *Mare Tenebrarum*. A list of Poe's sources for "Brevities" in *Collected Writings* (2:xxiv–xxv) illustrates how heavy is his use of Bryant.

concentralization: Poe's coinage (Pollin, *Poe: Creator of Words,* 25), which he repeats in paragraphs 85 and 86.

especiality: "Poe often italicized his own coinages, although sometimes erroneously." "Concentralization" (see previous item) is credited "solely to Poe by the *OED,* while 'especiality' is cited *solely* for 1460." The *OED* omits Poe's use (BRP) (Pollin, *Poe: Creator of Words,* 16). Because several italicized words in this passage are common terms (*sensitive, perception,* and *essential*), *especiality* might not indicate that Poe thought it a coinage.

phænomenon: "The spelling . . . seems eighteenth century or earlier, an apparent affectation in Poe, for all twelve instances in the *OED* for the nineteenth century drop the 'a' of the diphthong" (BRP). BRP suggests a search of John Herschel as a likely source of Poe's odd spelling, but Herschel consistently spelled it "phen." See, for example, the 1830 article "Sound," which Herschel contributed to the *Encyclopaedia Metropolitana: Physical Astronomy. Sound. Light* (n.p., n.d.), 820. See as well *Outlines of Astronomy* (Philadelphia, 1853, but unaltered in spelling from earlier editions), in which "Phenomena" is a page heading and forms of the word, so spelled, appear frequently. See also paragraph 178n, "excentrically."

67   wilderness: "A favorite word in Poe. (Pollin [*Word Index*] gives twenty-nine instances), often indicating [']multifold confusion['] as well as 'wild places'" (BRP).

68   mote: Nichol (*Views of Astronomy,* Lecture 3, p. 15) uses the same word in a very similar context (Hodgens typescript).

If I venture. . . . of their Creator: Thus every action alters the universe. In the poetic visionary fantasy "The Power of Words" (1845), Poe has one angelic spirit explain to another how each spoken word, through the vibrations it creates, literally and physically changes the world; the speaker shows his companion a star that he has spoken into existence (*Thirty-Two Stories,* 322, see also 318; *Short Fiction,* 116, see also 107–8; *Collected Works,* 3:1215). In *Eureka* and elsewhere, Poe gave spirituality the physical basis that people of his era were sure science would soon provide. See also Levine, *Edgar Poe,* esp. 155ff.

69   unthoughtlike thoughts: paragraph 29 and paragraph 29n.

soul-reveries: Poe's coinage (Pollin, *Poe: Creator of Words,* 65).

71   brotherhood: Compare Poe's letter to John Neal (Poe, *Letters of Edgar Allan Poe,* ed. Ostrom, 1:32, dates it Oct.–Nov. 1829): "the beauty of the . . . sky and the sunshiny earth—there can be no tie more strong than that of brother for brother . . . that they love the same parent" (TOM, notes). This is the letter that begins, "I am young—not yet twenty—*am* a poet—if deep worship of all beauty can make me *one.*"

omniprevalent: "This is Poe's coinage, as *OED* says for this usage; [it is] used also in the *Evening Mirror* of 1/13/1845. [It appears also] in 'Marginalia' item 134 [*Collected Writings,* 2:234], but spelled with a hyphen, 'omni-prevalent'" (BRP).

One: Poe *seems* to believe sincerely in ultimate unity and Oneness in the sense the New England Transcendentalists did. Yet as always in Poe, there was ambivalence, for he increasingly came to attack Transcendentalists in print. In "How to Write a Blackwood Article," his comic satire on magazine article writing, for example, he has "Mr. Blackwood" tell the aspiring incompetent author Psyche Zenobia, "Put in something about the Supernal Oneness. Don't say a syllable about the Infernal Twoness." (In early versions of the tale, he aimed satire at Goethe or Coleridge, and in 1845 he turned on *The Dial,* the Transcendentalist journal. See *Collected Works,* 2:359–60n21.) Where, then, did Poe stand, if he propounded this unity as eternal truth on one page yet mocked it on another?

this . . . *One:* Poe deliberately breaks grammatical rules for poetic emphasis. His meaning is clear: this absolute, irrelative, unconditional oneness.

73   sphericity: See Pollin, *Poe: Creator of Words,* 37. BRP suggests that the term, with a misspelling ("sphereicity"), was probably borrowed from Herschel (see ¶227n).

radiated: As our list of variants shows, Poe altered this word (and also "irradiate" and "irradiation") from the published "irradiated." Both words carry the sense of "sending forth from a center," but "irradiate" was more commonly used to mean "light up" or "illuminate." Poe's alterations were in the interest of precision.

75   Dr. Nichol. . . . "Geometry": Poe quotes either the *Tribune* report of Nichol's talk, which was printed on the morning of Poe's *Eureka* lecture, February 3 (Conner's idea), or the pamphlet reprint of the *Tribune* articles (Connor, "Poe and John Nichol"; Nichol, *Views of Astronomy,* [New York, 1848], Lecture 3, p. 20) (Hodgens typescript; TOM, notes). There are minor variations between the version Hodgens quotes and Poe's quotation. See also Pollin, "Contemporary Reviews of *Eureka,*" n5. John Pringle Nichol was Regius Professor of Astronomy at the University of Glasgow; Emerson helped arrange his lectures, which were unfortunate competition for Poe, who had hoped to raise enough cash from his talk to bankroll a proposed magazine, "The Stylus."

76   "ultimate principles," . . . God?: Pressed by the competition of Nichol and eager to show that he, too, is an authority, Poe both quibbles and deals with Nichol's ideas out of context. Nichol "was talking about discrepancies between the observed and calculated paths of Uranus." Poe distorts Nichol, too; his *Views of the Architecture of the Heavens* and the *Tribune* account of January 31 both make plain that he would agree with what Poe said about the "Volition of God" (Conner, "Poe and John Nichol," 201–2). There is no doubt that Poe knew much of the Nichol material well; see, for example, his note to paragraph 163.

self-evidence: paragraph 12n.

77   Magnetism . . . Transcendentalism: See our note to paragraph 57. Each of the "isms" Poe lists is concerned in part with unifying spiritual links between one person and another or between any person and the universe. Thus magnetism (or, for other speculators, electricity) was supposed to make possible the phenomenon now labeled as hypnotism. "Mesmerism," as hypnosis was then called, was felt to be based on "Animal Magnetism." Swedenborgianism (see Pollin, *Poe: Creator of Words,* 77) is the philosophy of the mystic philosopher and scientist Emanuel Swedenborg (1688–1772), who was supposed to have been clairvoyant (see Poe's story "The Fall of the House of Usher" [1839], in *Collected Works,* 2:392–422; *Short*

Fiction, 62, 64–65, 88–98, 104–6; *Thirty-Two Stories,* 87–103). Ralph Waldo Emerson, the principal voice of New England Transcendentalism, spoke of a "world-spirit" or "Oversoul." The liberated human spirit was capable of receiving direct inspiration through the Oversoul; it was, moreover, identical with the Oversoul—though Emerson often deliberately maintained an ambiguity about whether the Oversoul was literally "out there," permeating all things, or only within each person (see, e.g., the opening chapter of *Nature* [1836]). Poe's sarcasm in regard to "isms" is misleading, for *Eureka* plainly argues that some unifying spiritual force exists and that, moreover, it is susceptible to scientific analysis and explanation.

Laplace . . . attack it: See note to paragraph 22. Beaver, in a different context, quotes a passage from Laplace's *Mécanique céleste* (1798) in which Laplace came close to what Poe demands (Poe, *The Science Fiction of Edgar Allan Poe,* ed. Beaver, 406n). Laplace said that if one knew enough about forces and had enough data—in modern terms, if one could quantify the variables—one could, if intelligent enough to analyze them all, derive a formula that would remove uncertainty of past, present, and future. Poe's remark about Laplace's timidity, then, is somewhat unfair.

mathematico-physical: The term derives from Herschel's *A Preliminary Discourse on the Study of Natural Philosophy,* 3:iii:274 (*OED*).

Leibnitz: Gottfried Wilhelm Leibnitz (1648–1716) "held substance to be *force;* [and] space, matter [and] motion . . . [to be] phenomenal; he believed in the continuity and development of consciousness" (TOM, notes). Compare Poe's comment about Leibnitz in "Marginalia" item 38: "Leibnitz . . . was fond of interweaving even his mathematical, with ethical speculations, making a medley rather to be wondered at than understood" (*Collected Writings,* 2:146). Poe perhaps thought of Leibnitz in this context because Poe perceived a connection between his (Poe's) speculation about *"some* principle . . . behind the Law of Gravity" and what he termed "Leibnitz' *Law of Continuity."* See *Collected Writings* (2:190–91, 2:272) for discussions of Poe's—limited—knowledge of Leibnitz.

physico-metaphysical: Poe's coinage, following the pattern of "mathematico-physical" above. See Pollin, *Poe: Creator of Words,* 33, for Poe's parallel coinage: "Physico-mental" (BRP).

78 taken for a madman: Speaking in his own voice in a treatise, which, he says, he wants taken seriously as his most important pronouncement, Poe uses a favorite device from his fiction, in which often a narrator begins by telling the reader that he comes from a family noted for mental instability, or that people have called him mad, or even that "you may think me mad, but I am sane—see how cleverly I can reason?" Such passages offer rationalist readers the option of considering the narrative that follows merely a projection of a disordered mind and therefore credible as psychological fiction: the events may be incredible, but the "projection" is credible. Poe's use of the device here should trouble the reader who want to see *Eureka* as entirely serious.

I here declare . . . thing: Poe's certainty contrasts strikingly to Isaac Newton's great uncertainty. Newton wrote in a letter of February 25, 1692/3 that the idea of one body acting upon another through a vacuum and at great distance "without the mediation of anything else . . . is to me so great an absurdity that I believe no man who has in philosophical matters a competent faculty of thinking, can ever fall into it" (Poe, *The Science Fiction of Edgar Allan Poe*, ed. Beaver, 406–7n).

83 light-particles: Poe's coinage (Pollin, *Poe: Creator of Words*, 55).

light-impressions: Poe's coinage (ibid., 54).

84 particles: In this paragraph, Poe seems to be using a theory of light as particles. In contemporary (2004) science, light-as-particles accounts for certain phenomena, whereas others require light-as-waves. We do not have a single accepted theory to account for the nature of light. There is a summary of the ambiguous state of the issue in Poe's day in Beaver (Poe, *The Science Fiction of Edgar Allan Poe*, ed. Beaver, 397–403) that connects the uncertainty on this and related matters to Newton's puzzlement.

85 Conversing: The *OED* provides several very old (from 1551 on) instances of "conversion" being used to mean "turning around" but does not list "conversing" in that sense. BRP suggests, "Poe seems to be coining a verb from the mathematical term 'the converse of.'"

"concentralization": Poe provides an ad hoc definition here because his previous use of this coined word in paragraph 65 is different.

87 slight inspection . . . situated: This is a strangely naive statement for Poe to make. When the Milky Way is visible, a "slight inspection" in fact suggests just the opposite; the distribution of stars does look roughly even. Yet Poe is right that the distribution of matter in the universe is, as Twarog puts it, "lumpy," but seems roughly even. Poe visualizes an analogy between the "radiation" of atoms and heavenly bodies.

irrelation: Poe's coinage (Pollin, *Poe: Creator of Words*, 30). Compare De Quincey's 1848 usage cited in the *OED*: "The instinct of contempt . . . towards literature was supported by the irrelation of literature to the state."

89 Footnote: Poe's note refers the reader to a page and passage in *Tales by Edgar A. Poe*. At that point in "The Murders in the Rue Morgue," his detective (not Poe himself) explains that the Paris police have failed to solve a double murder because they "have fallen into the gross but common error of confounding the unusual with the abstruse. But it is by these deviations from the plane of the ordinary, that reason feels its way, if at all, in its search for the true." It was what was most bizarre about the case that made solving it easiest for Dupin. He says that the question to ask is not "'what has occurred'" but rather "'what has occurred that has never occurred before.' In fact," Dupin concludes, "the facility with which I shall arrive, or have arrived, at the solution of this mystery, is in the direct ratio of its apparent insolubility in the eyes of the police." Citing his fictitious charac-

ter in this context illustrates, first, the close ties of *Eureka* to the fiction and, second, Poe's incurable love of playing games as he wrote. The cross-reference is discussed in *Collected Works*, 2:573n33; see also Poe's cross-reference from "The Mystery of Marie Rogêt" to "The Murders in the Rue Morgue" (ibid., 3:737).

90 I do not say: Compare the conclusion of Thoreau's *Walden* (1854): "I do not say that John or Jonathan will realize all this. . . . The sun is but a morning star" (266). One should not claim that Thoreau had read *Eureka* or that there is a common source, although both are quite possible. But the similarities suggest another way in which *Eureka* is a transcendentalist document. There is even a surprising amount of shared rhetoric. See paragraph 97 for another example or examine *Walden* just five paragraphs before the passage quoted, where Thoreau uses the rare word *tintinnabulum*, suggesting again a tie to Poe, who coined "tintinnabulation" in his poem "The Bells."

I go on to say. . . . Nature: BRP suggests that "the word 'say' plus the anaphora in the verbs show the lecture-style origin of the treatise."

91 *ray-streams:* Poe's coinage (Pollin, *Poe: Creator of Words*, 61).

93–95 Read in isolation, this passage could be taken as Poe's anticipation of the current (2004) investigation of subatomic physics; he could be said to be talking about the "strong force" and the "weak force." He is not. He is constructing a model, analyzing what one might see if one could freeze the diffusing process at several stages and examine the distribution of "atoms." See paragraph 110 for further apparent but misleading evidence of Poe's prescience.

97 I . . . expect to find, lurking . . . the secret: See paragraph 90n. Compare the last paragraph of the chapter entitled "Where I Lived, and What I Lived For" in Thoreau's *Walden*, which is also about searching intuitively for truths buried "somewhere hereabouts" and rhetorically overlaps the passage in *Eureka*.

110 *strongest of forces:* Poe is not predicting the more recent subatomic physics (¶¶93–95n).

111 they can: Poe's intention is "can they."

satisfactions: BRP notes that "it is odd to find here the language of Bentham's Utilitarianism (the maximum of satisfactions or pleasures)" applied to atoms. Such anthropomorphic language, however, is consistent with Poe's general philosophic scheme, for he is arguing, after all, that matter and spirit are one and that the laws of physics are the will of God.

114 exactly . . . purposes: BRP notes Poe's discussion of *"the great* idiosyncrasy in the Divine system of adaptation," namely, "the complete *mutuality* of adaptation." Poe writes:

> In Divine constructions, the object is either object or purpose, as we choose to regard it, while the purpose is either purpose or object; so that we can never (abstractedly, without concretion—without reference to facts of the moment)

decide which is which. For secondary example:—In polar climates, the human frame, to maintain its due caloric, requires, for combustion in the stomach, the most highly ammoniac food, such as train oil. Again:—In polar climates, the sole food afforded man is the oil of abundant seals and whales. Now, whether is oil at hand because imperatively demanded?—or whether it is the only thing demanded because the only thing to be obtained? It is impossible to say. There is an absolute reciprocity of adaptation, for which we seek in vain among the works of man. ("Marginalia," item 18, in *Collected Writings,* 2:127–28)

Poe argues that his view of "Divine . . . adaptation" is absent from the "Bridgewater Treatises" (1833–40, see ¶133n). "Marginalia" item 18 is the one that ends with the famous statement "The Universe is a Plot of God." The connection with *Eureka,* then, is extremely likely.

116 surface: As the list of textual variants shows, Poe changed the printed "circumference" to "surface." The latter is preferable because Poe's perception is three-dimensional; he envisions a sphere, not a circle.

118 "In the beginning": Poe's quotation from Genesis starts a paragraph on the sustained effects of God's creation (*"continuous Volition"*). Compare the usual deistic model of a clockwork universe set in motion by God.

   "sub-principle": BRP notes Poe's fondness for the qualifying prefix *sub.* See Pollin, *Poe: Creator of Words,* 37, which includes "sub-sub-editor." One thinks of Melville's "poor devil of a Sub-Sub" librarian in the "Extracts" section of *Moby-Dick;* this must have been a popular gag.

122 To explain:—. . . . —unless: Poe's heavy use of dashes (seventeen in this paragraph alone, one of which is very much oversize) may lead readers to question his seriousness, for he had written satirically on the subject in a tale about a hack writer so full of self-importance that he considers calling his memoirs "Memoranda to serve for the Literary History of America." At the conclusion, the literary hack gives one reason for his "success": "The *style!*—that was the thing. I caught it from Fatquack—*whizz!*—*fizz!*—and I am giving you a specimen of it now." (See "The Literary Life of Thingum Bob, Esq." [1844], in *Thirty-Two Stories,* 284–302; *Short Fiction,* 353–54, 422–25; and *Collected Works,* 3:1124–48.) It is, of course, possible that Poe slipped into the rather shrill tone that so many dashes produce here for reasons other than stylistic whimsey, but there is other evidence that "Thingum Bob" was on his mind as he wrote *Eureka* (see ¶149n). For Poe on the "proper" use of the dash, see "Marginalia" item 191 (*Collected Writings,* 2:325–27). To BRP, dashes used this way also suggest oral presentation, attesting to the origin of *Eureka* as a lecture (see ¶90n). An enlightening discussion of Poe's more serious reasons for using dashes in *Eureka* appears in Dayan, *Fables of Mind.*

129 See paragraphs 94–96.

133 *The Body . . . hand:* In the February 1836 *Southern Literary Messenger,* Poe favorably reviewed Peter Mark Roget's *Animal and Vegetable Psychology, Considered with Reference to Natural Theology* (*Complete Works,* 8:206–11). To brief himself on the series of books of which Roget's formed a part, he read an anonymous article in the *Quarterly Review* (vol. 50, Oct. 1833–Jan. 1834), "The Universe and Its Author" (St. Armand), in which appears this suggestive passage: "[T]he time appears to have newly arrived, when science and conviction ought to walk hand in hand with faith." The context of the passage suggests a close tie to *Eureka,* because the author argues that science is about to confirm faith. There is, however, a notable difference; the *Quarterly Review* article is somewhat more religiously literal than is *Eureka.* St. Armand argues that the eight "Bridgewater Treatises" provided much of the philosophical frame for *Eureka,* that, indeed, *Eureka* can be understood as "an uncommissioned ninth Bridgewater Thesis." ("In 1829 the Rev. Francis Henry, Eighth Earl of Bridgewater, left £8,000 pounds to the British Royal Society for the purpose of commissioning . . . a book 'On the Power, Wisdom, and Goodness of God, as manifested in the Creation'" [St. Armand, "Seemingly Intuitive Leaps," 9]. Eight books, not just one, resulted. Mark Twain had the final word on the matter in *Adventures of Huckleberry Finn,* wherein "the rightful Duke of Bridgewater" is transmuted into "Bilgewater.") For more on Poe's use of these books, see ¶198nn ff. Interestingly, a section in J. S. Mill's *A System of Logic,* which Poe used in *Eureka,* also mentions the "Bridgewater Treatise" [*sic*]. See notes to paragraphs 13, 17, and 18. Poe's "Marginalia" item 18 is on the failure of the Bridgewater Treatises to notice *"the great* idiosyncrasy in the Divine system of adaptation," namely, "the complete *mutuality* of adaptation." A note to that item traces repetitions of Poe's remarks in different contexts (*Collected Writings,* 2:127–28).

BRP suggests comparing *"The Body and The Soul"* as walking hand in hand with "I roamed with my Soul" in line 12 of Poe's poem "Ulalume" (1847) (*Collected Works,* 1:416).

134 "Cosmogony": The term refers to the study of the origin of the universe. (It is contrasted to "cosmology," which is the study of philosophical constructs dealing with laws governing the universe.) Laplace, in fact, did not concern himself with such basic questions as why matter was present to begin with, matter, that is, to form the star from which his model generates the rest of the solar system. Poe quibbles because his argument in *Eureka* includes the history of matter itself.

Laplace: In *Exposition du système du monde* (1796) Pierre Simon, Marquis de Laplace (see ¶77n) presented the "Nebular Hypothesis," which sought "to give scientific form to a theory originally propounded by Swedenborg and Kant." Laplace's *Mécanique analytique* (1799–1825) helped provide incontrovertible mathematical proof of Newton's gravitational hypothesis (Poe, *The Science Fiction of Edgar Allan Poe,* ed. Beaver, 408n).

135 Poe is saying that if one accepts the law of gravity, Laplace's work is correct. Laplace visualized a vast gas cloud. As it collapsed, it rotated faster. (This model

"works"—visualize an ice skater spinning. Skaters spin faster as they concentrate their bodies at the center of a spin, spreading their limbs and bending their bodies to slow.) Two principles explain the phenomenon: the conservation of angular momentum and gravity. The paragraphs that follow are Poe's summary of Laplace. Laplace figured that as the sun collapsed and accelerated, the spinning would leave behind material in the shape of a disk from which planets would eventually form.

Laplace's scheme is felt today to be basically correct, although he ignored too many details for it to work mathematically. The sun, for instance, is not spinning nearly fast enough to match Laplace's visualization.

In a letter to Charles F. Hoffman of September 20, 1848, Poe wrote that *Eureka* gave *"Laplace's theory in full"* and spoke of his "firm conviction of its absolute truth *at all points."* He next pointed out—correctly—that his work dealt with a broader subject: "The *ground* covered by the great French astronomer compares with that covered by my theory, as a bubble compares with the ocean on which it floats" (Poe, *The Science Fiction of Edgar Allan Poe*, ed. Beaver, 408; Poe, *Letters of Edgar Allan Poe*, ed. Ostrom, 2:379–82, esp. 380). Poe's letter reacts to misrepresentations in Hoffman's review of *Eureka*.

137 The mass. . . . the mass: Nichol (*Views of Astronomy*, Lecture 5, p. 29) contains a passage very close to this (Hodgens typescript). Poe does not quote; perhaps he paraphrases, or both follow a common source. Hodgens notes that Nichol himself leans here on his own book, *The Views of the Architecture of the Heavens.*

138 non-increasing: Poe's coinage (Pollin, *Poe: Creator of Words,* 32).

—just as . . . presented: another passage very close to Nichol (*Views of Astronomy,* Lecture 5, p. 30) and, like the one in paragraph 137, dependent in turn on Nichol's *Views of the Architecture of the Heavens* (Hodgens typescript).

caoutchouc: rubber.

140 and Poe's handwritten note to it: Poe tried to make his work very timely. Neptune had only been discovered in 1846. Nichol gave it a good deal of attention in his lecture course; in the fifth lecture, he said that it had two moons. So had said also the May 1848 *Fraser's Magazine* (TOM, notes). (Yet the second moon, Nereid, was not discovered until 1949.) Triton should have caused Poe some difficulty in his amplification of Laplace's model, for it moves in a direction opposite to the orbital direction of the planet around the sun. The second moon mentioned in Nichol is probably the result of an unconfirmed sighting. Triton, the innermost moon, was discovered in 1846. Perhaps Nichol confused Neptune with Uranus, which was known to have two moons that went in the "right" direction. Partial rings of Neptune were not discovered until 1983. Information available in 1848 was somewhat ambiguous. Such details are not basic, however, to the theory of the formation of the solar system that Poe was illustrating.

141 spherification: Poe's coinage (Pollin, *Poe: Creator of Words,* 37).

147 As of 2002, planets and moons in the solar system are: Mercury, none; Venus, none; Earth, one moon; Mars, two moons (Deimos and Phobus); Jupiter, thirty-nine moons, most of them retrograde; there are also rings. Saturn has twenty-eight moons, at least one retrograde, in addition to rings; Uranus has twenty-one moons, five retrograde; and Neptune has eight moons, one retrograde, and more are likely. Pluto, not discovered until 1930, has one moon (Charon).

149 Uranus: Poe has the right answer; see his note below. Uranus *is* tilted. It turns on its axis like other planets, but we see it almost pole-on. Its satellites, then, spin in that odd orbital plane. There is thus a relationship between the way a planet spins and the way its moons do; it tells the observer that the moons were not "captured" but rather thrown off during the planet's own formation. Poe might be leaning on Nichol here. As Hodgens (typescript) and BRP note, the same information and argument appear in Lecture 5 (p. 27) of Nichol's *Views of Astronomy*.

bouleversement (in Poe's note): The French word means "somersault." The note is essentially correct. Poe's alteration (in the 1848 text the word was *inclination*) might be an evasion. A little unsure of himself, he perhaps substituted a word that is more obscure, less precise ("inclination" is just right) and has humorous associations for him. It is in his 1835 burlesque tale "The Unparalleled Adventure of One Hans Pfaall" (*Collected Writings,* 1:422, 1:486n), which deals with a balloon voyage to the moon. See also his use of it in "The Literary Life of Thingum Bob, Esq." (*Thirty-Two Stories,* 301; *Short Fiction,* 387, 425, *Collected Works,* 3:1144). Poe seems to have had that story in mind as he wrote this portion of *Eureka;* see our note to paragraph 122.

151 the finger of Deity itself: If one examined only one area of the universe, there would be no way to account for angular momentum without postulating some sort of "finger of God" to get "tangential velocity" started. In the larger view, apparent angular momentum in one sector will be counterbalanced by counteracting momentum far off. See note to paragraph 153, "rotation . . . aggregation."

151–53 Poe mocks the idea of divine intervention but retains it in the "one primary exercise of the Divine volition," a view logically compatible with, although different in tone from, the familiar idea that when physics progresses far enough, "God will turn out to be a formula." Poe intends more, as the next sentence explains, for his God is also all matter. God not only wills the primal particle into expansion but also *is* the particle. Thus Poe reconciles spirit with matter, or, to put it differently, tries to provide a physics for spirituality. God "became all things at once," so all parts of the universe are God. The beliefs of occultists and adherents of numerous Oriental, tribal, and mystical religions approximate this; often for such believers the goal of human life is attainment of full realization of one's own divinity. This is conceivable because one's matter is also the matter of the godhead. Related concepts in eastern religious thought attracted Transcendental writers such as Emerson to the Orient. Poe is philosophically often close to the Transcendentalists he professed to scorn; his ideas are spelled out explicitly in his fiction, although sometimes with humor and even satiric under-cutting of the ideas themselves. *Eureka* retains both doctrine and satire. For ex-tended discussion of Poe's paradoxical attitudes toward Transcendentalism, see Levine, *Edgar Poe,* 151–68, esp. 162. For the source of Poe's phrase "the finger of God," see Luke 11:20.

152 Nature . . . Nature: BRP points to the phrase in the letter from Henry St. John, Viscount of Bolingbroke (1687–1751) to Alexander Pope: "One follows Nature and Nature's God; that is, he follows God in his works and in his word." One thinks also of Pope's "Epitaphs Intended for Sir Isaac Newton" (1730): "Nature, and Nature's laws lay hid in night: / God said, *Let Newton be!* and all was light." Poe would have known it from Jefferson, for the Declaration of Independence (1776) speaks of "the laws of nature and of Nature's God."

153 rotation . . . aggregation: Poe's scheme is not too far removed from one widely believed in 2002. If the "Big Bang" theory of how the universe began is correct, it is assumed that turbulence would be the source of angular momentum. The analogy given by astronomy teachers is the behavior of water going downstream. Angular momentum is the result of the interaction of the pressure of the gas cloud against its own gravitational pull. The unevenness ("lumpy-ness") of the gas cloud would be sufficient to start the whirling.

imparticularity: See paragraph 45.

155 that our Moon is self-luminous: The perils of doing astronomy by what Profes-sor Hill in *The Music Man* called the "Think System." The moon is not luminous. Poe, however, is probably just repeating Nichol, who said in *Views of Astronomy,* Lecture 7, p. 40, that the moon gives off light of its own (TOM, notes; Hodgens typescript). See also Pollin (*Poe: Creator of Words,* 63), who lists "self-luminous" as Poe's coinage.

total eclipse: During a lunar eclipse, the earth blocks the sun. The moon appears reddish at such times, because some light coming through the earth's atmo-sphere does get to the moon.

flashes: There are no "flashes" during a lunar eclipse. Reports of them might be the result of observer error. Or Poe might have his eclipses confused. When there is a *solar* eclipse (the moon between earth and sun), there is a phenom-enon called "Bailey's beads," bright "beads" of light visible at the moment the light of the reemerging sun breaks through the rough edges of the lunar land-scape.

Auroras: These are believed to be the result of the interaction of solar discharg-es (sunspots) with atmosphere. The moon does not have them.

156 Auroras: There are auroras on Venus because it has an atmosphere. BRP sug-gests comparison with Poe's poem "Ulalume" (1847): "Astarte's bediamonded crescent, / Distinct with its duplicate horn" (*Collected Works,* 1:417, 11:37–38). "Astarte" is Venus; see also ibid., 1:422.

157 Melville islands . . . vegetation: Melville Island is in the Timor Sea, sixteen miles
off the northwestern coast of Australia. Beaver (409) speculates that the name
may have come to Poe because of the popularity of Herman Melville's two "ultra-
tropical" novels of South Seas adventure, *Typee* (1846) and *Omoo* (1847) (Poe,
The Science Fiction of Edgar Allan Poe, ed. Beaver, 409). Poe's immediate source,
however, is the newspaper account of Nichol's seventh lecture, in which he speaks
of "ultra-tropical vegetation" on Melville and Bathurst islands (TOM, notes).
Hodgens notes that Poe here repeats an error in Nichol (Lecture 7, p. 40):
"Nichol is referring to Melville Island, not island*s*" (Hodgens typescript).

whirling-off: Poe's coinage (Pollin, *Poe: Creator of Words*, 69).

159 In speaking: The book *Eureka* retains many characteristics of Poe's lecture on
"The Universe," which, in BRP's phrase, it "closely represents." See the Introduc-
tion for contemporary newspaper accounts of what Poe said.

160 the succession of animals on the Earth: Loosely evolutionary ideas were common
among educated people in the half century before Charles Darwin. Emerson,
for example, used evolution as an example of an "obvious" relationship in chapter
5 of *Nature* (1836). He speaks of "resemblances . . . in things whose analogy is
obvious, as when we detect the type of the human hand in the flipper of the fossil
saurus." The idea that evolution, whatever its cause, may produce not only new
but also "better" creatures and people is interesting to encounter in Poe, who
in general scoffed at the meliorist assumptions of most intellectuals of his era.
Poe's story "Mellonta Tauta" heavily overlaps *Eureka;* Poe used a good deal of the
same prose in both pieces. But "Mellonta Tauta" mocks the idea of progress of
any sort. Pundita, its narrator, is contemptuous of the nineteenth century, but
her own age, far in the future, is no wiser. A passage in Nichol (*Views of Astrono-
my,* Lecture 6, pp. 36–37) is a likely source for the idea that evolution on Earth
is tied to the development of the solar system, though Poe carried the idea fur-
ther (Hodgens typscript). Hodgens notes, correctly, that not many stages are
available in Poe's scheme: "There were just two discharges after Earth's—those
of Venus and Mercury." BRP adds "that improvement here comes through solar
and planetary changes, not man's technological advances."

vitalic: Poe's coinage (Pollin, *Poe: Creator of Words*, 40). BRP adds, "The seeming
coinage . . . [here and in paragraph 214], ascribed to Poe by the *OED,* must
reflect the widespread school of *Vitalism,* of French origin in the late eighteenth
century, overturned in the next century (see "Physiology," *Encyclopedia Britanni-
ca,* 11th ed., 21:554).

161 Comte: Auguste Comte (1798–1857). His *Traité d'astronomie populaire* was pub-
lished in Paris in 1845. Beaver (Poe, *The Science Fiction of Edgar Allan Poe,* 409)
thinks that Poe knew Compte's *Cours de philosophie positive* (1830–42) through
Sir David Brewster's review in 1838 of a two-volume Paris edition (1830–35) in
the *Edinburgh Review.* A serious and solid essay, this is the lead article in the July
1838 issue (36:271–308). It covers covers the sorts of connections between phys-

ical science and worldview with which Poe is concerned. See esp. 297f., where Brewster shows Comte summarizing Laplace and suggesting yet another way of verifying his hypothesis.

162 the Cloud-Land of Metaphysics: BRP notices that Poe uses the same phrase in "The Rationale of Verse" (para. 2). BRP also recalls "Cloudland" in Coleridge. In "Fancy in Nubibus, or the Poet in the Clouds" (1817), Coleridge wrote of making "the shifting clouds be what you please" (l. 3) in the evening sky, and of imagining "a traveller go / From mount to mount through Cloudland, gorgeous land!" (l. 9) (*The Complete Poetical Works*, ed. E. H. Coleridge, 1:435). See also *Collected Writings*, 2:66 and 2:255 ("Pinakidia," item 100, and "Marginalia," item 147) for a possible tie to Aristophanes' "The Clouds." Each deals with the question of whether "The Clouds" contained rhyme.

163 unfounded opinion . . . overthrown: Poe is correct; indeed, Laplace was not only challenged but actually fell into disfavor later in the nineteenth century (Kaufmann, *Exploration of the Solar System*, 516).

the large telescope of Cincinnati: "This magnificent telescope, one of the largest and most perfect in the world, was made at the Frauenhofer Institute, Munich, by Mssrs. Mertz & Mahler." Provided with a clockwork mechanism that a single observer could operate, it weighed about 2,500 pounds, had a focal length of roughly 17½ feet, an object-glass 12 inches diameter, and a magnifying power of from 100 to 1,400 x. The tone of contemporary accounts suggests why Poe could assume his listeners or readers would know of it; it was considered one of the marvels of the age: "This stupendous instrument, mounted on a stone pedestal of great strength and graceful figure, rises, when directed at the zenith, some 20 feet above the floor of the room in which it is located." The whole was located on a high hill above the Ohio River in a building whose walls were on wheels mounted on railroad tracks for easy movement. (Cist, *Sketches and Statistics*, 108.)

Lord Rosse: William Parsons, Earl of Rosse (1800–1867), was one of the first to see that there were other galaxies. His telescope had great resolution. Rosse's discoveries did, in fact, cause controversy for a century (see ¶213 and its notes). Details on Poe's probable source for this information and on his other use of it are in *Collected Writings*, 1:497–98.

the appearance of nebulosity: At this stage of astronomical history, "nebulae" meant any fuzzy-looking object. A modern definition is "any non-point source of light in the sky" (Twarog).

Twarog explains that distance is critical. The debate in that era was "Are all galaxies the same sort of object?" Rosse could see that *some* nearby galaxies were just clusters of stars and guessed that distant fuzzy objects with extended spiral features were galaxies, too. Rosse had seen stars in M51 and in the nebula in Orion. That nebula does not have a well-defined shape: One sees an extended gas cloud in which some stars are embedded. Rosse had no way to resolve stars in extra-galactic nebulae. The "Orion nebulosity" today refers to the gas surrounding the stars; any blobs Rosse saw were the star-clusters. Stars were not resolved in extra-galactic nebulae until the twentieth century. Poe, then, merely repeats an error of his age, that better telescopes would show nebulae to be galaxies.

nebulists: Poe's coinage (Pollin, *Poe: Creator of Words,* 32).

the great "nebula" . . . stars: The object Poe names was not one that better telescopes could resolve into a "simple collection of stars." It was *obviously* a gas cloud, although there are some stars associated with it. Better telescopes have since enabled astronomers to determine that some "fuzzy objects" are gas clouds, some are, in fact, galaxies, and others are a mixture of both.

letter (in the note): Poe refers apparently to Nichol's book, *Views of the Architecture of the Heavens,* the subtitle of which is *In a Series of Letters to a Lady.* The first American edition, "Republished from the last London and Edinburgh editions to which has [*sic*] been added notes and a glossary &c by the American Publishers," appeared in New York (A. H. Chapin & Co.) in 1840.

Dr. N. . . . hypothetical (in the note): Hodgens (typscript) locates the passage in Nichol's Lecture 5 (*Views of Astronomy,* p. 29): "The audience will perceive that these [Laplace's] are two great hypotheses, but we must begin with hypotheses. No calculation or deduction can ever enable the human race to track back our System to its origin. This being the case I would have the audience observe that LAPLACE's system rests entirely upon hypothesis. It is a hypothetical Cosmogony."

the late experiments of Comte (in the note): Comte worked out a mathematical means to verify Laplace's theory of how the solar system was formed. As Brewster's review of Comte (see ¶161n) put it, the question to be answered was "what was the duration of the rotation of the sun when the mathematical limit of his [the sun's] atmosphere extended to the different planets?" Comte tried his equation first on the relationship of the earth and moon. It worked; the "periodic time" of the moon "agrees within less than the tenth of a day with the duration which the revolution of the earth ought to have had at the time when the lunar distance formed the limit of our atmosphere" (299).

Maskelyne (in the note): See paragraph 62n.

165 *the primary processes* of Creation: Astronomers today do, in fact, attempt to observe at least the early results of *"the primary processes"* of creation; echoes of the "Big Bang" still resonate. Data gathered from a great distance are data from greatest antiquity, a principle Poe fully understands—see, for instance, paragraph 167, in which he says that the "processes" we observe today are "but the phantoms of processes completed long in the Past." Attempts to reconstruct the physics and chemistry of the new universe use such data.

nebulosity: First recorded with this meaning in Herschel's *Astronomy* (1833) (BRP; *OED*). Poe repeats it in paragraph 168.

166 hoary . . . age: Poe again echoes his own fiction. In "MS. Found in a Bottle," a very early (1833) tale (*Thirty-Two Stories*, 16–25; *Short Fiction*, 622, 623–29, 630–31; *Collected Works*, 2:143), he speaks of the sailors on board a ghost ship (he has in mind the Flying Dutchman) as follows: "They all bore about them the marks of a hoary old age." The connection in his mind is the projection of the past into the present. The Dutchman is doomed to sail for eternity.

167 Mass-constitutive: Poe's coinage (Pollin, *Poe: Creator of Words*, 56).

169 rendering . . . Cæsar's: Matthew 22:21 (BRP).

170 valid objections. . . . establish: Poe is correct. For Laplace's system to work, matter must be distributed in lumps rather than evenly. Laplace postulates the lumpiness but does not attempt to account for it; he merely "goes from there" (Twarog). That is not Laplace's error; it is more accurate to say, as Poe implies, that Laplace was not particularly concerned with the problem.

171 Epicurean atoms: The Greek philosopher Epicurus (341–270 B.C.E.) was a follower of Democritus in the matter of atoms. How close *Eureka* is to Poe's fiction is suggested by the passage in which Epicurus is mentioned in "The Murders in the Rue Morgue" (1841) (*Thirty-Two Stories*, 38–39n11; *Short Fiction*, 181, 245n9; *Collected Works*, 2:535), a passage, incidentally, in which Poe's detective, Dupin, is explaining how the mind proceeds via associations—exactly the process that for Poe connects the nebula in Orion with atomism and with the nebular cosmogony of Laplace. "I knew," Dupin says to the narrator, "that you could not say to yourself 'stereotomy' without being brought to think of atomies, and thus of the theories of Epicurus; and since . . . I mentioned to you how . . . the vague guesses of that noble Greek had met with confirmation in the late nebular cosmogony, I felt that you could not avoid casting your eyes upward to the great *nebula* in Orion." See also the note to paragraph 49.

inacumen: Poe's coinage (Pollin, *Poe: Creator of Words*, 29).

172 the ring. . . . *distances:* Poe's imaginative elaboration of Laplace alters Laplace, who never said that all the rings existed at once as rings. Indeed, Laplace never explained how planets condensed from rings at all. Poe here tries to invent a physical mechanism to explain what Laplace never tackled. Poe's theory is "pure numerology" (Twarog). See also "Postscript to a Letter about 'Eureka,'" note to paragraph 2.

173 seventeen planets: Poe counts the known planets and asteroids. See notes on Poe's revisions of *Eureka:* the 1848 edition had sixteen.

a number . . . *systems:* BRP writes, "G. P. Kuiper authoritatively postulated that through the contracting nebulosities of all the galaxies, 1 out of 100 form planetary systems like ours, numbering 10^9 (Ency. Brit., 1960, 6:501, 'Cosmogony')." For poetic accounts of the creation of planets, see the last stanza of Poe's poem "Ulalume" (1847) (*Collected Works*, 1:418–19) or "The Power of Words" (1845) (*Thirty-Two Stories*, 318–22; *Short Fiction*, 114–16; *Collected Works*, 3:1211–15).

(note): A similar thought appears in Nichol, *Views of Astronomy*, Lecture 5, p. 28 (Hodgens typescript).

174 Titanic: An unusual and clever use of the word. As the Titans were primal giants in Greek mythology, so these atoms are a primal form of cosmic matter.

Μελλοντα ταυτα: "Those things that are to be," or, as Poe translated it, "These things are in the future." (The Greek in *Eureka* was printed without accents.) Poe quotes the reply of the messenger to Creon at the end of Sophocles' *Antigone* (Pollin, *Poe: Creator of Words*). Poe used the quotation in two stories: as a motto added to the 1845 version of his apocalyptic tale "The Colloquy of Monos and Una" and as the title of his satiric fantasy about the distant future, "Mellonta Tauta." Since large portions of "Mellonta Tauta" are shared with *Eureka* (see notes ¶11ff.), Poe's use of the Greek quotation again here once more closely links *Eureka* with his fiction (see also ¶160n). It is likely that Poe's immediate source was Edward Bulwer-Lytton's *Ernest Maltravers* (1837) (TOM, notes), where it appears as a motto for Book 9: "These things are in the Future." See *Collected Writings*, 2:180; 2:257, 2:259, 2:378, for Poe's other uses of this book and the index to that volume for other levies on Bulwer.

175 *unequably,* with *clusters:* See note to paragraph 153 and also paragraph 50. Poe's universe contracts (see ¶174); modern astronomers believe it expands. In both, however, matter is distributed somewhat unevenly.

177 We have no reason . . . "nebulæ": Poe's statement is correct and matches the dominant theory that the earth's location in the universe is not "special," that data about our environment are probably average. There is a theological issue here, of course, the "Copernican principle" that once one moves man from the center of the universe, all other religious accounts of reality will collapse as well.

178 we must picture. . . . capital Y: Poe follows Humboldt's *Cosmos* closely here: "The stellar milky way . . . constitutes . . . an annulus, that is to say an independent zone, somewhat remote from our lenticular-shaped starry stratum, and similar to Saturn's ring. . . . Our planetary system lies in an eccentric ["excentric" in Maddison, "Poe's *Eureka*"; see "excentrically" below] direction nearer to the region of the Cross than to the diametrically opposite point, Cassiopeia." (Humboldt, *Cosmos* [1849 ed.], 1, 141. We follow the 1849 London edition translated by Elise C. Otté. See notes to paragraphs 9 and 231, and esp. 232.) Maddison refers to the same edition but omits the ellipsis after "constitutes," spells "annulus" with one *n*, and spells "eccentric" as "excentric," probably confused by Poe's spelling. (TOM, notes, following Carol Hopkins Maddison). As a matter of fact, Humboldt's view was advanced for the date; our location was not known to be near the edge of the galaxy until 1917. Poe's description of the shape of the galaxy seems reasonably close to the modern image of a spiral. Spiral galaxies are disks (lenticular objects) that have, superimposed on them, spiral structure. A modern composite picture of the galaxy (Berman and Evans, *Exploring the Cosmos*, 334–35) shows dark regions caused by interstellar dust (dust-lanes in the

spiral arms of the galaxy). Poe's "gash" is such a dark region. A diagram clarifies the relationship between the *Y* Poe visualizes, the spiral, and lenticular shape. Imagine a "top view" of a galaxy shaped like Saturn:

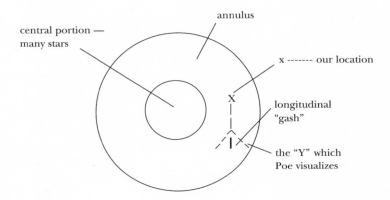

central portion —
many stars

annulus

x ------- our location

longitudinal
"gash"

the "Y" which
Poe visualizes

Although Poe was not above padding a work with extraneous information culled from reference works, the passage is germane: in it, he is addressing the issue of the roughly equal distribution of matter.

star-island: Poe's coinage (Pollin, *Poe: Creator of Words*, 87).

excentrically: Pollin (*Word Index*) shows that Poe usually spelled this work *eccentrically*, and we initially thought to change it to conform with his usual practice. BRP suggested, however, that Poe might have been following a source, possibly Rees's *Cyclopaedia* (Abraham Rees, *Cyclopaedia; or, Universal Dictionary of Arts, Sciences, and Literatures* [London, 1802–19]). In the portions of Rees we examined, BRP's surmise was correct. Rees consistently spells the word "exc." See, for example, the article "Steam Engine," in the 1972 facsimile reprinting of only the entries on engineering and manufacturing topics, Neil Cossons, ed., *Rees's Manufacturing Industry*. Another source, John F. W. Herschel, also was in the habit of using "exc"; we noticed it in his *Outlines of Astronomy*.

179 Maddison says that Poe's language here again is close to that of Humboldt, and points to *Cosmos* (1:72–73) in the London, 1845 edition (see notes to ¶178n and ¶232). Here, for comparison, is a portion of the passage from *Cosmos*. Like Poe's, it deals with visualizing earth's position in the Milky Way. Plainly, however, Poe was not copying. See also paragraph 209 and note.

In the direction of the longer axis, where the stars lie behind one another, the more remote ones appear closely crowded together, united, as it were, by a milky-white radiance, or luminous vapour, and are perspectively grouped, encircling as in a zone the visible vault of heaven. This narrow and branched girdle, studded with radiant light, and here and there interrupted by dark spots, deviates only by a few degrees from forming a perfect large circle round the concave sphere of heaven, owing to our being near the centre of the large starry cluster, and almost on the plane of the Milky Way. If our planetary system were far *outside* this cluster, the Milky Way would appear to telescopic vision as a ring, and at a still greater distance as a resolvable discoidal nebula.

Humboldt is correct that the Milky Way looks equally bright in all directions (even though our sun is near the edge of its ring). Humboldt (and Poe) did not know that this is merely because interstellar dust prevents us from seeing more than about a thousand parsecs in any direction in the plane of the galaxy. With only that range of vision, one gets the notion that one is in the center; one cannot see either to the near edge or to the distant edge. Instead, one sees a thousand parsecs of stars in either direction. Our galaxy is nearly ten times larger than nineteenth-century astronomers could envisage, and our sun is nearer to the edge than Humboldt thought. A chart to aid in visualizing the matter appears on page 3 of Mihalas and Binney, *Galactic Astronomy*. For Poe's earlier knowledge of Humboldt, see paragraph 9n and his story "Hans Pfaall" (see ¶149n), especially *Collected Writings*, (1:402, 1:474, 26e). BRP thinks that "lenticular shaped" comes from Herschel, *Treatise on Astronomy*, para. 626. See also the note to paragraph 178.

180 space-... power: BRP notes that although he ascribed it as a coinage to Poe (Pollin, *Poe: Creator of Words*, 65), he now finds that it has "another significant paternity. The *OED* lists it for the 1799 *Philosophical Transactions*, but more to the present point, it returned to Poe's texts in 1846, after its use in 'Hans Pfaall,' through the intermediation of a third popularizing text by Thomas Dick, his *Practical Astronomer* (England, 1845; Harpers, 1846)." Poe was relying on John Herschel's *Treatise on Astronomy*, an often-reprinted text of 1833 (America, 1834). Dick's several uses (*Christian Philosopher*, 298, 299, 302) brought it to Poe's awareness for "The Literati" papers and *Eureka*. It also helps prove that Poe relied on the third of Dick's science-made-easy texts (see note to ¶198).

181 Were the succession.... is so: Poe gives an accurate statement of what astronomers call "Olbers' paradox," referring to a theory argued by Heinrich Olbers in 1823: if the universe were infinite in extent, the night sky should be white. At any point at which we looked there would be at least one star, so that there would be no black background anywhere. A passage in Nichol, *Views of Astronomy*, Lecture 1, pp. 6–7, makes the same point (Hodgens typescript). But, as Poe says, even if the universe were infinite in size, we would only see light that has had time to reach us. Modern cosmology uses fifteen billion years as a rough estimate of the age of the universe, so were there stars more than fifteen billion light-years away, people on earth would not be able to see them. The sky would still seem black. Because we conceive of the universe as finite because of the curvature of space, however, the question is academic at present (Twarog).

182 Erebus: Mt. Erebus, an active Antarctic volcano discovered and named in 1841 by Sir James Clark Ross, whose explorations were reported in an *Edinburgh Review* article mentioned by Poe (*Complete Works*, 8:87). Poe alludes to it in his poem "Ulalume—A Ballad (1847), calling it "Yaanek," a name he apparently coined, for it is not in standard geographical sources:

> These were days when my heart was volcanic
>> As the scoriac rivers that roll—
>> As the lavas that restlessly roll
> Their sulphurous currents down Yaanek,
>> In the ultimate climes of the Pole—
> That groan as they roll down Mount Yaanek,
>> In the realms of the Boreal Pole.
> (*Collected Works*, 1:415–19, 1:416)

In mythology, Erebus, son of Chaos, begot Aether and Hemera (Day) by Nux (Night), his sister. The name signifies darkness and is applied to the dark space through which the shades pass into Hades. Poe uses it also in "The Spectacles" (1844) (*Collected Works*, 3:897; *Short Fiction*, 337, 349n9).

perpetual variation: Poe is wrong, in fact, for dark voids are areas of cosmic dust, and matter is, for all practical purposes, distributed evenly in the solar neighborhood. Only "local" bodies—those within the solar system—exert more than negligible force. One wonders, however, why, even before cosmic dust was known, Poe bothered to fuss with the gravitational pull of distant stars when he had the easily discernable tug of the moon at hand to make his point (Twarog). Perhaps he was attracted to the idea because of his general sense of the interconnectedness of all things— the same impulse which is behind his story "The Power of Words" (1845) (*Collected Works*, 3:1211–15; *Thirty-Two Stories*, 318–22; *Short Fiction*, 107–8, 114–16).

185 phantom . . . idea: Poe says in paragraph 29 that infinity "is by no means the expression of an idea—but of an effort at one. It stands for the possible attempt at an impossible conception." In paragraph 37, he says that infinity "belongs . . . to the class representing *thoughts of thought.*" See paragraphs 29–39.

187 Each . . . God: Extended discussion of philosophical precedent for Poe's vision of multiple gods appears in the Introduction.

190 This paragraph is a correct restatement of what are now known as Kepler's Three Laws of Planetary Motion (Twarog).

radius vector: The term had long been standard; the *OED* lists usage from 1753: "A variable line drawn to a curve from a fixed point as origin; in astronomy the origin is usually at the sun or a planet around which a satellite revolves."

191 moon-attended: Poe's coinage (Pollin, *Poe: Creator of Words*, 57).

immortal laws *guessed* . . . . "guess-work": See paragraph 23 and note. Poe is right about Kepler and Newton only in the most general sense (Twarog), though his feeling that guessing has been important in the development of science is sound. Poe expanded on this point in a letter to Charles Fenno Hoffman. See paragraph 135 note.

Plato . . . Alcmæon: Poe's statement is a play on a passage from Cicero's "Tusculan Disputations" (1:39, TOM): *"Errare mehercule malo cum Platone, . . . quam cum istis vera sentire"* (By Hercules, I prefer to err with Plato, . . . than to think the truth with "those"). "Those" refers to the Pythagoreans in general. Cicero does not name Alcmæon (see next item), but Alcmæon was a Pythagorean.

Alcmæon was a native of Crotona in the sixth century B.C.E., a pupil of Pythagoras. His *On Nature* (ca. 500 B.C.E.) may be the first work on natural philosophy. He argued that the gods alone had certain knowledge; men could, however, conjecture. Poe alluded to him in a satire on bad writing, "How to Write a Blackwood Article," in a passage in which "Mr. Blackwood" advises the aspiring but incompetent Signora Psyche Zenobia to stuff her writing with irrelevant but learned-seeming allusions: "The tone metaphysical is also a good one. If you know any big words this is your chance for them. Talk of the Ionic and Eleatic schools— of Archytas, Gorgias, and Alcmæon" (*Thirty-Two Stories,* 74, 74n10; *Short Fiction,* 360, 415n10; *Collected Works,* 2:341, 2:359n18). Poe had thought creatively about bad writing and knew of other authors who had as well. See Levine and Levine, "'How to' Satire."

193 distance. . . . 28 hundred millions: Modern figures are always given in kilometers: Earth to moon, 384,500 kilometers (ca. 238,928 miles, using 1 kilometer = .6214 miles). Distances from sun in 10^6 kilometers: Mercury, 57.9 (35,970,600); Venus, 108.2 (67,235,480); Earth, 149.6 (92,588,600); Mars, 227.9 (141,617,060); Jupiter, 778.3 (438,635,620); Saturn, 1427.0 (886,737,800); Uranus, 2871.0 (1,784,039,400); Neptune, 4497.1 (2,749,497,900); and Pluto, 5913.5 (3,674,338,200).

the nine Asteroids . . . and: Astræa actually had been discovered just in 1845; its discovery set off a boom in asteroid sighting. A ninth was found in April 1848 and named Higeia (Twarog). By 2002 more than twenty thousand asteroids had been named, among them asteroids called for our consultant, Bruce Twarog, and his astronomer wife, Barbara.

Neptune: Discovered only in 1846, the planet was still news in 1848. It had been noticed that the transit of Uranus was irregular. Astronomers hypothesized that the gravitational pull of another planet must be the cause. John Couch Adams in England and Urbain Jean Joseph Leverrier in France did the necessary mathematics in 1845 to predict its location, and Johann Gottfried Galle in 1846 found it exactly there. The first satellite, Triton, was detected a month later (Poe, *The Science Fiction of Edgar Allan Poe,* ed. Beaver, 410–11n42).

May not . . . *radiation?:* Hodgens (typescript) suggests that Poe here responds to a challenge posed in Nichol (*Views of Astronomy,* Lecture 4, p. 25): "Now the origin of Bode's law is entirely unknown: it is what is called an empirical law, because we do not understand the principle upon which it acts." Poe's explanation is nonsense. As of 2004 there was still no fully satisfactory explanation of the law (Twarog).

Bode: Johann Elert Bode (1747–1826), an important compiler of astronomical statistics and founder in 1774 of the *Astronomische Jahrbuch*. A formula for what Poe called the *"order of interval* among the planets" goes by his name, though it had earlier been noticed by Kepler, and announced by Johann Daniel Titius in 1772. One gets a rough estimate of the "order of interval" by writing a series of 4s; adding (in order) 0, 3, 6, 12, 24 (0 for Mercury, then 3 for Venus); and doubling the number for each planet outward (TOM, notes; Poe, *The Science Fiction of Edgar Allan Poe*, ed. Beaver, 411). This empirical law is called the Titius-Bode Law.

194 There are . . . ocean: Poe plays to his American audience, flattering readers with an unwarranted assumption about their experience as travelers. He also enjoyed implying that he himself knew Europe well; see his stories "The Assignation" (1834) and "The Murders in the Rue Morgue" (1841), for example. *Thirty-Two Stories* (26, 130–31) and *Short Fiction*, 471, 153) explain the real sources of Poe's "expertise" about Venice and Paris. It is in fact unlikely that, after a childhood sojourn in England (1815–20), he ever left the United States.

Sound passes. . . . latter: Poe's figures are good approximations. Calling the speed of sound roughly 1,100 feet per second gives a speed of sound of 750 m.p.h. (the contemporary figure at sea level is 1,087 feet per second, about 741 m.p.h.). Sound from the moon—were there an atmospheric carrier—would arrive in 13.1667 days, less about a second and a quarter to allow for the light to arrive.

198 If we ascend. . . . general survey: In these and subsequent paragraphs, Poe leans very heavily on Thomas Dick's *The Christian Philosopher: or, The Connection of Science and Philosophy with Religion* (Glasgow, 1823) (Alterton, *Origins*, 139–40). There were a number of subsequent editions, some pirated. We follow a New York edition (Solomon King, 1831). For comparison, here is the equivalent paragraph in Dick, from his chapter "Omnipotence of the Deity":

> Were we to take our station on the top of a mountain, of a moderate size, and survey the surrounding landscape, we should perceive an extent of view stretching 40 miles in every direction, forming a circle 80 miles in diameter, and 250 in circumference, and comprehending an area of 5,000 square miles. In such a situation, the terrestrial scene around and beneath us—consisting of hills and plains, towns and villages, rivers and lakes—would form one of the largest objects which the eye, or even the imagination, can steadily grasp at one time. But such an object, grand and extensive as it is, forms no more than the *forty thousandth part* of the terraqueous globe; . . . were a scene, of the magnitude now stated, to pass before us every hour, until all the diversified scenery of the earth were brought under our view, and were twelve hours a-day allotted for the observation, it would require nine years and forty-eight

days before the whole surface of the globe could be contemplated, even in this *general* and *rapid* manner. (Alterton, *Origins*, 139, quoting Dick, 17)

successiveness: The *OED* gives a 1676 usage, then James Mill's 1829 *"Human Mind* whence Poe may have derived it," although "Poe's Italics often indicate his belief that he is coining a new word" (BRP). See Pollin, *Poe: Creator of Words*, 16.

Dick was, like the authors of the "Bridgewater Treatises," a "populizer" (St. Armand, "Seemingly Intuitive Leaps," 12), trying to show how science could confirm faith. See paragraph 133 note for further discussion of the impact of these works on *Eureka*.

199 Here is the paragraph in Dick from which Poe obtained both his idea and his data (Alterton, *Origins*, 139):

> The earth contains a mass of matter equal in weight to at least 2,200,000,000,000,000,000,000,000, or more than 2 thousand trillions of tons, supposing its mean density to be only about 2½ times greater than water. To move this ponderous mass, a single inch beyond its position, were it fixed in a quiescent state, would require a mechanical force almost beyond the power of numbers to express. The physical force of all the myriads of intelligences within the bounds of the planetary system, though their powers were far superior to those of men would be altogether inadequate to the production of such a motion.

See paragraph 201 note.

201 The diameter. . . . circumference: Another illustration taken from Dick, this from his chapter "The Solar System": "Of this system, the SUN is the center and the animating principle. . . . This vast globe is found to be about 880,000 miles in diameter. . . . Were its central parts placed adjacent to the surface of the earth, its circumference would reach two hundred thousand miles beyond the moon's orbit, on every side. . . . Even at the rate of 90 miles a-day, it would require more than 80 years to go round its circumference" (Alterton, *Origins*, 140).

The close connection between *Eureka* and Poe's fiction is illustrated again in his use of Dick in his apocalyptic tale "The Conversation of Eiros and Charmion" (1839) (Alterton, *Origins*). Poe's tale avoids specific Christian implications: it uses Dick's physics, not his theology. A guide to Poe's use of Dick appears in *Collected Writings* (1:657). Poe used *The Christian Philosopher* six times and Dick's *Celestial Scenery* (1838) ten times there.

202 the tongue of an archangel: This may come from I Corinthians 12:4, "the tongues of men and of angels," or Milton's *Paradise Lost* (7:112–13): "To recount almighty works, / What words or tongues of seraph can suffice?" (BRP). Compare also the angel figure in paragraph 200.

Leverrier's planet: Neptune (¶193 and note).

the largest orbs . . . Space: Poe's statement is too simplistic. The mass of a star, not its size, would determine how vast a "vacancy" it would sweep clean of matter. In fact, high-mass, high-luminosity stars do have large cavities around them, but this is because of their radiation pressure, not their gravitational pull (Twarog).

203 the eye of the mind: "A recasting of Hamlet's 'in my mind's eye, Horatio' (1.2.line 185)" (BRP). Poe used it elsewhere (*Complete Works*, 8:144 [a review of William Gilmore Simms's *The Partisan* in the January 1836 *Southern Literary Messenger*] and *Collected Writings*, 3:44 [a column entitled "Literary Notices" in the *Broadway Journal* on September 20, 1845, discussing a weekly paper, the *New World*]). Poe sometimes further alters Shakespeare, as "in our mind's eye."

204 *Alpha Lyræ:* Further evidence of the close relationship between *Eureka* and Poe's satiric tale "Mellonta Tauta." Not only do the two works share several pages of nearly identical prose (see ¶11–¶24 above), they also share a good deal of common information. Alpha Lyræ is mentioned twice in "Mellonta Tauta," once in a passage in which Pundita, Poe's unreliable tourist-narrator, explains a special relationship between the sun and Alpha Lyræ. The idea is pure stardust, of course: all celestial bodies interact with one another, but Alpha Lyræ is too immensely distant to be in significant relationship with the sun. Pundita passes along this pearl of her husband's wisdom (he is a "pundit") in a context that suggests a connection with the thought of Immanuel Kant (*Thirty-Two Stories*, 356n14; *Short Fiction*, 618n14; *Collected Works*, 3:1300–1302), which is also suggestive for *Eureka*. Both *Eureka* and "Mellonta Tauta" contain disparaging allusions to Kant (see ¶12).

205 159————*miles:* Substituting modern values in Poe's illustration for the distance to Alpha Lyræ yields a very different distance; the figures Poe used were off by a factor of about 2. Now, one would use not 159 miles but 317 (Twarog).

202–5 As elsewhere noted, *Eureka* often shows its origin as a talk. These paragraphs strike BRP as especially oral in nature. In paragraph 205, "readers" in the first sentence could well read "listeners," and the deliberate error and correction regarding distance "is the sort of jest expected on the platform, not in a treatise." See also the opening of *Eureka*, especially paragraph 11 note.

209 19 trillions, 200 billions of miles: The distance is now reckoned at 11.214 light-years, a radically different value from the figures Friedrich Bessel (see next item) generated. Indeed, 61 Cygni is much closer to earth than is Alpha Lyræ—only 0.4 the distance (or as our astronomer consultant writes it, 0.4 D Lyr). A pocket calculator puts that at 6.5822968×10^{13} miles (Twarog).

Bessel. . . . 61 trillions of miles: Friedrich Wilhelm Bessel (1784–1846), director of the Koenigsberg Observatory, in 1838 published his study of the annual parallax of the star 61 Cygni. This was the first time anyone had succeeded in observing parallax of a star, and this yielded the first even approximately accurate figures for interstellar distance. Bessel's accomplishment was officially recognized in 1841 (Poe, *The Science Fiction of Edgar Allan Poe*, ed. Beaver). An account of this work by Bessel appears in Humboldt's *Cosmos*, in the same passage (2:72) in which the material alluded to in paragraph 179 also appears (see ¶179n). Humboldt writes that it follows from "Bessel's . . . excellent Memoir on the parallax of the remarkable star 61 Cygni . . . , (whose considerable motions might lead to the inference of great proximity), that a period of nine years and a quarter is required for the transmission of light from this star to our planet." Accounts of new scientific developments, however, were widely available and generally provided "context," explaining how the new work affected the "big picture" (Twarog). One cannot prove that Poe took this information from Humboldt.

210 Struve . . . second: Otto Struve (1819–1905), director of the Pulkovo Observatory in Russia. Struve's elegant method for measuring the speed of light used "stellar aberration," that is, the apparent change in position of a star that results from the motion of the earth about the sun. The size of the observed change depends upon

$$\frac{VE}{C} \text{ when VE = velocity of Earth and C = speed of light.}$$

If VE is known, one can derive C. VE was known from the length of our year, its orbital period, and the size of its orbit (2 AU). Encke had earlier determined 1 AU (the distance between the Earth and the Sun) by using solar parallax. These early calculations were quite accurate—off only about 3 percent from modern figures (Twarog).

A modern figure for the speed of light is 186,000 miles per second. So far as Poe's argument goes, all the material about the vastness of the universe is padding.

213 the elder Herschell . . . telescope: Sir William Herschel (1738–1822) did brilliant work on the motion of stars in space, concluding with a "pretty correct idea of which way the Sun moved" (Ronan, *Astronomers Royal*, 93). In the course of further work to catalog the brightness ("magnitude") of stars, he decided to produce the estimates of stellar distances to which Poe refers. He had at Slough in 1789 a telescope with "a 48-inch mirror and a focal length of 10 feet" (Poe, *The Science Fiction of Edgar Allan Poe*, ed. Beaver, 411). Herschel "tells us that his fortyfoot reflector will bring him light from a distance of 'at least eleven and threefourths millions of millions of millions of miles'—light which left its source two million years ago" (Williams, *The Great Astronomers*, 257). Herschel studied nebulae, discovering roughly two thousand new ones himself. The most distant he could see "was at least three hundred thousand times as distant from us as the nearest fixed star" (ibid., 259). Herschel, incidentally, could be a source for Poe's notion in paragraphs 185 and 186 and at the close of *Eureka* that there may be other universes, each "instinct with life" (Williams, *The Great Astronomers*). His were the first systematic attempts to use actual observations "to determine the extent of the stellar system" (Pannekoek, *A History of Astronomy*, 316).

Herschell: Poe's spelling error is discussed in *Collected Writings*, 1:471. The trail runs to his story "The Unparalleled Adventure of One Hans Pfaall" (1835) and to an item in Poe's "literati" series on Richard Locke.

magical tube of Lord Rosse: William Parsons, third earl of Rosse (1800–1867) (see ¶163 and its notes). From 1839 on, he had a thirty-six-inch reflector at Birr Castle. A six-foot reflector was completed in 1845. A news item about the earl's astronomy equipment ran in the January 10, 1845, *Evening Mirror* (TOM, notes). "Between 1845 and 1908 his Leviathan, 58 feet in length and 7 feet in diameter, was the largest telescope ever built" (P. Quinn, ed., *Edgar Allan Poe,* 1400). Poe wrote about it in a letter to the *Columbia Spy* (Letter 4 in the *Spy* for June 8, 1844). BRP suggests mention of Poe's boyhood use of a telescope from the upper porch of his Richmond home (A. H. Quinn, *Edgar Allan Poe,* 92–93). On a likely source for Poe's information on Rosse and the telescope, see the tale "Hans Pfaall" in *Collected Writings,* 1:430, 1:497–98. See also paragraph 82 (p. 428) of that story.

214 *Space and Duration are one:* The statement seems to be unambiguous evidence that Poe understood space-time in the modern sense. Although most of the more famous ways in which *Eureka* "anticipates" or "predicts" twentieth-century science turn out on close examination to be not quite the same as more modern concepts, or shrewd guesses based on not very solid data, this one seems to be a fine extrapolation from firm information that Poe thoroughly understood. It suggests how very good a mind Poe had (Twarog). The remainder of the paragraph, however, seems to be nonsense, because Poe never—despite the dramatic dashes he perhaps added to cover his logical tracks—says exactly why vast cosmic distances are necessary. The word "vitalic" perhaps provides a clue to what Poe had in mind; BRP suggests a link to the passage in paragraphs 159 and 160 in which Poe speculates very loosely (so loosely that he apologizes for doing so) on the possibility of a relationship between celestial events and the evolution of life and consciousness. Pollin writes, "The remainder of the paragraph seems to be a bow to theological propriety which the school of Vitalism was seeking to conciliate." See also 133 and note.

216 Divine adaptation: As ¶218n explains, in this portion of *Eureka* Poe echoes "Marginalia" item 18. BRP, who edited Poe's "Brevities" (*Collected Writings,* vol. 2), has provided detailed notes on how close the two passages are. "Item 18," he writes,

is devoted to "Divine adaptation" by contrast with "human constructions." The first three sentences of the earlier passage are close to the first three of paragraph 216, but do not use the term "reciprocity." This, however, is introduced at the end of the first of the three paragraphs. The texts are so similar as to warrant our regarding paragraphs 216–217 as variants of the passage from the "Marginalia." The ostensible point of Poe's 1844 article lay in the short paragraph, omitted, on the writers of the Bridgewater Tracts [see ¶218n and also ¶133] who avoid this "mutual adaptation" because it tends "to overthrow the idea of . . . First Cause—of God." Or else, they have "failed to perceive"

Poe's sole insight (expressed in the next paragraph below, q.v.). In the 12/ 44 set of "Marginalia" (item 82) Poe used "plot adaptation" for this one sentence article, and in the 8/45 "American Drama" article of the *American Whig Review* he incorporated all of Marginalia item 18 unchanged—a waystation to *Eureka*.

217 azotized: "Azote" was Lavoisier's term for nitrogen. Poe referred to it also in "Von Kempelen and His Discovery" (1849) (Pollin, *Discoveries in Poe*, 178–80; *Short Fiction*, 607–11, esp. 607–8, 620n6; *Collected Works*, 3:1355–67, esp. 3:1359, 3:1366n9) in "Hans Pfaall" (1835), in which tale Poe referred to Herschel, as he does so importantly in *Eureka*.

train-oil: Oil from blubber, or from seals and codfish. See note to paragraph 114.

reciprocity of adaptation: Poe is alluding to a phenomenon that he terms in "Marginalia" item 18 "mutuality of adaptation" (see *Collected Writings*, 2:127–28). (It is absent, he complains, from the "Bridgewater Treatises.") He is either being prescient or concealing his source in regard to an aspect of what is now termed coevolution; this is applied to the interdependence between plants and animals, enabling their continued living and reproducing together. Following a suggestion by BRP, we checked a number of histories of evolutionary theory without finding reference to the concept before Poe. The 1989 second edition of the *OED* and its supplements through 1997 did not list "coevolution." An excellent discussion of attempts to define coevolution appears in Schemske, "Limits to Specialization," 67–109. Building upon a definition by Jonathan Roughgarden in *Theory of Population Genetics and Evolutionary Ecology: An Introduction* (New York: Macmillan, 1979)—"the simultaneous evolution of interacting populations" (451)—Schemske notes that one needs to add that the process is the result of "interactions between taxa at the level of particular traits" (70). Close examination of what Poe says in paragraphs 216 and 217 in the light of those definitions suggests that Poe may not have had a secure grip on coevolution as it is now understood. His explanation in paragraph 216 perhaps promises more than his example in paragraph 217 delivers, for the example does not quite show "simultaneous evolution" or "interaction . . . on the level of particular traits." Poe does not argue, that is, that people of the cold north have evolved so that they can metabolize fats or that the animals they eat have mutually evolved in ways beneficial to both species. Our consultant in the history of biology (Professor Emeritus John A. Weir, University of Kansas), however, agreed with us that Poe's insight was nevertheless impressive and very unusual for the period—"profound," he called it.

218 In the construction. . . . God: Poe quotes himself again, repeating a passage previously used in "Marginalia" item 18 in 1844 and in his article "The American Drama" (1845) (Pollin, "Politics and History," 128; Poe, *The Science Fiction of Edgar Allan Poe*, ed. Beaver; see also ¶216 and ¶216n). In both places the "plot of God" passage is connected to mention of the "Bridgewater Treatises" (see ¶133). (Poe's

"depends" means "hangs from" or "is supported by.") The passage is important evidence of Poe's sense of unity. Artistic and scientific inspiration are of the same sort, man's efforts—flawed by his "finite intelligence"—to perceive the perfect beauty that underlies creation. Hence Poe's most astute analyst, the detective Dupin, is also a poet: see the story "The Purloined Letter" (1844). BRP kindly provides a table of variations. In each case, the "Marginalia" item 18 version appears first and the *Eureka* version is after the slash: the *approach / the approach;* reciprocity between cause and effect. / reciprocity.; the points / the incidents; that we cannot distinctly see, in respect to any one of them, whether that one / that we shall not . . . depends; perfection of plot / *perfection* of plot; unattainable in fact,—because Man is the constructor. / unattainable . . . constructs.

219 washer-womanish: Poe's coinage (Pollin, *Poe: Creator of Words,* 68). In this portion of *Eureka* he seems to be uncomfortable with his material. See note to paragraph 222.

220 Fourier: Authorities disagree on whether Poe intended to refer here to Jean Baptiste Joseph Fourier (1768–1830), a "French physicist noted for his researches on heat and numerical equations" (Poe, *The Science Fiction of Edgar Allan Poe,* ed. Beaver, 411) or to the French social theorist François Marie-Charles Fourier (1772–1837). There is considerable evidence that Poe had in mind the latter. *Eureka* heavily overlaps Poe's satirical story "Mellonta Tauta." In that tale, the narrator consistently misspells the names of any figures Poe intends to criticize. Poe elsewhere made snide remarks about F. M-C. Fourier, who was extremely well known in the United States because a number of American socialist utopian communities were deeply influenced by his theories. Brook Farm near Boston, which began as an idyllic Transcendentalist haven, eventually fell into the hands of Fourierist theorists who attempted to turn it into a phalanstery. Poe, who admired Hawthorne's stories (the feeling was mutual), nevertheless teased him in print for having involved himself in Brook Farm's "phalanx and phalanstery atmosphere" (Holman, "Splitting Poe's 'Epicurean Atoms,'" 2). "Phalanx" and "phalanstery" are Fourier's terms. In "Mellonta Tauta," Poe spelled Fourier as "Furrier." In *Eureka,* he spelled it "Fourrier" in 1848, correcting it later in a penciled note (see list of Poe's corrections). Poe's error was probably a carryover of the joke he was using in the story (see *Thirty-Two Stories,* 346, 347–60, esp. 349, 349n5; *Short Fiction,* 547–48, 588–96, esp. 589, 617n6; *Collected Works,* 3:1289–309, esp. 3:1293 and 3:1306n12). (See the next item for further evidence that Poe had the humor of "Mellonta Tauta" in mind.) On the other hand, Jean Baptiste Joseph Fourier was extremely famous and very important; his great work in theory of equations and in heat diffusion and partial differential equations was closely related to very general scientific and philosophical issues of the sort that interested Poe. He "rejected the prevailing Laplacian orthodoxy of analyzing physical phenomena through the assumption of imperceptible molecules connected by local Newtonian forces" (Ravetz and Grattan-Guiness, "Jean Baptiste Joseph Fourier," 97). The work of Descartes, Bernoulli, Newton, Laplace, Comte, Bessel,

and others intersects his. Indeed, several of those great figures were his contemporaries, and he dealt with them personally. Poe knew about this Fourier: he was one of the famous men of the age. His political adventures during the period of the French Revolution, his career as a Napoleonic administrator, and his work in Egypt during the French campaigns there make an extraordinary story that was well known. There is even a scrap of circumstantial evidence that Poe had read about him in some detail. In Poe's "The Mystery of Marie Rogêt" (1842), Poe mentions a street address, "Rue Pavée Saint André." That address does not appear in the novel from which Poe cribbed most of his geographical facts about Paris, *Pelham or Adventures of a Gentleman* by Edward Bulwer-Lytton (1828, 1840; the place names are in vol. 1, ch. 23). But until 1829, Fourier lived at 15 Rue Pavée St. André des Arts.

Jean Baptiste Joseph Fourier's fame, the relevance of his work to *Eureka,* and the chance that Poe borrowed a fact about him, however, do not point directly to what Poe says in paragraph 220 of *Eureka,* whereas the works of F. M-C. Fourier plainly do. Poe says "reveries," and "reveries" is appropriate language for his work, for although his thought has been surprisingly influential, his writing is marked by, in Edward S. Mason's words, "a great deal of the fantastic and ridiculous and a verbiage so luxuriant as to seem at times that of a madman." He does indeed offer wild speculation on the cosmos, as Poe suggests: the Milky Way, he allowed, is soon going to dissolve. Fourier felt that his work on the human passions was the true completion of the work of Newton. His writings, although notably chaotic, are, in fact, intellectually akin to *Eureka.* Charles Fourier believed in analogy. His work is dotted with tables to show correspondences among smells, planets, human passions, his coming state of "Harmony," phalanxes, the climate on earth, the oceans (which would become beverages), the solar system, the universe, and creation beyond the universe. For further examples of Poe on F. M-C. Fourier, see his scornful references in "Marginalia" item 165 (*Collected Writings,* 2:274–75, 2:275, 2:276n) and "Fifty Suggestions," notes 10 and 28 (ibid., 481, 482n, 493–94, 494n).

Mädler: Johann Heinrich von Mädler (1794–1874), the German astronomer, is also mentioned in Poe's "Mellonta Tauta" (see previous item), where Poe's narrator Pundita spells his name "Muddler." The misspelling indicates satirical intent ("a muddler"). Operating at the observatory in Dorpat (Tartu) in what is now Estonia after 1840 with the excellent astronomical equipment with which Struve had worked, Mädler tried to establish that the Milky Way had a central constellation—Alcyone, in the Pleiades. Later research effectively destroyed his hypothesis (Twarog). See paragraph 221 and note. Mädler, however, is not Poe's only source for the idea; it was current in intellectual circles as well. The idea of the rotation of stars around a common center is important in "Mellonta Tauta," wherein Poe develops an "analogy": stars move around a center as the planets move around the sun. This makes it likely that Poe connected the idea to Immanuel Kant as well, for in "Mellonta Tauta," Pundita expounds Kant, whose name she spells as "Cant" (*Thirty-Two Stories*, 351n8; *Short Fiction*, 617n7; *Collected Works*, 3:1295). BRP points out that Poe knew Kant only secondhand via summaries. See note to paragraph 12.

period . . . years: The modern figure for the time it takes the sun to orbit the center of the galaxy is larger: 230 million years. The "stupendous globe," of course, is nowhere in sight.

221 A point . . . Herculis: See note to paragraph 220. A passage in Nichol (*Views of Astronomy*, Lecture 2, p. 12) also explains that stars toward which the sun is moving appear to spread out, whereas those from which it moves away seem to cluster more closely. Nichol has the earth's solar system moving *toward* Hercules, however, and Poe, away. Hodgens (typescript) suggests that Poe had the direction wrong.

Mädler . . . performed: See note to paragraph 220. Note that Poe makes clear in paragraphs 224 and 225 that he rejects Mädler's idea.

222 "analogy": Poe's discussion of analogy in this and subsequent paragraphs *rejects* the hypothesis that there exists a vast central star around our sun and the rest of the galaxy revolve. It does not do so because reasoning from analogy is a logical fallacy. Like other high Romantics of transcendental leanings, Poe believed strongly in the importance of analogical inferences. He agreed on this matter with Emerson, who wrote in the chapter entitled "Language" in *Nature*, "there is nothing lucky or capricious in . . . analogies . . . they are constant, and pervade nature. These are not the dreams of a few poets, here and there, but man is an analogist, and studies relations in all objects." In "The American Scholar," Emerson put it even more simply: "[S]cience is nothing but the finding of analogy, identity, in the most remote parts." Poe rejects the argument for the vast star not because he is suspicious of analogical reasoning but rather because the analogy is incomplete. There is no evidence of a central "orb" or of the curved trajectory of the sun. The close correlation between *Eureka* and the satirical "Mellonta Tauta" continues: the narrator of the story also connects a central "orb," the rotation by the sun, Mädler, and analogy, the same range of ideas and associations (*Thirty-Two Stories*, 356n14; *Short Fiction*, 618n14; *Collected Works*, 3:1301).

223 non-luminosity: Poe's coinage (Pollin, *Poe: Creator of Words*, 86). The word *non-luminous* (see ¶222) is ascribed by the *OED* solely to the introduction to David Brewster's *Optics*. Poe was familiar with Brewster's *Letters on Magic* and *Edinburgh Encyclopedia* articles (see Pollin "'MS Found in a Bottle'"; *Collected Works*, index entries in 2:1415; and *Collected Writings*, 1:656, index entries).

227 Sir John Herschell: Sir John Frederick William Herschel (not Herschell; see ¶213n) (1792–1871), English astronomer. Poe quotes paragraph 615, chapter 12, of Herschel's *A Treatise on Astronomy* (TOM, notes). The *Treatise* was enormously popular. Carey, Lea and Blanchard of Philadelphia brought out editions in

1834, 1835 ("New ed." but not actually revised), 1836, 1838, 1839, 1842, 1844, 1845, 1846, and 1848. Poe said that he had read the Harper's edition of 1835 (*Short Fiction*, 615n26), but we have been unable to confirm its existence. (See *Collected Writings*, 1:471n23a, for discussion of Poe's use of Herschel in "Hans Pfaall.") We obtained copies of both the 1834 and 1835 Philadelphia editions, which do contain Poe's quotation with just enough minor variations to leave one uncertain about why they are present. Poe did frequently tinker with other people's words; it was a habit as marked as his odd practices regarding the digraph and dieresis (explained in *Collected Writings*, 2:xxxvi–xl). The text, identical in these two copies, was: "It is difficult to form any conception of the dynamical state of such a system. On the one hand, without a rotatory motion and a centrifugal force, it is hardly possible not to regard them as in a state of progressive collapse. On the other, granting such a motion and such a force, we find it no less difficult to reconcile the apparent sphericity of their form with a rotation of the whole system round any single axis, without which internal collisions would appear to be inevitable."

Later editions of Herschel's *Treatise on Astronomy* are different in chapter and paragraph numbering, but we have not found one with Poe's exact wording.

Collected Writings (1:658) indexes eighteen other references to Herschel. See also paragraph 73.

229 Poe quotes from Nichol's first lecture, the one given on January 25 and covered in the New York *Tribune* on January 27. See the note to the next paragraph. Oliver Dyer, "phonographic writer," transcribed Nichol's entire series of lectures for the *Tribune;* his texts were quickly published as *Views of Astronomy* (New York: Greeley and McElrath, 1848). Poe's quotation varies from that text in small details; among other things, Poe corrected obvious typographical errors:

Eureka	Dyer/Nichol
When	when
to bear upon	to bear to upon
which were thought	which which were thought
irregular,	spherical
which looked oval;	that looked oval,
Rosse's	Ross's
Now	¶Now,
comparatively	comparalively
reverse;	reverse,
stars,	stars
stretching . . . power	stretching . . . power

230 without . . . phænomena: One commentator remarks of Poe's critique of Nichol here, "One reads these words with a good deal of surprise. . . . [I]t is not unlikely that Poe owed the first suggestion of his 'stupendous truth' to the very man whom he now dismisses as not having the 'faintest suspicion' of it. At the very

least he knew that Nichol was thoroughly acquainted with the nebular cosmogony, for in his first reference to Nichol years before he had presented his name as an inevitable association of the theory" (Connor, "Poe and John Nichol," 203)." But Hodgens, in a note to us, points to a distinction: "As shown here [and elsewhere] . . . , Dr. N., following Herschel, was prepared to consider the collapse of clusters or galaxies and of solar systems, but not ready (shall we say) to say the entire universe of stars is collapsing." Connor slightly misreads Poe; Poe is not accusing Nichol of not knowing about the nebular cosmogony but of having "missed" Poe's "stupendous" idea of a universe beginning and ending in unity because of an initial action by God: *"In the Original Unity of the First Thing lies the Secondary Cause of All Things, with the Germ of their Inevitable Annihilation"* (¶5). Connor was correct in his general observation that Poe is unfair to Nichol, as we have discussed in the Introduction. Poe's first reference to Nichol was in "The Murders in the Rue Morgue" (1841) (*Collected Works*, 2:570n16, 2:571n21). He referred to him again in a review in the June 21, 1845, *Broadway Journal* of Tayler Lewis's *Plato Contra Athos . . . Extended Dissertations on Some of the Main Points of the Platonic Philosophy . . . Compared with the Holy Scriptures.* (Poe spelled the name "Nichols" in both places.) (See *Collected Writings*, 3:88, 4:67, 88/71–74, 3:154, 4:116, 154/67–69.)

231 Argelander: Friedrich Wilhelm Argelander (1799–1875), a Prussian astronomer who continued the pioneering work of F. W. Bessel (see above) ultimately publishing an extensive catalog of the motions of 560 stars, *DLX stellarum fixarum positiones mediae ineunte anno 1830* (Helsinki, 1835), "incontestably the most exact of the contemporary catalogs" (Sticker, "Friedrich Wilhelm August Argelander"). Poe here probably refers, however, to Argelander's *Über die eigene Bewegung des Sonnensystems. hergeleitet aus den eigenen Bewegungen der Sterne* (Concerning the Peculiar Movement of the Solar System as Deduced from the Proper Motions of the Stars) (St. Petersburg, 1837). This work verifies with superior data and instruments Herschel's brilliant work on the movement of the sun. Argelander asks but stops short of exploring the large question, "Are all bodies . . . subject only to their mutual attractions, or do all of them obey the attractive force of a large central body?" (Sticker, "Friedrich Wilhelm August Argelander," 241), a question of which Poe makes much in *Eureka*. BRP points out that Alterton and Craig (*Edgar Allan Poe,* 552) reached the same conclusion regarding Poe's reference to Argelander.

Mädler's basis: All astronomy subsequent to Argelander's work depends upon it (Sticker, "Friedrich Wilhelm August Argelander").

Humboldt: Recall that *Eureka* is dedicated to Alexander von Humboldt.

232 "When. . . . hypothesis": Poe quotes the first section, "Celestial Portion of the Cosmos," of Humboldt's *Kosmos* (Stuttgart, 1845). He apparently used an incomplete, pirated English-language edition published in New York by Harper and Brothers, because he referred to that edition in the *Broadway Journal* on August

30, 1845. His footnote quoting the German original he included to suggest that he knew German, although he did not: he had an English text open before him, which he altered somewhat, probably to make the translation seem his own work. Gruener ("Poe's Knowledge of German") reports that the 1845 edition is a sixty-six-page pamphlet, the first installment of a book the rest of which Gruener believes never appeared. We examined the copy owned by the Library of Congress in which the first sixty-four pages, ending in the middle of a sentence, are bound together with a photocopy of pages 65 through 128. BRP reports that Harper and Brothers did complete the volume. The photocopied pages likely came from the remainder of the Harper edition, which Gruener could not locate and the Library of Congress does not own. (There is a copy in Boston, BRP reports.) Harper promised a second volume but did not produce it. Because Poe so warmly praised *Kosmos,* we think it likely that he did not know even the remainder of the first volume, for the volume ends with a moving affirmation of "the unity of the human kind" that repudiates "all the unsatisfactory assumptions of higher and lower races of men" (108). Poe's racial ideas were not nearly so modern. Poe, at any rate, probably based his "translation" on this edition, although his alterations are considerable. The passage Poe adapted is on page 46. The Harper and Brothers text reads, "If the non-perspective proper motions of the stars be considered, many of them appear groupwise opposed in their directions; and the data hitherto collected make it at least not necessary to suppose that all the parts of our astral system, or the whole of the star-islands which fill the universe, are in motion about any great, unknown, luminous, or non-luminous central mass. The longing to reach the last or highest fundamental cause, indeed, renders the reflecting faculty of man as well as his fancy disposed to adopt such a supposition."

BRP notes an error in Maddison ("Poe's *Eureka*"), who discussed this passage using a later translation by Elise C. Otté, while the Harper volume uses the Augustin Pritchard translation. Poe's "rewrite" is closer to the latter. See also the *Broadway Journal,* July 12, 1845 (*Collected Writings,* 3:169) and the notes to it (4:127–28). The *Broadway Journal* item introduces four transplanted paragraphs from *Kosmos,* and the notes discuss Poe's rewording of the translation.

non-perspective: Poe's coinage (Pollin, *Poe: Creator of Words,* 86).

234 Herschell: See paragraphs 7 and 65 notes.

collapse: Poe believed that the universe is in its contracting phase. See paragraph 236 note.

orbitual: "An unexpected term for the common 'orbital' and half a dozen more adjectives for 'orbit.' The *OED*'s attribution as the first instance to Herschel's *Treatise on Astronomy* probably indicates Poe's further reliance upon that work" (BRP).

235 Herschell: See paragraphs 7 and 65 notes.

236 "if . . . obtain": Poe's quotation is hypothetical; he is not quoting anyone in par-

ticular. His general point is incorrect; the universe is known to be still expanding. The current standard view is that "in a finite universe with an edge, gravitational imbalance must draw matter away from the edge—i.e., a collapse must occur" (Twarog).

237 supremeness: The *OED* credits Poe with this coinage in his 1844 tale "The Premature Burial" (*Short Fiction,* 308; *Collected Works,* 3:953) (BRP). For a useful discussion of this paragraph, see Dayan, *Fables of Mind.*

238 *vortical:* Poe's coinage (Pollin, *Poe: Creator of Words,* 40). BRP adds that Poe "pays special attention" here and in several stories to "the movement and funnel-shape of the gyre." See "MS. Found in a Bottle," 1833 (*Thirty-Two Stories,* 16; *Short Fiction,* 623; *Collected Works,* 2:135); "A Descent into the Maelström," 1841 (*Thirty-Two Stories* 160; *Short Fiction,* 40; *Collected Works,* 2:577); *The Narrative of A. Gordon Pym,* 1837 (*Collected Writings,* 1:144); and "Hans Pfaall," 1835 (*Short Fiction,* 558; *Collected Writings,* 1:387–433).

239 gradual . . . comet: "Encke's comet" was named after Johann Franz Encke (1791–1865), who showed in 1819 that comet sightings in 1786, 1795, 1805, and 1818 were of the same comet. He calculated its orbit and period (about 1,204 days) and noted that it was accelerating, though not in the "perfectly regular" manner Poe claims. Its behavior, indeed, posed major problems for nineteenth-century astronomy. Its situation is, in fact, much like that of Halley's comet. Fuller discussion of Poe's use of Encke in "Hans Pfaall" and of comets in his work is in *Collected Writings* (1:463n9a, 1:473n26b).

242 Lagrange: Poe's science summary is good, but his science history is faulty. Lagrange (1736–1813) worked on planetary theory from 1774 to 1784 and again following 1808, but the breakthrough for which Poe credits him was actually Laplace's, not Lagrange's, although Lagrange figures in the story. Here is an account from a standard modern astronomy history:

> Halley had in 1693 perceived that the moon's period of revolution, hence also its distance from the earth, had gradually diminished. . . . If this diminution in the moon's orbit continued into the future, the moon would finally descend upon the earth. In 1770 the Paris Academy offered their prize for research as to whether the theory of gravitation could explain the phenomenon; Euler, in his prize treatise, [concluded] . . . 'that the secular inequality of the moon's motion cannot be produced by the forces of gravitation.' In . . . 1772 he . . . [supposed] that the term probably arose from the resistance of an ethereal fluid which filled celestial space. . . . After many fruitless attempts by Lagrange and Laplace, the latter at last, in 1787, succeeded in discovering the real cause. By the action of the planets upon the earth, the eccentricity of the earth's orbit was continually diminishing . . . ; because the orbit became more circular, the mean distance of the sun increased, and its perturbing effect decreased. By the attraction of the sun, the moon's orbit was enlarged; this enlargement now gradually diminished through the decrease of the sun's

NOTES TO PAGES 98–103

effect . . . Thus . . . uneasiness was removed, and the conviction that Newton's theory was capable of explaining all the movements in the solar system grew even stronger. (Pannekoek, *A History of Astronomy*, 304–5)

243 *an ether:* Compare what Poe says here to Agathos' explanation in Poe's story "The Power of Words" (1835) (*Thirty-Two Stories*, 318–22, esp. 321–22n5; *Short Fiction*, 107–8, 114–16, 145–46, esp. 146n5; *Collected Works*, 3:1210–17). Agathos speaks of an ether "which, since it pervades, and alone pervades all space, is thus the great medium of *creation.*" In "The Power of Words," the ether does seem to be "matter"; in *Eureka*, Poe says that it is not. Agathos explains that one must take seriously the *"physical power of words,"* acting first on the air and then upon the "ether" so that one can literally speak stars into being. The distinction between ether as "matter" or as spiritual medium is less critical than one might think. Poe's underlying point is the same: Spirit and matter, creation, perception, and nature are intertwined, unified, ultimately one. The inspired artist-scientist-poet-visionary will someday be able to account for spirituality in scientific terms. Emerson's phrase from "The Poet" is apt: "The Universe is the externalization of the soul." For a comparison between Poe's projections and the models of contemporary astrophysics, see the Introduction to this volume.

245 vortical: See note to paragraph 238.

indrawing: Poe's coinage (Pollin, *Poe: Creator of Words*, 29).

246 system-atoms: Poe's coinage (Pollin, *Poe: Creator of Words*, 66).

247 climacic: Poe's coinage (Pollin, *Poe: Creator of Words*, 24).

250 that God . . . all: See I Corinthians, 15:28, "that God may be all in all" (TOM, notes).

256 this Heart Divine . . . *is our own:* Central to many of the mystical, Oriental, and/or occult beliefs that seemed sympathetic to Romantic authors is the understanding that the individual is identical with the universe. Transcendence in such systems of thought is often defined as the realization of this unity, which is sometimes seen as identical to merger with the godhead. The idea is recurrent in Emerson, for example, and appears in Western thought at least as far back as Plato. It is in Poe as well, although not always with the bright implications it carries in *Eureka*. For a gloomier variant, see his poem "A Dream within a Dream" (1827 and repeatedly revised until 1849):

> O God! can I not save
> One [grain of sand] from the pitiless wave?
> Is *all* that we see or seem
> But a dream within a dream?

See paragraph 263, where merger with a world-spirit that sounds very much like the Emersonian Oversoul is made especially specific, and paragraph 266, in which another aspect of occult belief is spelled out.

259 We . . . awful: That the young retain some sense of "a Destiny more vast" from a time before their birth is an idea found frequently among the Romantic authors and poets whom Poe knew best. The intuitive, magical knowledge of the very young was generally felt to be buried gradually as the maturing child was "socialized." In paragraph 259 and the paragraphs that follow, Poe plays a special variation on the theme. Wordsworth wrote in the "Ode: Intimations of Immortality from Recollections of Early Childhood" (1807):

> . . . trailing clouds of glory do we come
> From God, who is our home.

But by the time we are older, the inspired poetic vision has become, as Wordsworth put it elsewhere, "a study" (see *Critical Theory*, note to ¶9 of Poe, "Letter to B——"). In Poe, in contrast, the clouds of glory are a sign that each soul is part of the godhead, "that each soul is, in part, its own God" (¶263).

world-existence: Poe's coinage (Pollin, *Poe: Creator of Words*, 69).

262 World-Reason: Poe's coinage (Pollin, *Poe: Creator of Words*, 69).

263 re-constitution: Poe's coinage (Pollin, *Poe: Creator of Words*, 35).

266 There was. . . . *Spirit Divine:* In such religions as those referred to in the note to paragraph 256, the universe is understood as alive, sensate, identical with the individual, and identical with God. BRP suggests comparison with a very similar passage in "The Island of the Fay" (1841): see *Collected Works*, 2:601 and 2:605n3.

Self-Diffusion: Poe's coinage (Pollin, *Poe: Creator of Words*, 63).

pain-intertangled: Poe's coinage (ibid., 59).

Appendix: Poe's Postscript
to a Letter about the Lecture "Eureka"

2   sun . . . he: BRP suggests that Poe assigns gender to heavenly bodies (see ¶6 below also) because that practice is followed in an unpaged article on "Moon" in volume 24 of Abraham Rees's *Cyclopaedia; or, Universal Dictionary of Arts, Sciences, and Literatures* (London, 1802–19). That seems likely, for there is other evidence of the influence of Rees upon him, for example, Poe's odd spelling of "eccentricity" discussed in the notes to paragraph 178 of *Eureka.*

Kepler's Third Law: "The square of the time of revolution of any planet about the Sun is proportional to the cube of its mean distance from the Sun" (*Collected Works*, 3:1323n2).

gaseous ring: See notes to paragraph 172 of *Eureka.* This is a passage in which *Eureka* itself is unsound. Indeed, Twarog, who generally praises Poe's summary of science theory, responded to it with the same pejorative he used for the "Postscript" in general: "numerology."

4   Moon . . . her: See note to paragraph 2.

5   *caloric:* An archaic scientific term used for the "subtle fluid" that was the stuff of heat.

    lonesome latter days: Mabbott, in *Collected Works,* 3:1323n4, suggests comparison with Poe's poem "The Conqueror Worm" (1843), "a gala night / Within the lonesome latter years."

    melt . . . scroll!: Mabbott writes, "Compare also Isaiah 34:4, 'And all the host of heaven shall be dissolved, and the heavens shall be rolled together as a scroll'; and Revelation 6:14, 'The heaven departed as a scroll when it is rolled together'" (*Collected Works,* 3:1323n5).

6   Venus . . . her: See note to paragraph 2.

    Mercury's . . . his: See note to paragraph 2.

8   Kepler's . . . Theory: Woodberry, relying upon his science consultant Irving Stringham, writes, "It is stated that Kepler's first and third laws 'cannot be explained upon the principle of Newton's theory;' but, in fact, they follow by mathematical deduction from it. Poe's own explanation of them is merely a play upon figures" (310).

9   Jupiter. . . . diameter: Woodberry and Stringham write, "The density of Jupiter, for example, in a long and important calculation, is constantly reckoned as two and one half, whereas it is only something more than one fifth, and the densities of the planets are described as being inversely as their rotary periods, whereas in any table of the elements of the solar system some wide departures from this rule are observable" (310).

12   "breadth": Woodberry and Stringham write:

    A striking instance of fundamental ignorance of astronomical science is his [Poe's] statement at various places that the planets rotate (on their own axes) in elliptical orbits, and the reference he frequently makes to the *breadth* of their orbits (the breadth of their paths through space) agreeably to this supposition. Such a theory is incompatible with the Newtonian law of gravitation, according to which any revolution in an elliptical orbit implies a source of attraction at the focus of the ellipse. Examples of bodies which have breadth of orbit in Poe's sense are found in the satellites of all the planets, each of which, however, has its primary as a source of attraction to keep it in its elliptical orbit; the primary by its revolution round the sun gives then the satellite a breadth of orbit. But to make the proper rotation of the planets themselves take place about a focus, which would be merely a point moving in an elliptical orbit about the sun, would be to give them an arbitrary motion with no force to produce it (310–11).

15   *truck:* Poe has in mind the nautical meaning of this word: a ring or disc through which ropes pass.

BIBLIOGRAPHY

Collections of Scholarly Notes

Hodgens, Richard M. Typescript notes graciously loaned to us. They deal with similarities between *Eureka* and a number of documents, especially the lectures of John Pringle Nichol.

Mabbott, Thomas Ollive (TOM). Mabbott Papers, University of Iowa, Iowa City. Preliminary notes that Mabbott had prepared with an eye to further volumes of his edition. The notes are in various forms, and often several stages exist for a single work. Many have been painstakingly typed, under Maureen Mabbott's supervision, we believe, sometimes from rough handwritten notes, sometimes from marginal jottings. Scholars using them should be aware that they are very preliminary; some are essentially notes by TOM to himself. The should not be trusted for the wording of quotations. TOM seems often to have made notations from memory and in haste, planning to check for exact wording at a later stage of his work. But the notes, which are in the hands of librarians sympathetic to scholarship, are very useful and saved us many hours.

Publications

Allen, Hervey. *Israfel / The Life and Times of Edgar Allan Poe.* 2d ed. rev. New York: Farrar and Rinehart, 1934.

Alterton, Margaret. *Origins of Poe's Critical Theory.* Vol. 2, no. 3 of University of Iowa Humanistic Studies. Iowa City: University of Iowa, 1925. Reprint. New York: Russell and Russell, 1965.

Alterton, Margaret, and Hardin Craig. *Edgar Allan Poe: Representative Selections, with Introduction, Bibliography, and Notes.* New York: American Book Company, 1935. Rev. ed. New York: Hill and Wang, 1962.

Atkinson, Charles Milner. *Jeremy Bentham: His Life and Works.* London: Methuen, 1905.

Benton, Richard P., ed. *Poe as Literary Cosmologer: Studies on* Eureka: *A Symposium.* Hartford: Transcendental Books, 1975.

Berman, Louis, and J. C. Evans. *Exploring the Cosmos.* 5th ed. Boston: Little, Brown, 1986.

Bielfeld, Jacob Friedrich. *Les premiers traits de l'erudition universelle ou analyse abrégée de toutes les sciences, des beaux-arts et des belles-lettres.* 3 vols. Leiden: Sam. and Jean Luchtmans, 1767.

BIBLIOGRAPHY

————. *The Elements of Universal Erudition, Containing an Analytical Abridgment of the Sciences, Polite Arts, and Belles Lettres, by Baron Bielfeld.* 3 vols. Translated by W. Hooper. London: G. Scott for J. Robson and B. Law, 1770. Translated from the last edition printed at Berlin, 1768.

Brandon, Ruth. *The Spiritualists: The Passion for the Occult in the Nineteenth and Twentieth Centuries.* New York: Knopf, 1983.

Brewster, David. Review of Comte, *Cours de philosophie positive. Edinburgh Review* 36 (July 1838): 271–308.

Browne, Sir Thomas. "Of Sneezing." Chapter 9 of *On Man*, book 4 of *Pseudoxia Epidemica; or, Enquiries into Very Many Received Tenents and Commonly Presumed Truths.* 6th ed. London: Printed for the assigns of Edward Dod.

Bryant, Jacob. *A New System or an Analysis of Antient Mythology: Wherein an Attempt Is Made to Divest Tradition of Fable and to Reduce the Truth to Its Original Purity.* London: Printed for T. Payne, 1774–76. There were additions of new material in later versions. We use the third edition, which is in six volumes: *A New System; or, An Analysis of Antient Mythology.* London: James Nunn, 1807.

Cantalupo, Barbara. *"Eureka:* Poe's 'Novel Universe.'" In *A Companion to Poe Studies.* Edited by Eric W. Carlson, 323-44. Westport: Greenwood Press, 1996.

Carlson, Eric W. "New Introduction." In *Selections from the Critical Writings of Edgar Allan Poe.* Edited by F. C. Prescott, vii–xxii. New York: Gordian Press, 1981.

————, ed. *The Recognition of Edgar Allan Poe/Selected Criticism since 1829.* Ann Arbor: University of Michigan Press, 1966.

Cist, Charles. *Sketches and Statistics of Cincinnati in 1851.* Cincinnati: W. H. Moore, 1851.

Coleridge, Samuel Taylor. *The Complete Poetical Works of Samuel Taylor Coleridge.* Vol. 1, ed. Ernest Hartley Coleridge. London: Oxford University Press, 1912. Reprint. London: Oxford University Press, 1975. There are several later reprints. We consulted a 1975 reprint.

Conner, Frederick W. "Poe and John Nichol / Notes on a Source of *Eureka.*" In *All These to Teach: Essays in Honor of C. A. Robertson.* Edited by Robert A. Bryan et al., 190–208. Gainesville: University of Florida Press, 1965.

Dayan, Joan. *Fables of Mind: An Inquiry into Poe's Fiction.* Oxford: Oxford University Press, 1987.

Dick, Thomas. *The Christian Philosopher; or, The Connection of Science and Philosophy with Religion.* Glasgow, 1823. The first American edition is New York, G. and C. Carvill, 1826.

Disraeli, Isaac. *Curiosities of Literature.* Various editions of this work, in part or whole, have appeared since the first (London: J. Murray, 1791). We refer to the 1853 edition: *Curiosities of Literature* and *The Literary Character Illustrated* by Disraeli along with *Curiosities of American Literature* by Rufus Griswold. New York: Leavitt and Allen, 1853.

Emerson, Ralph Waldo. "Blight." In *Poems,* ed. Edward W. Emerson, 140. Boston: Houghton Mifflin, 1904.s

Forrest, William Mentzel. *Biblical Allusions in Poe.* New York: Macmillan, 1928.

BIBLIOGRAPHY

Godwin, Parke. *A Biography of William Cullen Bryant.* 2 vols. New York: D. Appleton, 1883.

Gruener, Gustav. "Poe's Knowledge of German." *Modern Philology* 2 (June 1904): 124–40.

Hawking, Stephen W. *A Brief History of Time: From the Big Bang to Black Holes.* Toronto: Bantam Books, 1988.

Herschel, John F. *Outlines of Astronomy.* Philadelphia: Blanchard and Lea, 1853.

———. *A Preliminary Discourse on the Study of Natural Philosophy.* London: Printed for Longman and J. Taylor, 1830.

———. *A Treatise on Astronomy.* London, 1833. Philadelphia: Carey, Lea and Blanchard, 1834.

Holman, Harriet R. "Hog, Bacon, Ram, and Other 'Savans' in *Eureka:* Notes toward Decoding Poe's Encyclopedic Satire." *Poe Newsletter* 2 (Oct. 1969): 49–55.

———. "Splitting Poe's 'Epicurean Atoms': Further Speculation on the Literary Satire of *Eureka.*" *Poe Studies* 5 (Dec. 1972): 33-37.

Holt, Palmer C. "Poe and H. N. Coleridge's *Greek Classic Poets:* 'Pinikidia,' 'Politian,' and 'Morella' Sources." *American Literature* 34 (March 1962): 8–30.

Humboldt, Friederich Heinrich Alexander von. *Kosmos.* Stuttgart, 1845. *Cosmos.* New York: Harper and Brothers, 1845. A pirated translation. Poe had seen at least the first half of the first volume of this version (¶232n).

———. *Cosmos.* Translated by Elise C. Otté. London: H. G. Bohn, 1849.

Huxley, Aldous. *Vulgarity in Literature.* London: Chatto and Windus, 1930.

Irwin, John T. *American Hieroglyphics: The Symbol of the Egyptian Hieroglyphics in the American Renaissance.* New Haven: Yale University Press, 1980.

Kaufmann, William J., III. *Exploration of the Solar System.* New York: Macmillan, 1978.

Ketterer, David. "Protective Irony and 'The Full Design' of *Eureka.*" In *Poe as Literary Cosmologer: Studies on* Eureka: *A Symposium.* Edited by Richard P. Benton, 46–55. Hartford: Transcendental Books, 1975.

Krutch, Joseph Wood. *Edgar Allan Poe: A Study in Genius.* New York: Knopf, 1926.

Laplace, Pierre-Simon. *Exposition du système du monde.* Paris: lmpr. du Cercle-Social, An IV de la Republique francaise [1796]. Translation. London: Printed for Richard Phillips, 1809.

Levine, Stuart. *Edgar Poe: Seer and Craftsman.* Deland: Everett/Edwards, 1972.

———. "Masonry, Impunity, and Revolution." *Poe Studies* 17, 1 (June 1984): 22–23.

———. "Poe and American Society." *Canadian Review of American Studies* 9, 1 (Spring 1978): 16–33.

———. "Scholarly Strategy: The Poe Case." *American Quarterly* 17 (Spring 1965): 132–44.

Levine, Stuart, and Susan F. Levine. "History, Myth, Fable, and Satire: Poe's Use of Jacob Bryant." *ESQ: A Journal of the American Renaissance* 21 (4th Quarter 1975): 197–213.

———. "'How to' Satire: Cervantes, Marryat, Poe." *Modern Language Studies* 16 (Summer 1986): 15–26.

Maddison, Carol Hopkins. "Poe's *Eureka.*" *Texas Studies in Literature and Language* 2 (1960): 350–67. Examines possible links of *Eureka* to Roger Boscovich, S.J., *Theoria Philosophiæ Naturalis redacta, ad unicam legem virium in natura existentium* (Vienna, 1758, republished in Venice, 1763), to Alexander Humbolt, and to William Whewell's *Astronomy and General Physics Considered with Reference to Natural Theology* (?; Maddison gives no dates).

Mason, Edward S. "Fourier and Fourierism." In *Encyclopaedia of the Social Sciences.* Vol. 6, 402–4. New York: Macmillan, 1931.

Mihalas, Dimitri, and James Binney. *Galactic Astronomy: Structure and Kinematics.* San Francisco: W. H. Freeman, 1968, 1981.

Mill, John Stuart. *A System of Logic, Ratiocinative and Inductive; Being a Connected View of the Principles of Evidence and the Methods of Scientific Investigation.* New York: Harper and Brothers, 1846. We use this edition because of the likelihood that Poe had access to it.

Milton, John. "Comus." In *An Oxford Anthology of English Poetry.* Edited by Howard Foster Lowry, Willard Thorp, and Howard C. Horsford. New York: Oxford University Press, 1956.

Moldenhauer, Joseph J., comp. *A Descriptive Catalog of Edgar Allan Poe Manuscripts in the Humanities Research Library, the University of Texas at Austin.* Austin: University of Texas Press, 1973.

Montaigne, Michel de, *Essays.* Translated by Charles Cotton; edited by W. Carew Hazlett, book 2, ch. 27. New York: A. L. Burt, n.d.

Nelson, Roland, W. "Apparatus for a Definitive Edition of Poe's *Eureka.*" In *Studies in the American Renaissance.* Edited by Joel Myerson, 161–205. Boston: Twayne Publishers, 1978.

Nichol, John Pringle. *Views of the Architecture of the Heavens.* Edinburgh, 1837. Reprinted as *Views of the Architecture of the Heavens: In a Series of Letters to a Lady.* 2d ed. Edinburgh: Tait, 1838.

———. *Views of Astronomy.* New York: Greeley and McElrath, 1848.

Omans, Glen A. "'Intellect, Taste and the Moral Sense': Poe's Debt to Immanuel Kant." In *Studies in the American Renaissance.* Edited by Joel Myerson, 123-68. Boston: Twayne Publishers, 1980.

Pannekoek, Antonie. *A History of Astronomy.* New York: Interscience Publishers, 1961. London: G. Allen Unwin, 1961.

Pascal, Blaise. *Pensées et opuscules.* Edited by M. Léon Brunschvicg. Paris: Librairie Hachette 1923(?).

———. *Pensées / The Provincial Letters.* Introduction by W. F. Trotter. New York: Modern Library, 1941.

Poe, Edgar Allan. *Collected Works of Edgar Allan Poe.* Vol. 1: *Complete Poems.* Edited by Thomas Ollive Mabbott. Cambridge: Harvard University Press, 1969. Reprint. Urbana: University of Illinois Press, 2000. The Harvard volumes are numbered consecutively. Volume 1 contains Poe's poems, volumes 2 and 3, *Tales & Sketches.* In the Illinois reprint, there is no consecutive numbering. Thus a citation to "Collected

BIBLIOGRAPHY

Works 3" directs readers either to volume 3 of the Harvard or the second volume of "Tales and Sketches" in the Illinois edition. Contents of the two editions are identical.

———. *Collected Works of Edgar Allan Poe.* Vol. 2: *Tales and Sketches, 1831–1842.* Edited by Thomas Ollive Mabbott. Cambridge: Harvard University Press, 1978. Reprint. Urbana: University of Illinois Press, 2000.

———. *Collected Works of Edgar Allan Poe.* Vol. 3: *Tales and Sketches, 1843-1849.* Edited by Thomas Ollive Mabbott. Cambridge: Harvard University Press, 1978. Reprint. Urbana: University of Illinois Press, 2000.

———. *Collected Writings of Edgar Allan Poe.* Edited by Burton R. Pollin. Vol. 1: *The Imaginary Voyages: The Narrative of Arthur Gordon Pym / The Unparalleled Adventure of One Hans Pfaall / The Journal of Julius Rodman.* Boston: Twayne Publishers, 1981.

———. *Collected Writings of Edgar Allan Poe.* Edited by Burton R. Pollin. Vol. 2: *The Brevities: Pinakidia / Marginalia / Fifty Suggestions.* New York: Gordian Press, 1985.

———. *Collected Writings of Edgar Allan Poe.* Edited by Burton R. Pollin. Vols. 3 (text) and 4 (annotations): *Writings in the* Broadway Journal: *Nonfictional Prose.* New York: Gordian Press, 1986.

———. *Complete Works of Edgar Allan Poe.* Vols. 2–16. Edited by James A. Harrison. New York: Crowell, 1902.

———. *Edgar Allan Poe / Thirty-Two Stories.* Edited by Stuart Levine and Susan Levine. Indianapolis: Hackett Publishing, 2000.

———. *Essays and Reviews.* Edited by G. R. Thompson. New York: Library of America, 1984.

———. *Eureka: A Prose Poem / New Edition with Line Numbers, Exploratory, Essay, and Bibliographical Guide.* Edited by Richard P. Benton. Hartford: Transcendental Books, 1973. A facsimile edition.

———. *The Letters of Edgar Allan Poe.* Edited by John Ward Ostrom. Cambridge: Harvard University Press, 1948. 2 vols. Reprint with supplement. New York: Gordian Press, 1966.

———. *The Rationale of Verse.* Edited by J. Arthur Greenwood. Princeton: Wolfhart Book, 1968. Although Greenwood says modestly that he will withdraw his book when a good edition of the essay appears, he should not. His book is too useful and goes into matters which, although not appropriate for a general edition, are interesting. The volume is also charming, quirky, and frank.

———. *The Raven and Other Poems.* Edited by Thomas Ollive Mabbott. New York: Facsimile Text Society, 1942. A facsimile of the 1845 edition of Poe's poems: T. Lorimer Graham's copy with Poe's handwritten corrections.

———. *The Science Fiction of Edgar Allan Poe.* Edited by Harold Beaver. New York: Penguin, 1976.

———. *The Short Fiction of Edgar Allan Poe / An Annotated Edition.* Edited by Stuart Levine and Susan Levine. Indianapolis: Bobbs-Merrill, 1976. Reprint. Urbana: University of Illinois Press, 1990.

———. *Tales by Edgar A. Poe.* New York: Wiley and Putnam, 1845.

BIBLIOGRAPHY

————. *The Works of Edgar Allan Poe*. Edited by Edmund Clarence Stedman and George Woodberry. Chicago: Stone and Kimball, 1894–96. 10 vols. There are several later reprints; we used the 1896 volume.

Pollin, Burton R. "Contemporary Reviews of *Eureka:* A Checklist." Part 1. *American Transcendental Quarterly* 26 (Spring 1975): 26–30.

————. *Dictionary of Names and Titles in Poe's Collected Works*. New York: Da Capo Books, 1968.

————. *Discoveries in Poe*. Notre Dame: University of Notre Dame Press, 1970 (see esp. "Poe's Iron Pen," 206–29).

————. "Empedocles in Poe: A Contribution of Bielfeld." *Poe Studies* 12 (Dec. 1979): 8–9.

————. "'MS. Found in a Bottle' and Sir David Brewster's Letters: A Source." *Poe Studies* 15 (Dec. 1982): 40–41.

————. *Poe, Creator of Words*. Baltimore: Enoch Pratt Free Library, The Edgar Allan Poe Society and the Library of the University of Baltimore, 1974. Reprint, revised and augmented. Bronxville: Nicholas T. Smith, 1980.

————. "Poe's Use of Material from Bernardin de Saint-Pierre's *Etudes.*" *Romance Notes* 12, no. 2 (1971): 1–8.

————. "Politics and History in Poe's 'Mellonta Tauta': Two Allusions Explained." *Studies in Short Fiction* 8 (Fall 1971): 627–31.

————. *Word Index to Poe's Fiction*. New York: Gordian Press, 1982.

Posey, Meredith Neill. "Notes on Poe's 'Hans Pfaal.'" *Modern Language Notes* 45 (Dec. 1930): 501–7.

Quinn, Arthur Hobson. *Edgar Allan Poe: A Critical Biography*. New York: Appleton Century, 1941.

Quinn, Patrick, ed. *Edgar Allan Poe / Poetry and Tales*. New York: Library of America, 1984.

Ravetz, Jerome R., and I. Grattan-Guinness. "Jean Baptiste Joseph Fourier." In *Dictionary of Scientific Biography*. Vol. 5, 93–99. New York: Charles Scribner's Sons, 1972.

Rees, Abraham. *Rees's Manufacturing Industry, 1819–20: A Selection from The Cyclopaedia; or, Universal Dictionary of Arts, Sciences, and Literature*. Edited by Neil Cossons. [Newton Abbot, Eng.]: David and Charles Reprints, 1972.

Ronan, Colin A. *Astronomers Royal*. Garden City: Doubleday, 1969.

Roughgarden, Jonathan. *Theory of Population Genetics and Evolutionary Ecology: An Introduction*. New York: Macmillan, 1979.

Schemske, Douglas W. "Limits to Specialization and Coevolution in Plant-Animal Mutualisms." In *Coevolution*. Edited by Matthew H. Nitecki, 67–109. Chicago: University of Chicago Press, 1983.

Schofield, Robert E. *Mechanism and Materialism: British Natural Philosophy in an Age of Reason*. Princeton: Princeton University Press, 1970.

St. Armand, Barton Levi. "'Seemingly Intuitive Leaps': Belief and Unbelief in *Eureka.*" In *Poe as Literary Cosmologer: Studies on* Eureka: A Symposium. Edited by Richard P. Benton, 4–15. Hartford: Transcendental Books, 1975.

BIBLIOGRAPHY

Sticker, Bernhard. "Friedrich Wilhelm August Argelander." In *The Dictionary of Scientific Biography.* Vol. 1, 240–43. New York: Charles Scribner's Sons, 1970.

Walker, I. M., ed. *Edgar Allan Poe: The Critical Heritage.* London: Routledge and Kegan Paul, 1986. "[John Milton Evans], from a review in the Amherst College *Indicator,* Feb. 1849, 193-9."

Wheelwright, Philip, ed. *The Presocratics.* Indianapolis: Bobbs-Merrill, 1960.

Williams, Henry Smith. *The Great Astronomers.* New York: Simon and Schuster, 1930.

Wilson, James Southall. "Poe's Philosophy of Composition." *North American Review* 223 (Dec.–Jan.–Feb. 1926–27): 675–84.

Yannella, Donald. "Writing the 'Other Way': Melville, the Duyckinck Crowd, and Literature for the Masses." In *A Companion to Melville Studies.* Edited by John Bryant, 63-81. Westport: Greenwood Press, 1986.

INDEX

Items indexed from the text of *Eureka* are listed by page number. The paragraphs of the text are numbered. Items indexed from our notes to *Eureka* are listed both by page and paragraph number. Thus "162 229n" refers to a note to paragraph 229 on page 162. Items indexed from the "Introduction" to *Eureka* are by page. A small *n* in that portion of the book refers to a sequential note on the page indicated: "xv n2."

INDEX

INDEX

Goethe, Johann Wolfgang von, 135 n71

Graham's, 131 n57

"the great *Now*," 100

Gruener, Gustav, "Poe's Knowledge of German," 164 n232, 171

Halley, Edmund, 165 n242

Halley's comet, 165 n239

Happiness, 105

Harrison, James A., ed., *Complete Works of Edgar Allan Poe*, vols. 2–16, xxix, xxxiii, 173; vol. 8, 140 n133, 151 n182, 155 n203; vol. 13, 126 n20

Harris, Wilson, *Palace of the Peacock*, xi

Hawking, Stephen, *A Brief History of Time*, xxi n6, 171

Hawthorne, Nathaniel, xxv, 159 n220

Heart Divine, 103, 166 n256

Heat, 27, 28, 44, 62, 63, 64, 89, 99, 109, 131–32 n57, 159 n220, 168 n5. *See also* Electricity; Light; Magnetism

Heaven(s), 13, 39, 72, 73, 74, 75, 76, 90, 91, 92, 98, 149–50 n179, 168 n5

Hebe, 80. *See also* Asteroid(s)

Hemera (Day), 151 n182. *See also* Erebus

Henry, Rev. Francis, Eighth Earl of Bridgewater, 140 n133. *See also* *Bridgewater Treatises, The*

Hermes Trismegistus, 129 n39

Herschell (Herschel), Sir John, 93, 94, 95, 135 n73, 158 n217, 163 n230, 163 n231; *Outlines of Astronomy*, 134 n65, 149 n178; *A Preliminary Discourse on the Study of Natural Philosophy*, 136 n77; "Sound," in *Encyclopedia Metropolitana: Physical Astronomy. Sound. Light.*, n 134 n65; *A Treatise on Astronomy*, 118 n7, 146 n165, 150 n179, 150 n180, 161–62 n227, 164 n234, 164 n235

Herschell (Herschel), Sir William (father of Sir John), 87; discussion of Poe's spelling error, 156–57 n213

Heterogeneity, 24, 27, 53, 62, 64, 88, 98, 101

Heterogeneous, the, 28, 64

Hieroglyphics, 15, 126 n23. *See also* Champollion, Jean François; Irwin, John T., *American Hieroglyphics*

Higeia, 152 n193. *See also* Asteroid(s)

"highway of the *Constant*," xvi, 15

Him, 22, 61. *See also* God; Spirit

Himself, individualizations of, 105. *See also* Being, Divine; God

Hodgens, Richard, 126 n23, 134 n68, 135 n75, 141 n137, 141 n138, 142 n149, 143 n155, 144 n157, 144 n160, 146 n163, 148 n173, 150 n181, 152 n193, 161 n221, 163 n230, 169

Hoffman, Charles F., 141 n135, 152 n191

Hog(s), 10, 11, 14; Francis Bacon and, 121–22 n13

Hogg, James, 121–22 n13

Hog-ites, 11, 12, 121–22 n13, 123 n15

Holman, Harriet, "Splitting Poe's Epicurian Atoms," 118 n7, 159 n220; "Hog, Bacon, Ram," 121 n13, 124 n18, 171

Home Journal, The, xxv

Homogeneity, 24. *See also* Heterogeneity

Hooper, W. (M.D.), 129 n40, 170. *See also* Bielfeld, Baron Jacob Friedrich

Hopkins, John H., Jr., review, xxv. *See also* *Literary World*

"How to Write a Blackwood Article," xiv, 124 n17, 130 n50, 134 n71, 152 n191

Humboldt, Baron Friedrich Heinrich Alexander von, xi, xii, xiv, xvi, xx, xxiv, xxvii, 8, 93, 117, 118 n9, 126 n23, 148 n178, 149–50 n179, 155–56 n209, 163 n231, 163–64 n232, 171; dedication, 3; note to dedication, 117

INDEX

Neal, John, 134 n71

Nebular Cosmogony/Hypothesis/Theory. *See* Laplace, Pierre Simon

Nelson-Mabbott copy of *Eureka*, xxxii, xxxiv

Nelson, Roland, "Apparatus for a Definitive Edition," xxxi, xxxii, xxxiii, 172

Neptune, 55, 56, 57, 63, 70, 80, 81, 83, 84, 109, 114, 115, 141 n140, 142 n147, 152 n193, 154 n202

Nereid (moon of Neptune), 141 n140

"Neuclid." *See* Euclid; "Mellonta Tauta" (in Greek)

Newton, Sir Isaac/Newtonian Gravity, xx, xxiii, xxiv, 15, 27, 29, 30, 31, 34, 35, 36, 37, 39, 41, 43, 45, 49, 51, 52, 54, 59, 60, 61, 62, 63, 65, 67, 68, 71, 79, 80, 90, 91, 95, 96, 109, 111, 125 n19, 126 n23, 127 n23, 132 n57, 133 n62, 136 n77, 137 n78, 137 n84, 140 n134, 140–41 n135, 143 n152, 151 n182, 151 n191, 153 n193, 155 n202, 159–60 n220, 165 n236, 165–66 n242, 168 n8, 168 n12

Nichol, John Pringle, xii, xx, xxv, 35, 36, 67, 93, 126–27 n23, 135 n75, 135 n76, 141 n137, 141 n138, 141 n140, 142 n149, 143 n155, 144 n157, 144 n160, 146 n163, 162 n229, 162–63 n230, 172; "Architecture of the Heavens," 35; Poe's note to, 126 n23, 135 n76, 141 n137, 141 n138, 146 n163; *Views of the Architecture of the Heavens*, 67; *Views of Astronomy: Seven Lectures*, 127 n23, 135 n75, 141 n137, 141 n138, 142 n149, 143 n155, 144 n160, 146 n163, 162 n229

"Night of Time," 9, 105

Nihility, 22, 103, 129 n44, 132 n58

Nine Great Powers, 115. *See also* Asteroid(s)

No-difference, 27, 131 n56. *See also* Difference; Unity

Nothing, 22

Noumena, 10

Nubian Geographer, 9, 119 n11. *See also* Idrisi, al

Nux (night), 151 n182. *See also* Erebus

Olbers, Heinrich, 150 n181

Omans, Glen A., "Intellect, Taste and the Moral Sense: Poe's Debt to Immanuel Kant," 121 n12, 128 n35, 172

Omnipotence, 23, 47

Omniscience, 47

One, xvii n3, xxiii, 9, 23, 24, 25, 26, 33, 35, 51, 68, 72, 87, 95, 96, 97, 102, 106, 131 n52, 134–35 n71, 138 n111, 166 n243. *See also* Many; Matter; Poetry; Spirit; Truth(s)

Oneness, xv, xvii, xx, 7, 23, 26, 29, 100, 102, 129 n41, 130 n50, 134–35 n71

Oriental, tribal, and mystical religions, 142 nn151–53; mystical, Oriental and/or occult beliefs, 166 n256

Orion, 67, 145 n163, 147 n171

Osborne copy of *Eureka*, xxxii, xxxiv

Ostrom, John Ward, ed., *Letters of Edgar Allan Poe*, xxvi, 108, 134 n71, 141 n135, 173

Otté, Elise C., 164 n232, 171

Oversoul, 136 n77, 166 n256. *See also* Emerson, Ralph Waldo

Pagan fables, 31

Pallas, 80. *See also* Asteroid(s)

Pannekoek, Antonie, *A History of Astronomy*, 156 n213, 166 n242, 172

Parallax, 85, 155 n209, 156 n210

Parmenides of Elea, xii, xiii, 124 n17

Parsons, William, third earl of Rosse, 157 n213. *See also* Rosse, Lord

Particle(s), xxi, xxii; absolute particle, 42, 44, 48; light, 38, 137 n84; Parti-

INDEX

STUART LEVINE, professor emeritus of English, University of Kansas, A.B., Harvard University, and M.A. and Ph.D., Brown University, is the founding editor of *American Studies* and founding chair of the American studies department at the University of Kansas. He has published books of original fiction and volumes on technical writing, on Poe, on Native Americans (with N. O. Lurie), on American painting, and, with Susan F. Levine, annotated editions of Poe's work. His writing awards include the Gross-Woodley Award in Fiction, the Anisfield-Wolf Award in Race Relations, and a citation from the National Council of Christians and Jews. A Fulbright lecturer in Argentina, Costa Rica (twice), Mexico, and Italy, he has also taught at Brown, the University of the West Indies, the University of Wisconsin, Kansas State University, and the University of Missouri–Kansas City. A professional musician, he was principal French horn of the Rhode Island Philharmonic Orchestra and had a weekly network radio program of music commentary.

SUSAN F. LEVINE, B.S.Ed., M.A., Southern Illinois University, is a former university administrator at the University of Kansas, where she completed a Ph.D. in Spanish with an emphasis on Latin American literature. She has taught Spanish language and literatures and has held a Fulbright lectureship in American literature in Asunción, Paraguay. She has published articles on Latin American and Spanish authors and has collaborated for many years with Stuart Levine on editions and scholarly studies of the works of Edgar Allan Poe.

The University of Illinois Press
is a founding member of the
Association of American University Presses.

Composed in 10.5/13 New Baskerville
by Celia Shapland
for the University of Illinois Press
Manufactured by Thomson-Shore, Inc.

University of Illinois Press
1325 South Oak Street
Champaign, IL 61820-6903
www.press.uillinois.edu